The Central Eskimo

The Central Eskimo

Franz Boas

Introduction by Henry B. Collins

UNIVERSITY OF NEBRASKA PRESS · Lincoln

Introduction by Henry B. Collins © 1964 by the University of
Nebraska Press
All rights reserved
Library of Congress Catalog Card Number 64–63593

The Central Eskimo originally was published as part of the Sixth
Annual Report of the Bureau of Ethnology, Smithsonian Institution, Washington, 1888.

Manufactured in the United States of America

*Bison Book edition reprinted by arrangement with the Smith-
sonian Institution.*

INTRODUCTION TO THE BISON BOOK EDITION

The Central Eskimo is Franz Boas' first major contribution to American anthropology and one of the two first scientific monographs on the Eskimo. This distinction is shared with that other classic of Eskimo ethnology—Gustav F. Holm's *Ethnologisk Skizze av Angmagsalikerne,* Meddelelser om Grønland, Vol. 10, 1888 (published in English as *Ethnological Sketch of the Angmagsalik Eskimo,* Meddelelser om Grønland, Vol. 39, 1914). Both appeared in the same year and reported on field explorations conducted in the same period, Boas' in 1883–1884, and Holm's in 1883–1885. Both works were by-products of geographical exploration—Holm's cartographic survey of the East coast of Greenland and Boas' similar survey on Baffin Island.

Franz Boas was born in Minden, northwestern Germany, on July 9, 1858. He received his University training at Heidelberg, Bonn, and Kiel, specializing in physics, mathematics, and geography. He received his Ph.D. at Kiel in 1881, his dissertation being *Beiträge zur Erkenntniss der Farbe des Wassers.* In 1882 Boas was busy with plans for an expedition to the Arctic, and in preparation had familiarized himself with the literature on the area and had acquired some knowledge of the Eskimo language. Seeking the assistance of the German Polar Commission, he was granted passage on the schooner *Germania,* which was to sail in June, 1883, for Cumberland Sound, Baffin Island, to bring back the personnel of a German polar station that had been established there the previous year. He also was offered the use of a house at the station, a good supply of provisions, hunting gear and some surveying instruments.

On June 20, 1883, the *Germania* sailed from Hamburg with Boas and his servant, Wilhelm Weike, on board. On July 15, after crossing Davis Strait, the vessel encountered heavy pack ice about 200 miles off Cape Mercy at the entrance to Cumberland Sound, and it was not until August 25 that she was able to enter the Sound. As the polar station at the head of the Sound could not be reached because of the pack ice, the *Germania* anchored at a Scotch whaling station in Kikkerton harbor, about midway up the Sound. It was from this base, instead of the German polar station as originally planned, that Boas set out on his explorations on foot, by boat, and by dog sled, during the twelve months that followed.

Although much has been written about Franz Boas' contributions to ethnology, physical anthropology, linguistics, folklore, statistics, etc., there is virtually nothing in the anthropological literature about his geographical explorations. For this, Boas himself was largely responsible. His Baffin Island work was something past and done, and he had directed his energies immediately to a new field, the study of the Northwest Coast Indians.

In *The Central Eskimo,* as in Boas' other publications on Arctic anthropology, there is no mention whatsoever of the difficult and often hazardous journeys up and down the shores of Cumberland Sound and Davis Strait. This aspect of the work was described in two geographical publications: "A Journey in Cumberland Sound and on the West Shore of Davis Strait in 1883 and 1884," *Bulletin of the American Geographical Society,* No. 3, pp. 241–272, 1884; and "Baffin-Land. Geographische Ergebnisse einer 1883 und 1884 ausgeführten Forschungsreise," *Ergänzungsheft No. 80 zu Petermanns Mitteilungen,* pp. 1–100, 1885. These are the most detailed of some fifteen geographical articles which Boas published in various German and American journals. Boas' field explorations in themselves represented a major contribution to Arctic geography. As they also provided an essential background for his ethnographic research it may be well to summarize them briefly.

A few days after the *Germania* arrived at Kikkerton a party of Eskimos came down by boat from the German polar station on Sirmilling Bay at the upper end of Cumberland Sound. They reported that the upper part of the Sound was full of ice and that they had had great difficulty in getting through. On September 4 Boas set out on the first of his Arctic journeys when he left with the Eskimos for the Polar station to bring news of the arrival of the *Germania*. After three days of difficult travel through the ice floes they reached the station, returning to Kikkerton once arrangements had been made for evacuation of the station personnel on a whaling vessel.

During the time he was at Kikkerton, Boas stayed in the home of Mr. James Mutch, local agent for the Scottish whaling company. He is generous in acknowledging the aid and assistance of Mutch and the owner of the whaling station, Mr. Noble:

> . . . it is with the greatest pleasure, I state here, that it was only their kindness which enabled me to accomplish a great part of the work I did. . . .
>
> His [Noble's] agent, Mr. James Mutch, who has wintered seventeen times in the Cumberland sound, was a most welcome and willing help to me in my long and tedious conversations with the Esquimaux, until I was myself able to talk with them. It was with his dogs and sledges that I made a' great number of my journeys; by his help I managed to get my skin clothing ready in time to start the winter travelling. In short, in every way I am indebted to the liberal aid of these gentleman. ("A Journey in Cumberland Sound and on the West Shore of Davis Strait in 1883 and 1884," p. 247)

From the latter part of September through October, Boas surveyed the coasts, islands and fjords on the north shore of Cumberland Sound by boat, returning from the last trip on October 26, only two days before Kikkerton harbor was frozen in. By this time most of the Eskimos, who had spent the summer in the interior hunting caribou, had returned to their winter homes around Kikkerton. Boas was now brought into closer association with the Eskimos, from whom he obtained valuable ethnographical and geographical information:

> Now I began in earnest to make my ethnographical studies, and was greatly helped by Mr. Mutch, of the Scotch station. Every night I spent with the natives who told me about the configuration of the land, about their travels, etc. They related the old stories handed over to them by their ancestors, sang the old songs after the old monotonous tunes, and I saw them playing the old games, with which they shorten the long, dark winter nights. In the month of November I had gathered sufficient information about the configuration of the country to form a more accurate plan of exploration. (Ibid., p. 253)

Later in the winter as he traveled by dog sled he added to his knowledge of the people and the country:

> Afterwards, when I travelled all over the sound and visited all the settlements of the country, I saw quite a number of old men and women who remembered the old time thoroughly, when they were more numerous and no white men

visited their land, when they hunted the whale and pursued the deer with bow and arrow only.

By their help I filled up the lacunae of my knowledge and learned about the old wanderings of these tribes. (Ibid., p. 255)

From the accounts of Charles Francis Hall and Ludwig Kumlien, Boas had been led to believe that the Cumberland Sound Eskimos were in the habit of traveling westward every year to the east shore of Foxe Basin. He had planned, with their help, to survey this unknown region. This was, in fact, the primary objective he had in mind when planning his expedition. But he was soon to find that this information was incorrect. None of the Cumberland Sound people had even been to Foxe Basin. Boas nevertheless hoped to carry out his original plan by hiring two Eskimos from the upper part of the Sound, with two dog teams, to accompany him to Nettilling Lake and then on to Foxe Basin. However, in the fall of 1883 a dog disease broke out and spread throughout the Sound, killing most of the Eskimos' dogs, so that it was impossible for Boas to assemble a team. Instead, he borrowed Mr. Mutch's team and with his servant and one Eskimo, started out on the 11th of December to survey the upper end of Cumberland Sound.

For fourteen days they traveled from one island and fjord to another in temperatures ranging from 40° to 55° below zero, building a snow house for shelter each night. A few extracts from Boas' account of the trip will afford some idea of the difficulties and hardships involved:

The 14th it suddenly became warmer and a heavy snowfall covered the ice with about two feet of snow. It was impossible to travel faster than three miles a day, though we worked as hard as possible. . . . By the severe cold a spring in one of our guns broke and the cartridges of the other were spent, so there was no chance of getting a seal which would furnish our lamp with a fresh supply of blubber. We had to stop with the thermometer at F–55° in the cold snow-house with no chance to melt ice for drinking or cooking anything. . . . The ice we had to pass was very rough, slabs of one to two feet thickness being piled up on one another to more than man's height. The holes between the pieces were filled up with soft snow, and we were obliged to crawl and stumble over the projecting points and edges of the slabs. . . . We had to turn, and at last we arrived in the morning in Anarnitung after a walk of twenty-five hours, tired and hungry. We crawled into the snow-house of one of the natives, and in less than no time we were asleep in the comfortable bed of deer skins. A few hours after our arrival a sledge came in from Kikkerton, which had been delayed by the heavy snow and arrived at Ussuadlu half a day after we left. The next day I began to survey the mouth of Kingnua, but had to return to Anarnitung, as my servant's feet grew very bad and he only told me then that he had frozen his feet. I left him in the snow-hut with the Esquimaux and went back myself to Kikkerton for provisions the 24th. (Ibid., p. 258, 259, 260)

The rest of the winter of 1883 and the early spring of 1884 was spent in traveling under equally difficult conditions, as he extended his surveys the whole length of Cumberland Sound from its upper end to Davis Strait. On one of these trips Boas was able at last to reach Nettilling Lake, being the first white man to see this largest lake in the Canadian Arctic Archipelago and the sixth largest in all of Canada.

Boas finally succeeded in acquiring from Eskimos in the Davis Strait area fifteen dogs which had escaped the dog disease. On May 5 he left Cumberland Sound for Davis Strait with two heavily loaded sleds and all his equipment. This was a long, difficult overland journey, up the large Kignait fjord, then along rivers and lakes connecting with Padli fjord and finally to Padloping on Davis Strait which was reached on the twenty-second of May.

During the next two months Boas surveyed the west coast of Davis Strait as far north as Cape Raper, latitude 69° 50′ N. Traveling conditions here were even more difficult and laborious than in Cumberland Sound. Summer was approaching and the condition of the ice grew worse daily. Heavy snow falls made hard going for dogs and men alike, and later in the summer as the snow cover melted, the ice was covered with several feet of water through which the dogs had to struggle. Wide leads had now developed in the ice, requiring detours of sometimes as much as forty miles before they could be crossed. There were frequent long delays as fog obscured the landmarks that had to be surveyed. To add to their troubles, both dogs and men were hungry most of the time. These were the conditions which Boas faced and surmounted as he made the first scientific survey of this 250 miles of unknown coastline. It is probably no exaggeration to say that Boas experienced more real dangers and hardships in his one year of Arctic field work than most anthropologists do in a lifetime.

Boas spent the last month of his Arctic year with the Eskimos at their summer settlement at Kivitung, between Cape Hooper and Broughton Island. On August 28 he boarded a whaling ship, the *Wolf*, and arrived at St. Johns, Newfoundland, on September 7, 1884.

Boas' cartographic work on Baffin Island—his first and only venture in this field—was carried out with the professional competence and skill that characterized his later and better known investigations in such diverse fields as ethnology, archeology, linguistics, folklore, physical anthropology, and statistics. In his travels of some 2,400 miles he had surveyed, under the most difficult conditions, a large part of the largest island in the Arctic Archipelago, comparable in size to the island of Sumatra. He established the existence of and gave their native names to two enormous lakes, Amadjuak and Nettilling, in the interior of Baffin Island, represented on the older charts as a single and incorrectly located Lake Kennedy. His own surveys of Cumberland Sound and the western coast of Davis Strait, based on sixty-one astronomical observations and a great number of magnetical bearings, showed that the existing charts were hopelessly inadequate, bearing "only a small resemblance to the true outlines of the country." Nonexistent fjords, bays, and islands were shown and existing ones omitted. The deeply indented and island-studded west coast of Davis Strait was represented by more or less straight lines. The map accompanying "A Journey in Cumberland Sound and on the West Shore of Davis Strait" shows the great difference between the true configuration of the country as determined by Boas' surveys and that given on the English Admiralty chart. In the map of northern Canada published in 1939 by the Hydrographic and Map Service of the Canadian Department of Mines and Resources, the Cumberland Sound–Davis Strait area is shown just as Boas recorded it.

The distinguished Canadian geologist-geographer, Dr. Robert Bell, Director of the Geological Survey of Canada, comments as follows on Boas' Baffin Island explorations:

Dr. Franz Boaz spent the years 1883–84 in Baffinland, and in winter he travelled extensively by dog-sleigh all along its north-eastern side. We are indebted for most of what we know of

INTRODUCTION

these parts to his observations and maps, published in 1885.
According to these, the mountains form three principal ranges,
all trending north-west, or parallel to the longer measurement
of the island. The highest runs along the north-east coast, facing Baffin bay; the middle range is between Cumberland and
Frobisher sounds, while the third, or southern one, extends
along the north-east side of Hudson strait from Resolution
island to Fox basin. ("A Survey in Baffinland, with a short
Description of the Country," *The Geographical Journal*, Vol.
18, No. 1, pp. 25–43, 1901)

In the maps accompanying *The Central Eskimo*, Boas drew
heavily on information supplied by Eskimo informants for those
parts of Baffin Island and other Arctic areas which he himself had
not visited. One of the most valuable features of these maps are
the red, blue, and black lines indicating the routes of travel followed by the Eskimos in different seasons of the year. The seasonal
movements of the Central Eskimos are essential to an understanding of the distribution, mode of life, and interrelationships of the
various tribal groups. Detailed discussions of these and related subjects are to be found in the introductory sections of this volume
called "Distribution of the Tribes, Influence of Geographical Conditions upon the Distribution of the Settlements, and Trade and
Intercourse between the Tribes." This thoroughgoing analysis of
the relationship between the Eskimos' way of life and the country
in which they live is in itself an admirable study in human geography, and a fitting introduction to the ethnographic sections that
follow.

In the foregoing I have chosen to emphasize Boas' geographical
explorations on Baffin Island mainly for the reason that this important aspect of his work has been largely ignored by those who have
written of his accomplishments in other fields. It is understandable
that Boas' anthropological colleagues should be little interested in
the details of his geographical work. For to anthropologists the primary significance of Boas' year in the Arctic was that this was the
crucial turning point in his career, that here on his first contact
with a primitive people he made the decision to move from study
of the physical sciences, in which he had been trained, to the study
of man, which in the future he was so largely to shape.

HENRY B. COLLINS
Bureau of American Ethnology
Smithsonian Institution

CONTENTS.

CONTENTS.

CONTENTS.

ILLUSTRATIONS.

The Central Eskimo

Introduction

The following account of the Central Eskimo contains chiefly the results of the author's own observations and collections made during a journey to Cumberland Sound and Davis Strait, supplemented by extracts from the reports of other travelers. The geographical results of this journey have been published in a separate volume.[1] A few traditions which were considered unsuitable for publication by the Bureau of Ethnology may be found in the Verhandlungen der Berliner Gesellschaft für Anthropologie, Ethnologie und Urgeschichte, 1887. The linguistic material collected during the journey will be published separately.

Owing to unfortunate circumstances, the larger portion of the author's collections could not be brought home, and it has therefore been necessary, in preparing this paper, to make use of those made by C. F. Hall, 1860–1862 and 1865–1869; W. Mintzer, 1873–'74, and L. Kumlien, 1877–'78. Through the kindness of Professor Otis T. Mason, I was allowed to make ample use of the collections of the National Museum and have attached its numbers to the specimens figured. The author's collection is deposited in the Museum für Völkerkunde at Berlin. I am indebted to the American Museum of Natural History; to Mr. Appleton Sturgis, of New York; to Captain John O. Spicer, of Groton, Conn.; and to Mrs. Adams, of Washington, D. C., for several figures drawn from specimens in their possession.

---

[1] Baffin-Land. Geographische Ergebnisse einer in den Jahren 1883 und 1884 ausgeführten Forschungsreise. Von Dr. Franz Boas. (Ergänzungsheft No. 80 zu „Petermanns Mitteilungen".) Gotha: 1885.

AUTHORITIES QUOTED.

In citing the various authorities, I have used abbreviations as indicated at the end of titles in the following list of works consulted :

De | Martini | Forbisseri | Angli navigati | one in regiones occi | dentis et septen | trionis | Narratio historica, | Ex Gallico sermone in La | tinum translata | per | D. Joan. Tho. Freigivm. | [Design.] | Cum gratia & privilegio Imperiali. cio. io. xxc. [Colophon :] Noribergæ | Imprimebatur, in officina Ca | tharinæ Ger-lachin, & Hære | dum Iohannis Mon | tani. Anno cio io xxc. (Cited, Frobisher.)

A | voyage of discovery, | made under the orders of the Admiralty | in | His Majesty's ships | Isabella and Alexander, | for the purpose of | exploring Baffin's Bay, | and inquiring into the probability of a | north-west passage. | By John Ross, K. S. Captain Royal Navy. | London: | John Murray, Albemarle-street. | 1819. (Cited, Ross I.)

Journal | of a voyage for the discovery of a | north-west passage | from the Atlantic to the Pacific; | performed in the years 1819–20, | in His Majesty's ships | Hecla and Griper, | under the orders of | William Edward Parry, R.N., F.R.S., | and commander of the expedition. | With an appendix, containing the scientific | and other observations. | Published by authority of the lords commissioners | of the admiralty. | London: | John Murray, | publisher to the admiralty, and board of longitude. | 1821. (Cited, Parry I.)

Journal | of a | second voyage for the discovery of a | north-west passage | from the Atlantic to the Pacific; | performed in the years 1821–22–23, | in His Majesty's ships | Fury and Hecla, | under the orders of | Captain William Edward Parry, R.N., F.R.S., | and commander of the expedition. | Illustrated by numerous plates. | Published by authority of the lords commissioners | of the admiralty. | London : | John Murray, | publisher to the admiralty, and board of longitude. | 1824. (Cited, Parry II.)

The | private journal | of | Captain G. F. Lyon, | of H. M. S. Hecla, | during | the recent voyage of discovery under | Captain Parry. | With a map and plates. | London: | John Murray, Albemarle-Street. | 1824. (Cited, Lyon.)

A | brief narrative | of | an unsuccessful attempt | to reach | Repulse Bay, | through | Sir Thomas Rowe's " Welcome," | in | His Majesty's ship Griper, | in the year | 1824. | By Captain G. F. Lyon, R. N. | With a chart and engravings. | London : | John Murray, Albemarle street. | 1825. (Cited, Lyon, Attempt to reach Repulse Bay.)

Narrative | of a | second voyage in search of | a | north-west passage, | and of a | residence in the Arctic regions | during the years 1829, 1830, 1831, 1832, 1833. | By | Sir John Ross, C. B., K. S. A., K. C. S., &c. &c. | captain in the Royal Navy. | Including the reports of | Commander, now Captain, James Clark Ross, R. N., F. R. S., F. L. S., &c. | and | The Discovery of the Northern Magnetic Pole. | London: | A. W. Webster, 156, Regent street. | 1835. (Cited, Ross II.)

A narrative | of some passages in the history of | Eenoolooapik, | a young Esquimaux who was brought to Britain in 1839, in the ship " Neptune " | of Aberdeen. | An account of the | discovery of Hogarth's Sound : | remarks on the northern whale fishery, | and suggestions for its improvement, &c. &c. | By Alexander M'Donald, L. R. C. S. E. | Member of Cuvieran Natural History Society of Edinburgh. | Edinburgh : Fraser & Co. | And J. Hogg, 116 Nicolson Street. | 1841. (Cited, Eenoolooapik.)

Narrative | of | the discoveries | on | the north coast of America; | effected by the | officers of the Hudson's Bay Company | during the years 1836–39. | By Thomas Simpson, esq. | London: | Richard Bentley, New Burlington Street. | Publisher in Ordinary to Her Majesty | 1843. | (Cited, Dease and Simpson.)

Narrative | of an | expedition to the shores | of | the Arctic sea | in 1846 and 1847. | By John Rae, | Hudson Bay Company's service, commander of the expedition. | With maps. | London: | T. & W. Boone, 29, New Pond Street. | 1850. (Cited, Rae I.)

Further papers | relative to the Recent Arctic expeditions | in search of | Dr. John Franklin, | and the crews of | H. M. S. "Erebus" and "Terror." | Presented to both houses of Parliament by command of Her Majesty, | January, 1855. | London: | Printed by George Edward Eyre and William Spottiswoode, | Printers to the Queen's most excellent Majesty. | For Her Majesty's stationery office. | 1855. (Cited, Rae II.)

Same volume: Observations on the Western Esquimaux and the country they inhabit; from Notes taken during two years at Point Barrow, by Mr. John Simpson, Surgeon R. N., Her Majesty's Discovery Ship "Plover." (Cited, Simpson.

The voyage of the 'Fox' in the Arctic seas. | A narrative | of the | discovery of the fate | of | Sir John Franklin | and | his companions. | By Captain M'Clintock, R. N., LL.D. | honorary member Royal Dublin Society. | [Portrait.] | With maps and illustrations. | London: | John Murray, Albemarle street, | publisher to the admiralty. | 1859. (Cited, M'Clintock.)

Life with the Esquimaux: | a narrative of Arctic experience in search of | survivors of Sir John Franklin's | Expedition. | By | Captain Charles Francis Hall, | of the whaling barque "George Henry," | From May 29, 1860, to September 13, 1862. | Popular Edition. | With Maps, | Coloured illustrations, and one hundred wood cuts. | London: | Sampson Low, son, and Marston, | Milton House, Ludgate Hill. | 1865. (Cited, Hall I.)

Tales and traditions | of the | Eskimo | with a sketch of | their habits, religion, language | and other peculiarities | by | Dr Henry Rink | knight of Dannebrog | Director of the Royal Greenland board of trade, and | formerly Royal Inspector of South Greenland | author of 'Grönland geographik og | statistick beckrevest, etc. | Translated from the Danish by the author | Edited by | Dr Robert Brown | F. L. S., F. R. G. S. | author of 'The races of mankind,' etc. | With numerous illustrations, drawn and | engraved by Eskimo | William Blackwood and Sons | Edinburgh and London | 1875. | All rights reserved. (Cited, Rink.)

Eskimoiske | Eventyr og Sagn | oversatte | efter de indfødte fortælleres opskrifter | og meddelelser | af | H. Rink, | inspektør i Sydgrønland. | Kjøbenhavn. | C. A. Reitzels Boghandel. | Louis Kleins Bogtrykkeri. | 1866. (Cited, Rink, Eventyr og Sagn.)

Eskimoiske | Eventyr og Sagn. | Supplement | indeholdende | et Tillæg om Eskimoerne | af | H. Rink. | Kjøbenhavn. | C. A. Reitzels Boghandel. | Louis Kleins Bogtrykkeri. | 1871. (Cited, Rink, Eventyr og Sagn, Supplement.)

Narrative | of the | second Arctic expedition | made by | Charles F. Hall: | his voyage to Repulse Bay, sledge journeys to the Straits [sic] of Fury | and Hecla and to King William's Land, | and | residence among the Eskimos during the years 1864–'69. | Edited under the orders of the Hon. Secretary of the Navy, | by | Prof. J. E. Nourse, U. S. N. | U. S. Naval Observatory, | 1879. | Trübner & Co., | Nos. 57 and 59 Ludgate Hill, | London. (Cited, Hall II.)

Als Eskimo unter den Eskimos. | Eine Schilderung der Erlebnisse | der | Schwatka'schen Franklin-Aufsuchungs-Expedition | in den Jahren 1878–80. | Von | Heinrich W. Klutschak, | Zeichner und Geometer der Expedition. | Mit 3 Karten, 12 Vollbildern und zahlreichen in den Text gedruckten Illustrationen | nach den Skizzen des Verfassers. | Wien. Pest. Leipzig. | A. Hartleben's Verlag. | 1881. | Alle Rechte vorbehalten. (Cited, Klutschak.)

Schwatka's Search | sledging in the Arctic in quest of | the Franklin records | By | William H. Gilder | second in command | with maps and illustrations | London | Sampson Low, Marston, Searle, and Rivington | Crown Buildings, 188, Fleet Street. | All rights reserved. (Cited, Gilder.)

Eskimoisches Wörterbuch, | gesammelt | von den Missionaren | in | Labrador, | re-
vidirt und herausgegeben | von | Friedrich Erdmann. | Budissin, | gedruckt bei
Ernst Moritz Monse. | 1864. (Cited, Wörterbuch des Labradordialectes.)

David Cranz | Historie | von | Grönland | enthaltend | Die Beschreibung des Landes
und | der Einwohner &c. | insbesondere | die | Geschichte | der dortigen | Mis-
sion | der | Evangelischen | Brüder | zu | Neu-Herrnhut | und | Lichtenfels. |
Mit acht Kupfertafeln und einem Register. | Barby bey Heinrich Detlef Ebers,
und in Leipzig | in Commission bey Weidmanns Erben und Reich. | 1765.
(Cited, Cranz.)

Bruchstükke | eines Tagebuches, | gehalten in | Grönland | in den Jahren 1770 bis
1778 | von | Hans Egede Saabye, | vormaligem ordinierten Missionar in den
Destrikten Claushavn | und Christianshaab, jetzigem Prediger zu Udbye | im
Stifte Fühnen. | Aus dem Dänischen übersetzt ⊦ von | G. Fries, | beabschiedig-
tem königlich dänischen Capitaine. | Mit einer Vorrede des Uebersetzers, |
enthaltend einige Nachrichten von der Lebensweise der | Grönländer, der
Mission in Grönland, samt andern damit | verwandten Gegenständen, und
einer Karte | über Grönland. | Hamburg. | Bey Perthes und Besser. | 1817.
(Cited, Egede.)

Baffin-Land. | Geographische Ergebnisse | einer | in den Jahren 1883 und 1884 aus-
geführten Forschungsreise. | Von | Dr. Franz Boas. | Mit zwei Karten und neun
Skizzen im Text. | (Ergänzungsheft No. 80 zu ,,Petermanns Mitteilungen".) |
Gotha: Justus Perthes. | 1885. (Cited, Baffin-Land.)

Die Amerikanische | Nordpol-Expedition | von | Emil Bessels. | Mit zahlreiche Illus-
trationen in Holzschnitt, Diagrammen und | einer Karte in Farbendruck. |
Leipzig. | Verlag von Wilhelm Engelmann. | 1879. (Cited, Bessels.)

Contributions | to the | Natural History | of | Arctic America, | made in connec-
tion with | the Howgate Polar expedition, 1877–'78, | by | Ludwig Kumlien, |
Naturalist of the expedition. | Washington: | Government Printing Office. |
1879.

Report | of the | Hudson's Bay expedition, | under the command of | Lieut. A. R.
Gordon, R. N., | 1884.

Traditions indiennes | du | Canada nord-ouest | par Émile Petitot | Ancien mission-
naire. | Paris | Maisonneuve frères et Ch. Leclerc, | 25, Quai Voltaire, | 1886.

The following is a list of the papers published by the author on
the results of his journey to Baffin Land and of studies connected
with it. The ethnological remarks contained in these brief commu-
nications have been embodied in the present paper. The method of
spelling in the first publications differs from that applied in the
present paper. It was decided to use the latter after a conference
with Dr. H. Rink.

" Reiseberichte aus Baffin-Land." Berliner Tageblatt, August 4, October 28, November 4, November 25, 1883; September 28, October 19, November 2, November 9,
November 16, November 23, December 28, 1884; January 4, April 3, April 27, 1885.

"Unter dem Polarkreise." New-Yorker Staats-Zeitung, February 1, February 22,
March 2, 1885.

"The configuration of Ellesmere Land." Science, February 27, 1885.

" A journey in Cumberland Sound and on the west shore of Davis Strait in 1883
and 1884, with map." Bull. Am. Geogr. Soc., pp. 241–272, 1884.

" Die Wohnsitze und Wanderungen der Baffin-Land Eskimos." Deutsche geogr.
Blätter, p. 31, 1885.

"Cumberland Sound and its Esouimaux." Popular Science Monthly, p. 768, May,
1885.

"Die Eskimos des Baffin-Landes." Verh. des V. deutschen Geographentags zu Hamburg. Berlin, 1885.

"Reise im Baffinlande, 1883 und 1884." Verh. der Ges. für Erdkunde zu Berlin, 1885, Nos. 5, 6.

"Die Sagen der Baffin-Land Eskimos." Verh. der Berlin. anthrop. Gesellschaft, 1885, p. 161.

"The Eskimo of Baffin Land." Transactions of the Anthropological Society of Washington, Vol. 3, pp. 95–102.

"Sammlung aus Baffin-Land." Original Mittheilungen aus der ethnol. Abtheilung der Kgl. Museen zu Berlin, 1886, p. 131.

ORTHOGRAPHY.

In the spelling of Eskimo words the author has adhered as closely as possible to Kleinschmidt's orthography, as he did not deem it proper to introduce a linguistic alphabet after so much has been published in another and almost sufficient one.

Accents and lengths have been marked where it seemed to be desirable. In quotations Eskimo words are spelled according to this system where it is possible to recognize their meaning and derivation. In other cases the original spelling of the authors has been retained. The alphabet used in this paper is as follows:

Vowels: a — a in father.
e — ey in they.
i — ee in feel.
o — o in nose.
u — oo in pool.
au — ow in how.
ai — i in hide.

Consonants: q — a hard, guttural sound (Kleinschmidt's κ).
r — the German guttural r.
rn — a guttural and nasal r.
χ — the German ch in Buch; Scotch ch in loch.
g — English g in go.
k — English k.
ng — English ng in during.
b — English b.
p — English p.
v — pronounced with the lips only.
f — pronounced with the lips only.
m — English m.
d — English d.
t — English t.
s — English s in soul.
n — English n.
(g) dl — ḍ of Lepsius's standard alphabet.
(g)dtl — ṭ of Lepsius's standard alphabet.
l — English l.
j — German j in jung; English y.
ss — š of Lepsius's standard alphabet, sounding between s and sh.

GEOGRAPHY OF NORTHEASTERN AMERICA.[1]

The Eskimo inhabit almost the whole extent of the coast of Arctic America. A large part of this country is occupied by the Central Eskimo, one of the great groups into which that people is divided. They live in the northeastern part of the continent and on the eastern islands of the Arctic-American Archipelago. In Smith Sound they inhabit the most northern countries visited by man and their remains are even found at its northern outlet. The southern and western boundaries of this district are the countries about Fort Churchill, the middle part of Back River, and the coast west of Adelaide Peninsula. Along the whole extent of this line they are the neighbors of Indian tribes, with whom they are generally on very bad terms, a mutual distrust existing between the two races.

The geography of the whole country is known only in outline, and a great portion of it awaits its explorer. Following is a sketch of what is known about it, so far as it is of importance to the ethnologist.

The vast basin of Hudson Bay separates two large portions of the American continent: Labrador and the region of the large Arctic rivers. The southern shore of the bay is inhabited by Indian tribes who interrupt the communication between the Eskimo of both regions. Hudson Bay, however, has the character of a true mediterranean sea, the northern parts of its opposite shores being connected by a number of islands and peninsulas. The low and narrow Rae Isthmus, which presents an easy passage to the Arctic Ocean, unites Melville Peninsula to the main body of the continent. From this peninsula Baffin Land stretches out toward the north of Labrador, with only two narrow channels intervening: Fury and Hecla Strait and Hudson Strait. Another chain of islands, formed by the parts of Southampton Island and Mansfield Island, stretches from Repulse Bay to the northwest point of Labrador, but the distances between the islands and the roughness of the sea prevent communication.

On the western part of the continent the great bays, Chesterfield Inlet and Wager River, are of importance, as they allow the Eskimo, though they are a coast people, to penetrate into the interior of the continent. A narrow isthmus separates the head of the bays from the lakes of Back River. At Coronation Bay the latter approaches the Arctic Ocean very closely, and it is probable that the coast west of Adelaide Peninsula, which is skirted by innumerable islands, is indented by deep inlets extending towards the lakes of Back River. Thus communication between the Arctic Ocean and Hudson Bay is facilitated by this large river, which yields an abundant supply of fish. From Wager River an isthmus leads to its estuary.

Boothia Felix, the most northern peninsula of the continent, is united to it by two narrow isthmuses, the former extending from

---

[1] A glossary of Eskimo geographic terms will be found on p. 254.

Pelly Bay to Shepherd Bay, the latter from Lord Mayor Bay to Spence Bay. It is separated from North Somerset by the narrow Bellot Strait. Farther west Adelaide Peninsula and King William Land form the continuation of the continent toward the western extremity of Boothia, thus outlining a spacious bay sheltered from the currents and the pack ice of Melville Sound and the adjoining bays. The eastern sides of Boothia and North Somerset and the western coasts of Melville Peninsula and Baffin Land form a gulf similar to Fox Basin.

Farther north, between Baffin Land and Greenland, North Devon and Ellesmere Land are situated. Thus Baffin Land forms a connecting link for three regions inhabited by Eskimo: the Hudson Bay Territory, Labrador, and Greenland.

The orography of the western coast of Hudson Bay is little known. Most of this coast seems to form a hilly land, consisting generally of granite. Between Wager River and Chesterfield Inlet it rises to a chain of hills of about one thousand feet in height, extending to a plateau farther north. Another chain seems to stretch in a northeasterly direction from Back River to the source of Hayes River. West of Back River Silurian strata prevail. The granite hills form a favorite haunt for the musk ox and reindeer.

Melville Peninsula consists chiefly of a chain of granite hills, sloping down to a Silurian plain in the eastern part of the peninsula. The northeastern part of Baffin Land is formed by a high chain of mountains stretching from Lancaster Sound to Cape Mercy. Long fjords and deep valleys divide them into many groups. Bylot Island, which stands high out of the sea, is separated from the mainland by Pond Bay and Eclipse Sound. The next group stretches from Pond Bay to the fjord of AnaꞮlereë′ling. Farther to the southeast the groups are smaller, and in Home Bay they are separated by wide valleys, particularly near Eꭓalualuin, a large fjord on the southern side of that bay.

From this fjord an enormous highland, which I named Penny Highland, extends as far as Cumberland Sound, being terminated by the narrow valley of Pangnirtung. The eastern boundary runs through the fjords Maktartudjennaq and Narpaing to Nedluqseaq and Nudlung. In the interior it may extend to about fifteen miles east of Issortuqdjuaq, the most northern fjord of Cumberland Sound. The whole of the vast highland is covered by an ice cap sending forth numerous glaciers in every direction. In Pangnirtung and on Davis Strait they reach the level of the sea.

Penny Highland, which forms the main body of Cumberland Peninsula, has attached to it a few mountain groups of moderate extent: the peninsula of Nudlung and the highland of Eꭓalualuin and that of Qivitung.

Farther southeast, between the valleys of Pangnirtung and Kingnait-Padli, is situated the highland of Kingnait, with sharp peaks emerging from the ice cap which covers the lower parts of the plateau. The rest of Cumberland Peninsula is formed by the highland of Saumia, which much resembles that of Kingnait. Near Cape Mercy the ice covered highland slopes down to a hilly region, which falls abruptly to the sea.

The southern parts of this range of mountains are composed of gneiss and granite. It may be that Silurian strata occur in some places, but they have not yet been found anywhere in situ. The northern parts are too imperfectly known to enable us to form an idea of their geological character.

The mountains just described slope down to a hilly region, which farther to the west levels off to a plain. The hills are composed of granite, the plains of Silurian limestone, which extends from Prince Regent Inlet to the head of Frobisher Bay.

The peninsula between Cumberland Sound and Frobisher Bay is formed by a plateau, which slopes down gradually to the northwest. It is drained by a great river flowing into Auqardneling, a fjord on the western shore of Cumberland Sound. Near Lake Nettilling the country is very low, the level of the lake being only forty feet above that of the sea. Here the watershed between Cumberland Sound and Fox Basin closely approaches the eastern shore, coming within five miles of the head of Nettilling Fjord. It is formed by a narrow neck of land about a quarter of a mile wide and sixty-five feet above the level of the sea.

From Eskimo reports I conclude that the plateau of Nugumiut, as we may call the peninsula between Frobisher Bay and Cumberland Sound, is comparatively level. Only a single mountain south of Qasigidjen (Bear Sound) rises into the region of eternal snow.

The peninsula between Frobisher Bay and Hudson Strait is formed by a granite highland, the Meta Incognita of Queen Elizabeth. It is covered with ice and sends a few glaciers into the sea. Farther west, near Lesseps Bay and White Bear Sound, the country becomes lower. The narrow isthmus leading from Hudson Strait to Amaqdjuaq cannot be very high, as the Eskimo carry their kayaks to the lake, which I believe is about two hundred feet above the level of the sea.

Last of all I have to mention the highlands of King Cape. The rest of the land is taken up by a vast plain in which two large lakes are situated; the southern, Amaqdjuaq, empties by a short river into Lake Nettilling, whence the long and wide Koukdjuaq runs to the shallow sea. From observations made by Captain Spicer, of Groton, Conn., and information obtained from the Eskimo, we learn that the whole of the eastern part of Fox Basin is extremely shallow and that there are many low islands scattered about in those parts of the sea. The plains of Baffin Land, Fox Basin, and the eastern half of Melville Peninsula may be considered a wide basin of Silurian strata bordered by granitic elevations on every side.

Besides the configuration of the land, the extent of the land ice formed during the winter is of vital importance to the inhabitants of the Arctic region, because during the greater part of the year it affords the only means of communication between the tribes, and because in winter the seal, which constitutes the principal food of the Eskimo, takes to those parts of the coast where extensive floes are formed. Therefore the state of the ice regulates the distribution of the natives during the greater part of the year and must be considered in studying the habits of the Eskimo. The extent of the land ice principally depends on the configuration of the land and the strength of the currents. On a shore exposed to a strong current an extensive floe can only be formed where projecting points of land form deep bays. We find the distribution of ice regulated in accordance with this fact all around the shores of the Arctic Ocean.

The strong current setting out of Lancaster Sound and Smith Sound generally prevents ice from forming under the steep cliffs of the land. Sometimes the pack ice of the sounds is stopped and freezes together into rough floes; a smooth plain is never formed. By far the largest land floe is formed from Bylot Island to Cape Dyer (Okan). In Home Bay it extends to a distance of about eighty miles from the mainland. The formation of this floe is favored by a number of shoals which extend from the peninsulas of Cape Eglinton (Aqojang), Cape Aston (Niaqonaujang), and Qivitung, for the large floes drifting south are stopped by the icebergs aground on these banks. The greater part of the floe is very rough, smooth ice prevailing only in the bays.

The strong southerly current passing through the narrowest part of Davis Strait between Cape Walsingham (Idjuk) and Holsteinborg breaks up the ice all along the shore from Cape Dyer to Cape Walsingham, Exeter Sound alone being covered by a larger floe. The bay between Cape Mickleham (Nuvuktirpang) and Cape Mercy is well covered with ice, which extends to the islands farthest out toward the sea.

Near Cape Mercy the strong tides caused by Cumberland Sound prevent the ice from consolidating in the entrance of the gulf. As the sound widens greatly behind the narrow passage formed by Nuvukdjuaq and Qaχodluin, the tide sets in with great force. For this reason the floe never extends beyond that narrow entrance. Often the head of the open water runs from Qeqerten to Nuvujen, and instances are known where it even reaches the line of Pujetung-Umanaq.

The southwestern shore of Cumberland Sound from Qaχodluin to Cape Brevoort (Qeqertuqdjuaq) is always washed by water, because a strong current, which often breaks up the ice of Field and Grinnell Bay (the bays of Ukadliq and Nugumiut), sets along the coast.

The floe seldom extends to Lady Franklin and Monumental Islands (Kitigtung and Taχolidjuin), but usually runs from point to point, compelling the natives to pass across the land in order to reach the floe of the neighboring bay. Most of the time the edge of the floe covering Frobisher Bay extends to a line from Countess of Warwick Sound (Tuarpukdjuaq) to about fifteen miles southeast of Gabriel Island (Qeqertuqdjuaq), whence it runs south to Kingnait. Sometimes Aqbirsiarbing (Cape True) is the most eastern point inclosed by the ice. A dangerous current sets through the strait between Resolution Island (Tudjaqdjuaq) and the mainland, forming whirlpools which menace every ship that attempts the passage.

Hudson Strait never freezes over. The greater part of the year it is filled with an immense pack which never consolidates into a continuous floe. As there are no large bays along the northern shore of that strait, no land floes of great importance are formed. Only the Bay of Qaumauang, North Bay, and Behm Bay (the bay of Quaiirnang and that east of Akuliaq) are covered with floes which are of importance to the natives. The bays east of Akuliaq and the large fjords of that region form a comparatively large body of ice.

Probably no land ice is formed between King Cape ₍Nuvukdjuaq₎ and the northern parts of Fox Basin. According to Parry and the reports of the natives, Fury and Hecla Strait and the bay which forms its eastern outlet are covered by land ice which is connected with the floe of the bays of Fox Basin as far as Piling.

In Hudson Bay there are very few places in which the land ice extends to a considerable distance from the shore. Neither Frozen Strait nor Rowe's Welcome freezes over, each being kept open by the swiftly running tides. The most extensive floes are formed in Repulse Bay, Wager Bay, and Chesterfield Inlet.

The drifting ice of the Gulf of Boothia never consolidates and even Committee Bay is rarely covered by a smooth land floe. Pelly Bay and the sea on the east coast of Boothia as far as Victoria Harbor (Tikeraqdjuq) freeze over, since they are sheltered by numerous islands. Still larger is the sheet of ice which covers the bay formed by the estuary of Back River, King William Land, and Boothia. The western shore of this peninsula farther north is skirted by a border of land ice the extent of which is unknown.

It is a remarkable fact that, although the extreme western and eastern parts of the country abound with extensive floes, the Hudson Bay region and the Gulf of Boothia are almost devoid of them.

This brief sketch will enable one to understand the geographical distribution and the migrations of the Eskimo tribes who inhabit this country.

DISTRIBUTION OF THE TRIBES.

GENERAL OBSERVATIONS.

The mode of life of all the Eskimo tribes of Northeastern America is very uniform ; therefore it is desirable to make a few general observations on the subject before entering into a detailed description of each tribe. All depends upon the distribution of food at the different seasons. The migrations or the accessibility of the game compel the natives to move their habitations from time to time, and hence the distribution of the villages depends, to a great extent, upon that of the animals which supply them with food.

As the inhospitable country does not produce vegetation to an extent sufficient to sustain life in its human inhabitants, they are forced to depend entirely upon animal food. In Arctic America the abundance of seals found in all parts of the sea enables man to withstand the inclemency of the climate and the sterility of the soil. The skins of seals furnish the material for summer garments and for the tent; their flesh is almost the only food, and their blubber the indispensable fuel during the long dark winter. Scarcely less important is the deer, of whose heavy skin the winter garments are made, and these enable the Eskimo to brave the storms and the cold of winter.

That the mode of life of the Eskimo depends wholly on the distribution of these animals will therefore be apparent, for, as already observed, they regulate their dwelling places in accordance with the migrations of the latter from place to place in search of food.

When the constraint of winter is broken the natives leave their old habitations. The warm rays of the sun melt the roofs of their snow houses, the strong vaults which afforded shelter and comfortable warmth during the long cold winter begin to break down, and new houses must be built. They therefore exchange the solid snow houses for light tents, which are very small and poor, until a sufficient number of sealskins for better structures is secured.

As at this time seals are found in abundance everywhere, basking in the warm sunshine and enjoying the beginning of the spring, a great supply is easily secured. As the season advances food becomes more plentiful, and with the breaking up of the rivers and ponds the salmon leave the latter and descend to the sea. About this time the Eskimo establish their settlements at the head of the fjords, where salmon are easily caught in the shallow rivers. In July the snow, which has covered the land for nine months, has melted away and the natives undertake hunting trips inland, in order to obtain the precious skins of the reindeer and the meat of the fawns, which is always highly prized. With the breaking up of the ice the variety of food is further increased by the arrival of the walrus and the ground and harp seals, which leave the country during the winter. Birds are also found in abundance, and no cares afflict the natives.

Before the sea begins to freeze over again the Eskimo return from deer hunting and gather at places where there are the best chances for obtaining food in the autumn. A few weeks are spent in making short excursions near the settlements, as longer journeys would be too dangerous during this tempestuous season. The colder it grows the more the natives are confined to their huts and the more they become dependent on the seal. While in summer shrubs of various kinds are available for cooking purposes, in winter blubber affords the only fuel for cooking and for heating their huts.

At last the smaller bays are sufficiently frozen to permit a new way of pursuing the game. The hunters visit the edge of the newly formed floe in order to shoot the seals, which are secured by the harpoon.

The process of freezing goes on quickly and the floating pieces of ice begin to consolidate. Only a few holes are now found, in places where icebergs, moved by the tides or the strong currents, prevent the sea from freezing. During a short time these openings form the favorite hunting ground of the natives. Though the walrus and the ground seal migrate to the edge of the floe as soon as the ice begins to form, the common seal (*Pagomys fœtidus*) remains, and this is always the principal food of the natives. In the autumn the fjords and the narrow channels between the islands are its favorite haunt; later in the season it resorts to the sea, frequently appearing at the surface through breathing holes, which it scratches in the ice. As winter comes on it is hunted by the Eskimo at these holes.

The foregoing observations will serve as a preliminary to the description of the distribution of the tribes of Northeastern America. The object of this section is to treat of the immediate relations between the country and its inhabitants, and a detailed account of their habits will be found in subsequent pages.

According to Dr. H. Rink, the Inuit race may be divided into five groups : the Greenlanders; the central tribes of Smith Sound, Baffin Land, the west shore of Hudson Bay, the Back River region, and Boothia; the Labradorians, on the shores of that peninsula; the Mackenzie tribes of the central parts of the north shore of America; and the tribes of Alaska. I am somewhat in doubt whether the central tribes and those of Labrador differ enough to justify a separate classification, as the natives of both shores of Hudson Strait seem to be closely related. A decisive answer on the division of these tribes may be postponed until the publication of Lucien M. Turner's excellent observations and collections, which were made at Fort Chimo.

BAFFIN LAND.

The Sikosuilarmiut.— I shall begin with the enumeration of the tribes in the southwestern part of Baffin Land. This country is inhabited by the Sikosuilarmiut, i. e., the inhabitants of the shore without an ice floe. They are settled in two places: Nurata, east of King Cape, and Sikosuilaq, within the peninsula (or island?) which projects east of King Cape. The large fjords Sarbaq and Sarbausirn, which belong to their territory, are known to me only by a description which I received in Cumberland Sound. In summer they visit the upper parts of this long fjord to hunt deer on the plains which reach to the shore of Fox Basin. Probably they do not extend their migrations very far to the north or northeast; otherwise, they would reach Lakes Amaqdjuaq and Nettilling, the region about the latter being the hunting ground of the natives of Cumberland Sound.

I know of only a single meeting between the Eskimo visiting Lake Nettilling and others who are supposed to have come from Hudson Strait. It occurred in 1883 south of the lake.

The Akuliarmiut.—This tribe is settled on the northern shore of Hudson Strait. Their winter resort lies west of Qeqertuqdjuaq (Parry's North Bluff). In summer they travel through White Bear Sound or Lesseps Bay to Lake Amaqdjuaq, which they reach after crossing a neck of land about ten miles in width. The exact direction of the road cannot be ascertained, as the position of their starting point, which is called Tuniqten, is doubtful. Crossing a short portage they ascend to Lake Amitoq, whence on a second portage they pass the watershed between Lake Amaqdjuaq and Hudson Strait. From the small Lake Mingong a brook runs into Sioreling and thence into Lake Amaqdjuaq (Baffin-Land, p. 67). On the southern shore of the large lake they erect their summer tents. Farther east, in North Bay, there is another winter residence of the same tribe. Unfortunately, I cannot specify the place of this settlement, which is called Quaiirnang.

The Qaumauangmiut.—East of the Akuliarmiut live the Eskimo so frequently met near Middle Savage Islands. Their principal residence is near Lake Qaumauang, from which they take their name Qaumauangmiut. My investigations concerning these tribes were much embarrassed by the want of trustworthy charts. If charts are tolerably well delineated, the Eskimo understand the meaning of every point and island and can give detailed accounts of the situation of the settlements and the migrations of the inhabitants.

Between Sikosuilaq and Akuliaq but a moderate amount of intercourse is kept up, as the settlements are separated by a wide and uninhabited stretch of land. Notwithstanding this many members of one tribe are found to have settled among the other. An American whaling station which was established in Akuliaq a few years ago may have had some influence upon the distribution and the life of these tribes. The greater importance of Akuliaq, however, cannot be ascribed to the presence of the whalers alone, as a few harbors near Sikosuilaq are also frequently visited by them. The whalers report that there are about fifty inhabitants in Sikosuilaq, about two hundred in Akuliaq, and farther east fifty more. Thus the population of the north shore of Hudson Strait probably amounts to three hundred in all.

The Qaumauangmiut are probably closely related to the Nugumiut of Frobisher Bay.

The Nugumiut.—I can give a somewhat more detailed description of this tribe, among the families of which Hall passed the winters of 1860–'61 and 1861–'62 (Hall I). Unfortunately, he does not give any coherent account of their life, only meager information being furnished in the record of his journeys. Besides, generalizations cannot be made from his two years' experience. My own observations in Cumberland Sound may serve as a complement to those of Hall. As he gives only a few native names of places, it is sometimes difficult to ascertain the exact position of the localities to which he alludes.

According to Hall and my own inquiries four places are inhabited by this tribe almost every winter: Tornait (Jones Cape of Hall), about thirty-five miles above Bear Sound, in Frobisher Bay; Operdniving and Tuarpukdjuaq, in Countess of Warwick Sound; Nugumiut, in (Cyrus W.) Field Bay; and Ukadliq, in (Cornell) Grinnell Bay. As these bays open into Davis Strait the formation of the ice is retarded and its extent diminished, and consequently some peculiarities in the arrangement of the life of the Eskimo are observed here. The only occupation of the Nugumiut and the inhabitants of Ukadliq is sealing with the harpoon on the floe of the inner parts of the bay. Near Ukadliq the tide holes east and west of Allen Island abound with seals. In winter, when the seals take to the open ice, the village of this group of families is established near Roger's Island, where the floe of the bay forms the hunting ground of the natives.

During the autumn the Nugumiut stay in Field Bay. The women are then busy preparing the deerskins; for, on account of the requirements of their religion, the walrus hunt cannot be begun until the deerskins which were taken in summer have been worked up for use. As soon as this is done they travel across Bayard Taylor Pass (so called by Hall) to Frobisher Bay, and in the latter half of December or in the beginning of January settle on Operdniving or on Tuarpukdjuaq in company with the natives who stay here during the fall. In Cumberland Sound I learned that this changing of the habitations takes place almost regularly and that sometimes the settlement is moved to Aqbirsiarbing (Cape True) if the bay is frozen over beyond Operdniving. In traveling to Aqbirsiarbing the tide holes of Ikerassaqdjuaq (Lupton Channel) are avoided by using the pass of Chappell Inlet. Here and in Tornait the natives go sealing on the ice or walrusing at the edge of the floe, which in most cases is not very far off.

About the latter half of March part of the Eskimo begin to travel up Frobisher Bay. In the middle of April, 1862, Hall found a settlement on Qeqertuqdjuaq (Gabriel Island), from which island the floe edge was visited and young seals were caught in the narrow channels between the numerous islands. Towards the end of the month a portion of the natives went farther to the northwest in pursuit of the basking seals (I, p. 470), intending to reach the head of the bay in July. Hall found summer habitations at Ukadliq (I, p. 468); on Field Bay (p. 296); and on Frobisher Bay at Agdlinartung (p. 308), Opera Glass Point (p. 341), Waddell Bay (p. 341), and Nuvuktualung, on the southern point of Beecher Peninsula (p. 348).

A very important hunting ground of the inhabitants of Tiniqdjuarbiusirn (Frobisher Bay), of which I received some detailed accounts, is Lake Amaqdjuaq. In the foregoing remarks on the Akuliaq tribe I described the course which leads from Hudson Strait to the lake. Another route is followed in traveling from the head of Frobisher Bay to Lake Amaqdjuaq, a distance of about fifty miles. Probably the men leave Sylvia Grinnell River and ascend to Lake Amartung, from which lake a brook runs westward to Lake Amaqdjuaq (Baffin-Land, p. 68). The women take a different route and arrive at Aqbeniling after a tramp of six days, near a small bay called Metja. Here the summer huts are erected and birds and deer are killed in abundance.

The facility in reaching the lake from Hudson Strait and Frobisher Bay is a very important consideration, as the Akuliarmiut and the Nugumiut meet here, and thus an immediate intercourse between the tribes is opened. The inhabitants of Hudson Strait leave Tuniqten in spring, arrive at the head of Frobisher Bay in the fall, and after the formation of the ice reach the Nugumiut settlements by means of sledges. When Hall wintered in Field Bay a traveling party of Sikosuilarmiut which had accomplished the distance from King Cape in one year arrived there (I, p. 267).

Another route, which is practicable only for boats, connects Qaumauang with Nugumiut. It leads along the shore of Hudson Strait. The traveler sails through the dangerous passage between Tudjaqdjuaq (Resolution Island) and the mainland and crosses Frobisher Bay either at its entrance or in the shelter of the group of islands farther up the bay.

In their intercourse with the Nugumiut, the inhabitants of Cumberland Sound generally follow the long coast between Ukadliq and Naujateling, passing through the numerous sounds formed by long, narrow islands. I can describe this region from personal observations.

The Oqomiut.—The Eskimo of Davis Strait call the tribes of Cumberland Sound and Saumia by the name of Oqomiut. The whole of the land from Prince Regent Inlet to the plateau of Nugumiut is divided by the Eskimo into three parts, Aggo, Akudnirn, and Oqo—i. e., the weather side, the center, and the lee side—and accordingly the tribes are called the Aggomiut, Akudnirmiut, and Oqomiut.

Unquestionably the whole of Cumberland Sound and the coast of Davis Strait from Cape Mercy to Exeter Sound belong to the Oqo of the Northern Eskimo. Farther north, the inhabitants of Padli extend their migrations from Qarmaqdjuin to Qivitung. These people occupy an intermediate position between the Akudnirmiut and the Oqomiut, having easy communication with both, and consequently it is doubtful to which they belong, so that the determination of the boundary between Oqo and Akudnirn remains arbitrary. In regard to their customs and from the position of the land, however, they may be more properly joined to the Akudnirmiut, of whom they would form a subdivision.

The names Oqo, Akudnirn, and Aggo must not be understood as respectively meaning a region strictly limited: they denote rather directions and the intervals between the localities situated in these directions. In asking for the position of Oqo one would be directed southeast, as this is considered the lee side; in the same way, if asking for Aggo, one would be directed to the shore of Prince Regent Inlet, the farthest land in the northwest, the weather side. In Cumberland Sound the natives of Iglulik are considered Aggomiut, while in Pond Bay they are known as a separate tribe. In the southern parts the whole of the northern region is comprised in the name Aggo; in the north Oqo means the whole of the southeastern regions.

Formerly, the Oqomiut were divided into four subtribes: the Talirpingmiut, on the west shore of Cumberland Sound; the Qinguamiut, at the head of it; the Kingnaitmiut, on the east shore; and the Saumingmiut, on the southeastern slope of the highland of Saumia. The names are derived from the districts which they inhabit, respectively. As the head of every fjord is called "qingua" (its head), the upper part of the large Cumberland Sound is also so named. The Qingua region may be limited by Imigen on the western shore and Ussualung on the eastern shore, though the name is applied to a region farther north; indeed, the name covers the whole district at the head of the sound. In looking from the head to the entrance of the sound the coasts are called according to their position: the southwestern Talirpia, i. e., its right one, and the northeastern Saumia, i. e., its left one; between Saumia and Qingua the highland Kingnait, i. e., the higher land as compared to the opposite shore, is situated.

Although at the present time this division is hardly justifiable, the names of these four tribes are often mentioned on the shore of Davis Strait. Their old settlements are still inhabited, but their separate tribal identity is gone, a fact which is due as well to the diminution in their numbers as to the influence of the whalers visiting them.

In my opinion a great difference between these tribes never existed. Undoubtedly they were groups of families confined to a certain district and connected by a common life. Such a community could more easily develop as long as the number of individuals was a large one. When the whalers first wintered in Cumberland Sound the population may have amounted to about 1,500. In 1840, when Penny discovered the sound, he met 40 Eskimo in Anarnitung (Eenoolooapik, p. 91). The greater number of the inhabitants were at the head of the fjords fishing for salmon, others were whaling in Issortuqdjuaq, and some were inland on a deer hunting expedition. The whole number at that time probably amounted to 200. A few years later the Kingnaitmiut of Qeqerten were able to man eighteen whaleboats. Assuming five oarsmen and one harpooner to each boat, the steersman being furnished by the whalers, and for each man one wife and two children, we have in all about 400 individuals. The inhabitants of Nettilling Fjord may have numbered as many, and 100 are said to have lived in Imigen. Penny found in Ugjuktung about 30 individuals who belonged to the Saumingmiut and had come thither from Davis Strait. Accordingly I estimate the whole tribe at 150 individuals. On the southwestern coast of the sound between Nuvujen and Naujateling a large number of natives were reported. They lived in three settlements and numbered about 600. These estimates are not absolutely reliable, as they are compiled largely from hearsay and conjecture. Many of the natives being away in the summer, at the time when these estimates were made, accuracy in their preparation was impossible. From inquiries which were made among American whalers who had visited this sound since 1851, the population of Qeqerten must have been larger than that of any of the settlements contiguous to the sound. The estimation is the more difficult as a few settlements were sometimes deserted; for instance, Ukiadliving, in Saumia, and Qarmaqdjuin (Exeter Bay). Probably eight settlements, with a population of 200 inhabitants each — i. e., 1,600 in the sound — would be about the true number in 1840. At first I was inclined to believe in the existence of a larger number, but from later reports I should consider this number too large rather than too small. Since that time the population has diminished at a terrible rate. In 1857 Warmow, a Moravian missionary who accompanied Penny, estimated it at 300. If this was correct, the rapid diminution must have occurred during the first years after the rediscovery of the sound. In December, 1883, the Talirpingmiut numbered 86 individuals, the Qinguamiut 60, the Kingnaitmiut 82, the Saumingmiut 17; total, 245. These were distributed in eight settlements. Beginning with the most southern settlement, the Talirpingmiut lived in Umanaqtuaq, Idjorituaqtuin, Nuvujen, and Qarussuit; the Qinguamiut, in Imigen and Anarnitung; the Kingnaitmiut, in Qeqerten; the Saumingmiut, in Ukiadliving. Accordingly the population of the settlements numbered as follows:

Name of the settlement.	Married.		Unmarried.						Total.
	Men.	Women.	Widowers.	Widows.	Men.	Women.	Boys.	Girls.	
Naujateling	6	6	1	..	......	1	3	3	20
Idjorituaqtuin ..	3	3	....	1	1	....	2	1	11
Nuvujen	8	8	1	2	1	....	4	2	26
Qarussuit.......	10	10	....	2	......	....	2	5	29
Imigen.	6	6	....	....	....	....	4	1	17
Anarnitung.....	12	12	1	1	1	....	8	8	43
Qeqerten........	26	26	....	6	4	....	9	11	82
Ukiadliving.....	6	6	....	1	......	1	2	1	17
Padli...........	11	13	2	2	1	....	7	7	43
Akudnirn	8	12	....	....	2	....	(18)		40
Total......	96	102	5	15	10	2	(98)		328

I have included in the foregoing table the inhabitants of Davis Strait and may add that the Nugumiut number about 80, the Eskimo of Pond Bay about 50 (?), those of Admiralty Inlet 200, and of Iglulik about 150. The total number of inhabitants of Baffin Land thus ranges between 1,000 and 1,100.

The reason for the rapid diminution in the population of this country is undoubtedly to be found in the diseases which have been taken thither by the whalers. Of all these, syphilis has made the greatest ravages among the natives. Of other diseases I am unable to give a full account and can only refer to those which came under my observation during the year that I passed in this region. In Qeqerten a man died of cancer of the rectum, two women of pneumonia, and five children of diphtheria, this disease being first brought into the country in 1883. In Anarnitung I knew of the death of two women and one child. On the west shore a number of children died of diphtheria, while the health of the adults was good. In the year 1883–'84 I heard of two births, one occurring in Qeqerten, the other in Padli. At Qarussuit and Anarnitung there were two abortions.

The opinion that the Eskimo are dying out on account of an insufficient supply of food is erroneous, for, even though the natives slaughter the seals without discrimination or forethought, they do not kill enough to cause any considerable diminution in numbers. The whalers do not hunt the seal to any extent, and when one realizes how small the population of the country is and how vast the territory in which the seal lives it is easy to understand that famine or want cannot arise, as a rule, from the cutting off of the natural food supply. In fact, in the spring enormous numbers of seals may be seen together basking in the sun or swimming in the water.

The causes of the famines which occur somewhat frequently among the Eskimo must be sought in another direction. Pressing need often prevails if in the latter part of the autumn the formation of the floe is retarded; for in that case hunters are not able either to go hunting in boats or to procure the necessary food at the edge of the floe, as new ice is attached to its more solid parts and the seals do not yet open their breathing holes. Such was the case at Niaqonaujang, on Davis Strait, in the fall of 1883. Gales of wind following in quick succession broke the floe. The new ice which had formed immediately prevented the natives from sealing, and in November and December a famine visited the settlement. Very soon the supply of blubber was exhausted, and being unable to feed the dogs the inhabitants were obliged to kill them one after another and to live upon their frozen carcasses. Only two dogs survived these months of need and starvation. Consequently the hunting season was a very poor one, since the natives missed the services of their dogs, which scent the breathing holes, and could not leave their settlement for any great distance.

In winter a long spell of bad weather occasions privation, since the hunters are then prevented from leaving the huts. If by chance some one should happen to die during this time, famine is inevitable, for a strict law forbids the performance of any kind of work during the days of mourning. When this time is over, however, or at the beginning of good weather, an ample supply is quickly secured. I do not know of any cases of famine arising from the absolute want of game, but only from the impossibility of reaching it.

Sometimes traveling parties that are not acquainted with the nature of the country which they visit are in want of food. For instance, a large company, consisting of three boat crews, were starved on the eastern shore of Fox Basin, their boats being crushed by the heavy ice and the game they expected to find in abundance having left the region altogether. On one of the numerous islands of Nettilling a number of women and children perished, as the men, who had been deer hunting, were unable to find their way back to the place in which they had erected their huts.

Another case of starvation is frequently mentioned by the Eskimo. Some families who were traveling from Akuliaq to Nugumiut passed the isthmus between Hudson Strait and Frobisher Bay. When, after a long and tedious journey, they had reached the sea, the men left their families near Qairoliktung and descended with their kayaks to Nugumiut in order to borrow some boats in which they could bring their families to the settlements. On the way they were detained by stormy weather, and meanwhile the families were starved and resorted to cannibalism. One woman especially, by the name of Megaujang, who ate all her children, was always mentioned with horror.

Generally food is plentiful between the months of April and October and an ample supply may be secured without extraordinary exertion. During the winter sealing is more difficult, but sufficiently successful to prevent any want, except in the case of continuous bad weather.

I shall now proceed to a description of the single settlements of Cumberland Sound. Separated from the Nugumiut by a long and uninhabited stretch of land we find the settlement of Naujateling, the most southern one of the Talirpingmiut. In the fall the natives erect their huts on the mainland or on an island near it, as the seal, at this season, resort to the narrow channels and to the fjords. Besides, the shelter which is afforded by the islands against the frequent gales is an important consideration, and in these protected waters the natives can manage their frail boats, which would not live for a moment in the tempestuous open sea. Later in the season the ice consolidates in the shelter of the islands, while beyond the bays and channels drifting floes fill the sea.

After the consolidation of the pack ice the natives move their huts to the sea. They leave Naujateling about December and move to Umanaqtuaq. I do not know exactly where they live if the water reaches that island. Should this happen, the floe between Qaχodluin, Umanaqtuaq, and Idjorituaqtuin would offer a productive hunting ground.

About the middle of March the season for hunting the young seal opens. The hunt is prosecuted with much energy over the entire extent of Cumberland Sound, because the white coat of the young animal is of prime importance for the inner garments. The pregnant females take to the rough ice, where deep snowbanks have been formed by the winter gales, and dig large excavations, in which parturition takes place. Another favorite place is the ground ice on gradually declining shores, where large caves are found between the broken pieces of ice. Therefore the fjords and islands which offer a long coast line furnish a good hunting ground, and in the latter part of March and in April the Eskimo either visit these regions or the floes of rough ice. At such times they sometimes live for a long period on the ice of the open sea in order to be nearer to their hunting ground. As the success of the hunt depends on the extent of ice visited, the Eskimo scatter over a large area, almost every one traveling over a separate tract.

At this time the winter settlements are almost totally broken up.

Some of the natives of Naujateling go bear hunting instead of "young sealing," but only a few polar bears lose their way into Cumberland Sound. They are generally found within a few miles of the floe edge, and even if the water reaches pretty far up the sound they do not travel beyond Qaχodluin and Miliqdjuaq, nor does the pack ice carry them far up the sound in summer. On one occasion, in the year 1880, three bears were seen near Qeqerten, about five years earlier one was killed in Qingua, and almost twenty years earlier another one near Anarnitung. Every occurrence of this kind is considered an event of such importance that it is talked about for years afterwards. I myself saw bear tracks in Kouaqdjuaq in March, 1884, and also at Miliqdjuaq. In February a bear was killed between Kautaq and Naujateling.

If the water washes the foot of the cliffs between Kautaq and Sulung, the Eskimo cross the isthmus which lies between Ijelirtung, the eastern branch of Qasigidjen, and Qaχodluin Bay on a sledge road and hunt among the islands that are scattered along the shore south of Qaχodluin. In summer they visit the same region on their hunting excursions.

The principal summer settlements are at the head of Qasigidjen and Kangertlung Fjords, which are situated near Idjorituaqtuin and Qimissung.

From here they ascend the plateau of Nugumiut and hunt on the level highlands. I think it takes them but a day to travel to the top of the plateau. They travel from Qasigidjen to Agdlinartung, a fjord of Frobisher Bay, whence the Nugumiut ascend the highland. Another route leads from Kangertlung to Eχaluin, near the head of Frobisher Bay.

Farther up the sound we find the winter settlement of Idjorituaqtuin. The same relation exists between this place and Qimissung as between Umanaqtuaq and Naujateling. On Qimissung, which lies near the mainland, the natives gather in the fall after returning from deer hunting, and only move to Idjorituaqtuin after the freezing up of the sea. Deer are hunted inland, the summer settlements being at the head of one of the numerous fjords of the west shore. Favorite places are Kangertlung, which is also visited by the Naujateling Eskimo; Eχaluin, which can be reached from Kangertlung by a short overland road; Auqardneling; and Utiqimitung, at the entrance of Nettilling Fjord. A large river, which, according to Eskimo reports, runs through the greater part of the peninsula, empties into Auqardneling. As it is very deep and wide it cannot be crossed without a vessel of some character, and thus it puts a stop to the migrations from Kangertlung and Eχaluin. In traveling from Kangertlung to Frobisher Bay the river must be crossed. To accomplish this the natives fill a deerskin with shrubs, sew it up, and float themselves across. Only the road leading from Qasigidjen to Frobisher Bay avoids the river.

North of Idjorituaqtuin we find the winter settlement of Nuvujen with the fall settlement, Nuvujalung, a high cliff at the entrance of Nettilling Fjord, belonging to it.

By far the most interesting branch of the Talirpingmiut are the inhabitants of Nettilling Fjord. Among all the tribes of Baffin Land this one claims particular attention, as it is the only one whose residence is not limited to the seashore. From Greenland to the mouth of the Mackenzie only two Eskimo tribes are known who do not live all the year round on the coast of the sea. These are the Talirpingmiut and the Kinipetu of Chesterfield Inlet. Back and Anderson and Stewart say that the latter tribe spend a great part of the year at the lakes of Back River.

Formerly the Talirpingmiut had three or four settlements on Lake Nettilling: at Tikeraqdjung, near the south point of the lake; at the outlet of Koukdjuaq, on the left bank of the river, opposite to Nikosiving Island; at Qarmang ; and probably a fourth one, on the north shore. As the lake abounds with seals, they could live here at all seasons. Its western part seems to have been particularly fitted for winter stations. In the winter of 1877–'78, three families staid near Koukdjuaq without encountering any considerable difficulty in procuring food. This was the last time that natives passed the winter at the lake; the greater portion of the tribe may have retreated to Nettilling Fjord about twenty years ago.

Though the Eskimo assert that the discovery of Lake Nettilling is of recent date, naming two men, Kadlu and Sagmu, as those who first reached it, this assertion is not trustworthy, for with them almost every historical tradition is supposed to have originated a comparatively short time ago. I was told, for instance, that an event which is the subject of the tale Igimarasugdjuqdjuaq the cannibal occurred at the beginning of this century, and yet the tradition is told almost word for word in Greenland and in Labrador.

Just so with Kadlu and Sagmu. According to the assertion of the natives the lake was discovered by the generation before the last — i. e., about 1810 — and yet an old woman about seventy-five years of age told me that her grandfather when a young man, starting from Nettilling, had visited Iglulik and that he had lived on the lake. The customs and habits of the Eskimo would have led to the discovery of the lake very soon after the first visit to Cumberland Sound, and no doubt their attention was then called to the abundance of game in this region.

The greater part of the natives spent the winter in Nettilling Fjord, starting on their way inland about the beginning of May, and returning to the sea about December. I suppose that cases in which men spent their whole life on the lake were exceptional, for they are referred to by the natives as remarkable events. For instance, a man called Neqsiang, who had two wives, lived on a small island near

Koukdjuaq and never descended to Cumberland Sound. A few times only he is said to have sent his son to barter with the Talirpingmiut of Nettilling Fjord. He came to Qarussuit in the spring, but returned after a short stay. It may be remarked here that the total absence of salt does not prevent the natives from staying on Lake Nettilling.

About 1850 the mode of life of the Talirpingmiut was as follows: In November they gathered in Isoa, the easternmost bay of the lake, descended toward the sea, and lived during the following months at the entrance of Nettilling Fjord. There they lived in the same manner as the other Oqomiut, pursuing the seals at their breathing holes. In the spring they hunted young seals; but, when the other natives began to prepare for whaling, they traveled on sledges westward. They avoided the large tide holes of the long fjord by making use of a few passes. Although the fjord is impassable in spring, a safe road leads along its northern shore to its northern branch, Kangertlukdjuaq, where the water hole Sarbaqdualung may be avoided by crossing the land at Tunukutang. In the spring large water holes are formed near Neqemiarbing and at the entrance of Audnerbing, compelling travelers to pass over the island which separates the two passages of Sarbaqdualung. The pass Tunukutang, which is used in winter, consists of a steep and narrow neck of land, which separates a small lake from Kangertlukdjuaq, and a short and winding river, the outlet of the lake. The second tide hole of the fjord may be passed by the branches Qasigidjen and Sarbaqdjukulu and the adjoining flat isthmus. The holes of Qognung, yet farther up the fjord, do not hinder the natives, as they do not occupy the whole width of the floe.

At length they reached Kangia, and from here a chain of small lakes was ascended, the watershed Ujaraqdjuin was crossed, and finally they arrived at Amitoq. Cairns are everywhere erected on prominent points for way marks. After they had come to Lake Nettilling, they rested a short time at Isoa, where the skin boats and the necessary household goods had been left the preceding fall. These were lashed upon the sledges and then they traveled as quickly as possible to the west. After following the southeastern shore to Tikeraqdjuaq they crossed the lake to a point near Tikeraqdjung, whence they went along the southern shore of the lake, reaching Koukdjuaq in about a fortnight. Here their tents were established on the left bank of the river, opposite to Nikosiving, where they staid until the breaking up of the ice. Then the men descended the river in their kayaks. Four days they followed the coast, passing the bay of Aggirtijung before they reached Qudjitariaq, a long and deep river, which they ascended. For a few weeks they hunted deer among the lakes of this region, which is called Majoraridjen, and then slowly turned southward. At last, about the latter half of August, they reached Qarmang, where at the beginning of summer the women and old men had arrived in their large boats. Here the whole party stopped until the lake was frozen up. Then they returned on sledges to Isoa and to the sea.

It would be very interesting to learn how far the natives formerly extended their migrations along the shore of Fox Basin and whether a regular intercourse existed between Iglulik and Cumberland Sound. According to reports of some old Eskimo, who had themselves passed the winter on the lake, there was always a small settlement at Qarmang. From here the shore of Fox Basin was reached with great ease. If, however, the route through Koukdjuaq had to be taken, a long, roundabout way was necessary. According to all reports, even in olden times expeditions to Iglulik were very rare. It is said that one was made about 1750 by a party under the leadership of an Eskimo, Makulu. About 1800 another party left, in which Kotuko assumed the leadership. About these a more detailed account exists. With a few boats and four kayaks they left Nettilling and followed the coast. Alone in his kayak, Kotuko visited Sagdlirn, an island east of Iglulik, but he did not see any people, as they were on a hunting excursion. He found one hut and a large dog. There were a great number of deerskins and walrus tusks, which proved the existence of an abundance of game. He returned, but on account of the prevailing fog could scarcely find his kayak. The absence of the party is said to have lasted three years.

About 1820 another party left for Iglulik, among whom two women, Amaroq and Sigjeriaq, were the most prominent. When they returned, after an absence of three years, they praised the country (Piling), where they had spent some time, as a land of plenty and abundance, and by these tales, in 1835, induced three boat crews to leave Nettilling in order to visit this happy land. They were grievously disappointed and after many misfortunes they perished on the narrow isthmus of Ipiuting. Their bodies were found by the Iglulik Eskimo, who related that the poor fellows had resorted to cannibalism. Among those who perished was a sister of the famous Hannah (Taqulitu), the companion of Hall in his travels in the Arctic. I must mention here that Hall, in 1868, met a native at Iglulik who was said to belong to Cumberland Sound. As, however, in Iglulik Cumberland Sound and Davis Strait are often confounded, I am inclined to think he was a native of the latter region.

From these facts it appears that a regular intercourse between the tribes along the shore of Fox Basin never existed, though formerly interviews were more frequent than they are at present. Since the last mentioned expedition no Eskimo has visited Piling, nor have any gone by the way of Lake Nettilling to Iglulik. Accordingly the ideas of the Oqomiut about that region are very indefinite. An old man was the only person whom I could find who knew Iglulik by name and remembered Ingnirn and Piling, two places which had been inhabited by many Eskimo. He mentioned another inhabited region beyond Iglulik, Augpalugtijung, which I was not able to identify. It was described as a large peninsula.

It is worth remarking that the Talirpingmiut seem never to have traveled over the country south of Koukdjuaq. I have not even heard mentioned a single hunting excursion made in this direction.

In the foregoing paragraphs I have described the mode of life of the greater part of the Talirpingmiut. Still another part staid in Cumberland Sound until the ice had gone and went away in the latter half of July. The passage through the rapids of the fjords was very dangerous, as in the whirlpools and overfalls the bulky boats were easily capsized. Therefore the changing of the tides had to be considered in order to effect a safe passage. The men preferred carrying the kayaks over the passes in order to avoid the dangers imminent to their frail crafts. Even up to this day tradition tells of a disaster which happened when the stubborn owner of a boat, against the warning of his friends, tried to pass Sarbaqdualung when the spring tide was running swiftly. The boat was upset and the crew were drowned, with the exception of one woman, who was saved on a bundle of deerskins.

From Kangia boats had to be carried over the portages Igpirto, Igpirtousirn, and Ujaraqdjuin. The rapids of Angmartung were also avoided by a portage over the level bottom of the valley. After passing Taquirbing, Lake Nettilling was reached, on the shore of which the huts were erected. In the fall the party returned before the beginning of the cold season. It has been already mentioned that only a few of the natives staid at the lake during the entire year, and even among these there were some who descended to the sea in March to take part in the young sealing, for the skins of the young seal cannot be altogether replaced by deerskins.

At the present time it is exceptional for any one to remain inland during the entire year. There may be seals enough in the lake to prevent hunger or starvation, but they are taken much more easily from the sea. In case of a lack of blubber, deer's marrow may be used for fuel. It is probable that the high mortality of recent years has induced the Eskimo to band together more closely than they formerly did and to adopt the plan of returning to Nettilling Fjord at the beginning of winter. In the fall the boats and other articles which are of no use in winter are left in Isoa, and some time is spent in Kangia, where snow houses are built. Here the kayaks are left, and in December, when the sealing begins to be more successful near the sound, the Eskimo turn to the entrance of Nettilling Fjord, where Tininiqdjuaq and Neqemiarbing are favorite places. Seals are hunted there with the harpoon in the same way as in the other settlements or Sarbaqdualung is visited for the purpose of shooting seals which frequent the tide holes. This, however, is not a favorite way of hunting, as the ice near the tide holes is very rough and treacherous.

In March and April young seals are caught on the shores of the numerous islands between Tininiqdjuaq and Nuvujalung, and at the same time the old settlements are left, as large water holes begin to appear. Qarussuit and Qingaseareang are the favorite places about this time of the year.

As soon as the young sealing is finished the hunt of the basking seal is opened, which is very successful here. Nowhere else did I see such large numbers of animals enjoying the warmth of the sun as in Nettilling Fjord. In April, when on the east shore scarcely any dared to leave the water, hundreds might be seen here. By the first of May all the natives have procured a sufficient number of sealskins for their summer dress, the skins being then in the best condition, as the first moulting has just occurred. This done, they eagerly prepare for the journey to the lake.

The natives start in the first week of May, and in two or three days arrive at Kangia, whence they reach Isoa in one day's journey. Following the southern shore of Lake Nettilling they sleep the first night on Tikeraqdjuausirn, the second on the island Manirigtung, near Tikeraqdjuaq, and five days after leaving Qarussuit arrive at Tikeraqdjung, where they settle for the summer. As numerous deer are found in this region, they live without any care or trouble. Very soon after their arrival the birds return. While moulting great quantities of these are caught. The geese are so abundant here that they are fed to the dogs. Many deer are caught while passing the deep river which runs from Lake Amaqdjuaq to Lake Nettilling. Frequently they visit the southern plains, which are filled with lakes and lakelets. Sometimes they go as far as Amaqdjuaq, which, as the older natives report, was formerly a summer settlement.

In the river whose outlet is near Padli salmon are caught in abundance. In this district the Talirpingmiut stay until the eastern part of the lake is frozen over.

In the shelter of the islands the floe is more quickly formed than in the open water of the western part, and in November the natives return by sledges to Isoa.

As they take with them heavy loads of deerskins they make very slow progress and generally arrive at their place of destination after six days of traveling. Sometimes they make a short trip to Isoa in March or April to hunt deer or to look for the things which were left behind in Kangia and Isoa at the time of their last departure.

Besides the Talirpingmiut quite a number of Cumberland Sound natives visit the lake by means of boats. They cross the sound after the breaking up of the ice and go to Nettilling, carrying the boats over the portages between Kangia and Isoa. As the Talirpingmiut have no boats they stay at Tikeraqdjuaq; the other natives, however, sometimes change their habitations and even visit Qarmang and the north shore of the lake. These journeys, however, are rare, for in the eastern part an inexhaustible supply of food may be obtained; therefore long excursions are quite unnecessary. At the beginning of October the boats leave the lake and the natives return to the fall settlements in the sound.

Nettilling Fjord, with its numerous islands, forms the northern boundary of Talirpia. Farther north we come to Qingua, the head of Tiniqdjuarbing (Cumberland Sound). It extends from Imigen to Ussualung. The winter settlement on the island of Imigen is situated in the midst of one of the best winter hunting grounds, for the southern portion of the island, on which the huts are erected, projects far out into the sea. The hunt is often rendered somewhat difficult by the rough ice which is due to the strong currents between Pujetung, Imigen, and Nettilling Fjord. Towards spring the natives sometimes resort to a place yet nearer the open sea, the largest island of the Pujetung group. Young seals are caught near Imigen, at the Kilauting Islands, and in Qaggilortung. This district, however, cannot be visited every year, as almost every spring the whole area west of a line from Imigen to Anarnitung is covered with very deep and soft snow, which prevents the Eskimo from using their dog sledges. When this condition prevails the natives settle on the sea ice between Augpalugtung and Imigen, or a little farther north, and remain there from the middle of March until the latter part of April.

These natives go deer hunting either to Issortuqdjuaq—where they live at Eχaluaqdjuin, Sirmiling, or Midlurieling—or to Eχaluqdjuaq, near Ussualung, where they hunt in the hilly land adjoining the ice-covered Penny Plateau. As the land farther northwest is said to consist of irregular hills and disconnected valleys, the skins and the meat of the killed deer would have to be carried up and down hills before the settlement was reached. Therefore the natives dislike hunting in this part of the country.

Eχaluaqdjuin and Eχaluqdjuaq, as is denoted by the names, are productive salmon rivers. In starting from the former and ascending a narrow valley, Lake Eχoleaqdjuin is reached, whence a pass leads to the valley adjoining Eχaluaqdjuin. Taking another road the long Lake Imeraqdjuaq is reached, which borders upon the glaciers of the highland. From here, after a four days' tramp following a large river, the traveler comes to Midlurieling. From Issortuqdjuaq a narrow isthmus offering a good sledging road is used in visiting the head of Qaggilortung. Another route, which is suitable only for foot passengers, leads by a chain of lakes to the head of Kangertlukdjuaq. It is not necessary to enumerate the overland routes in this district, as numerous valleys permit the traveler to pass from the east to the west and from the south to the north. In the fall the natives resort to Saunirtung or to Saunirtuqdjuaq, two islands northwest of Imigen, where they stay until January, when they return to the sea.

The second settlement of the Qinguamiut is Anarnitung, at the northern entrance of Qaggilortung. The small island and the neighboring point of Igdlungajung are, next to Qeqerten, the seat of the most important settlement of Cumberland Sound. On the southern and eastern declivity of the low hills which form this island are a number of very old stone foundations (see p. 141), such as are found everywhere on the Arctic shores of North America (Baffin-Land, p. 77).

If the ice in the upper parts of the sound is smooth, families belonging to this community settle on Kilauting, the largest island of a group running from northwest to southeast a few miles north of Imigen. Here they go sealing with the harpoon. If the ice, however, is rough (as it happened to be during my stay in Cumberland Sound), they remain in Anarnitung, whence some go to the water holes at the entrance of Issortuqdjuaq and shoot the blowing seals, while others go hunting on the ice near Anarnitung.

During the young sealing season they almost always leave the island. The favorite resort at this season is Sakiaqdjung, near Manituling, in Qaggilortung, but heavy snowfalls often compel them to exchange this region for the open sea. If they insist upon stopping there, snowshoes are used as the only means of traveling in the deep and soft snow. In 1878, when the Florence wintered in Anarnitung Harbor, the greater part of the natives remained near the ship; but her presence is accountable for this exception, as some of the families were in her service and others staid near her in order to barter seals, skins, &c.

Of some importance are the passes leading around the numerous water holes at the head of Cumberland Sound. The narrow island of Nudnirn, which separates Sarbuqdjuaq from Putukin, offers a good passage by way of a deep valley. Should the passage be made in a mild winter or in spring, when the water holes of Sarbuqdjuaq have enlarged, they must avoid the latter by passing over the inconvenient isthmus of Itidliaping, west of the steep cliff Naujan.

In spring the tide holes of Kangidliuta extend over the passage between that island and Surosirn, preventing sledges from passing to Issortuqdjuaq or to Tessiujang. Then Qaχodlualung is crossed by the way of Naqoreang or the more southerly Tappitariaq, which leads into the sound near Siegtung. Both passes are very inconvenient. From Tessiujang, Issortuqdjuaq may be reached by the fjords Ugjuktung and Itijareling and by the adjoining passes.

Lastly, I have to mention the road formerly used by the natives of Anarnitung in traveling to Nettilling. They crossed the entrance of Qaggilortung and ascended Tarrionitung, whence they came by the Lakes Qamusiojodlang and Irtiujang to Missirtung, in Nettilling

Fjord, thus avoiding a much longer journey around the large peninsula projecting to the eastward. A similar pass farther east connects Tornait and Kangertlukjuaq.

The ruins of a third settlement of the Qinguamiut are found at Tulukan on Qeqertelung.

The next subtribe to be treated is the Kingnaitmiut, who are now located exclusively upon Qeqerten. Formerly they lived in several places — for instance, near Pangnirtung and on Miliaqdjuin — but for a long time they have gathered on Qeqerten, as two whaling stations are established here, many natives being in the service of the whalers. The island is the largest settlement of the sound. It is a favorite resort during the fall and the first part of winter. In November and December, before the ice of the sound consolidates, the ice east of the islands is the best hunting ground. Later that west of the islands is preferred. There is one disadvantage peculiar to Qeqerten which is not shared by the other settlements, namely, the fohn-like winds which often blow for many days from Kingnait Fjord with irresistible violence. These confine the natives to their huts, though a few miles north or south calm weather prevails. Should fair weather ensue, the snow, which has been firmly packed by these gales, affords a good hunting ground ; but if, on the other hand, long spells of bad weather follow, want and hunger may be the result. The young seals are eagerly pursued all about Qeqerten.

In Pangnirtung and in the little valley Niutang, in Kingnait, well up in these fjords, are the ruins of two large, ancient settlements. The conditions which formerly enabled the natives to live here will be mentioned later.

The Kingnaitmiut go deer hunting to Kitingujang, at the head of Kingnait Fjord; to Nirdlirn, in the bay behind Augpalugtung and Sednirun; to Pangnirtung; or to the more southern fjords Eχaluaqdjuin and Kangertlukdjuaq.

I shall describe the districts occupied by the Kingnaitmiut, Saumingmiut, and Padlimiut together, as they all bear a uniform character.

From Nirdlirn the mountains of Ussualung or the highland near Ukiuqdjuaq are visited. The same country is traveled over from Pangnirtung, where the settlement is established either above Qordlubing or opposite Aulitiving. The deep valley, with its numerous glaciers, adjoining Pangnirtung and connecting Cumberland Sound and Davis Strait is rarely visited.

The favorite place for the settlement is Kitingujang in Kingnait. In the river which empties here many salmon are caught, and the declivities of the neighboring highlands, which are less steep than those of Pangnirtung, afford ample opportunity for long hunting excursions. Deer are found on the mountains, for here they escape the mosquitoes which swarm in the valleys. The natives do not go beyond Padli, but most of them have been there. They often travel through the valleys of Nerseqdjuaq and Tunussung to Pangᴄirtung, of Davis Strait, down the eastern shore of which they go a considerable distance. Sometimes they make boat excursions during the summer from Kitingujang, visiting the brooks which empty into Kingnait Fjord, or they settle in Tornait, whence Tupirbikdjuin in Pangnirtung is accessible by the wide valleys surrounding Angiuqaq.

I may omit the description of the separate summer habitations farther south, for the head of every fjord and every valley that is a means of reaching the interior are used for erecting the tents. The interior of the region, which is covered with ice, remains unvisited, no game being found there. Therefore it may be said in general that the Eskimo are limited to the peninsulas formed by the numerous fjords.

The Saumingmiut visit the southern fjords of Cumberland Peninsula, where I have marked the settlements on the chart. Here they pursue deer and polar bears, which frequently come down to Cape Mercy during the summer.

An important summer settlement of the Saumingmiut is Touaqdjuaq, from which place they visit the peninsula limited by Exeter Sound and Touaqdjuaq. An important summer station of both Saumingmiut and Padlimiut is Qarmaqdjuin, while Eχaloaping (Durban Harbor of the whalers), near the entrance of Padli, is visited only by the latter tribe.

The number of deer on Cumberland Peninsula is so variable that the result of the hunt is often unsatisfactory. Although in some seasons numerous herds are met, in others scarcely enough animals are killed to afford a sufficient stock of skins for the winter clothing. Early in the spring the deer pass quite regularly through Itidlirn (the lower part of Padli Valley, between Ikaroling and Padli), in their migrations from Narpaing to Qarmaqdjuin. I was told that in both the latter districts many deer can be found at all times.

Lastly, I have to describe the winter settlements of the Saumingmiut. They are in the habit of separating in the fall, part of them staying during winter on Qeqertaujang, in Ugjuktung, and the remainder at Ukiadliving, on Davis Strait.

Strange as it may seem, walrus are not found in the upper part of the sound, while farther south they are abundant. Akuliaχating, east of Qeqerten, is the most northern point that they visit. It is said that in former times they were met with everywhere in the sound, and indeed some of the local names give evidence of the truth of these traditions; for instance, the name of Uglirn (which is always applied to walrus islands), in the fjord Qaggilortung, and that of Anarnitung (a place having a bad smell from walrus excrement), at the head of the sound.

Before Cumberland Sound begins to freeze up, the Eskimo of Ug-juktung take walrus on the islands Uglirn, south of Qeqertaujang, and at Qeqertaq in Anartuajuin. The animals killed during the fall are buried under stones, and with this stock of provisions the Saumingmiut do not suffer want during the winter. In addition, however, they go sealing at the entrance of Ugjuktung, or travel overland to Kangertloaping, a branch of Kouaqdjuaq, as Nuvukdjuaq is almost always washed by water and cannot be passed in winter. The young sealing is here of little importance, as the bears visit the fjords about this season and frighten the animals away. In March the natives go bear hunting or move up the sound to join the King-naitmiut during the time of young sealing. In the spring the settle-ment is always abandoned, as most of them go to Davis Strait and join the other part of the tribe. Crossing the country, they travel over a pass leading from Anartuajuin to Ujaradjiraaitjung.

The favorite settlement on the east coast is Ukiadliving. There are several stone foundations in this place which are frequently reconstructed and used as dwellings. Here walrus are hunted in the summer and in the fall and a great stock of provisions is laid up. In winter the floe offers a good hunting ground for sealing and in the spring the bears visit the land and the islands to pursue the pupping (i. e., pregnant or parturient) seals. At the same time the she bear brings forth her young, the meat and skin of which are highly prized. Many old bears and cubs are killed at this season and the precious skins are prepared for sale.

Besides the beforementioned route another and longer one leads to Cumberland Sound. In taking this course the sledges start from Nedluqseaq, west of Ukiadliving, and follow a river which rises in a small lake whence the inland ice is ascended. Farther on the valley leading to Eχaluaqdjuin and Kangertlukdjuaq is reached. This is the only overland route on which the inland ice is crossed. Cape Mercy can be passed by a number of short isthmuses. In the shelter of the bay formed by the cape and Muingmang a floe is formed reach-ing to the foot of Uibarun (Cape Mercy). The pass Tappitaridjen, which cuts off two peninsulas, leads into the sound. The bays farther west are frozen up and the projecting points are avoided by short passes. Unfortunately this road was unknown to me during my stay in Saumia, else I could have easily visited Cape Mercy. At last Anartuajuin is reached. The water rarely extends to Nuvuk-djuaraqdjung, the point between Anartuajuin and Ugjuktung. It may be passed by a difficult road leading across the peninsula. If the water extends to Iliqimisarbing a pass is used which is ascended from Eχalualuin, in the bay of Naujaqdjuaq.

On Davis Strait a few important isthmuses must be mentioned. One is used by the inhabitants of Ukiadliving in traveling to Exeter Sound. They leave the sea at the head of Touaqdjuaq and by a difficult overland route cross to the southern shore of Exeter Sound. Much of the time the ice and snow near Udlimaulitelling make the route almost impassable in that direction. If, therefore, this route is impracticable or that through Touaqdjuaq is too difficult on account of the absence of snow, the journey is postponed until late in spring, when the hummocks begin to be leveled off and the snow becomes harder as it settles; then the rough ice can be passed, and after reaching Ituatukan, a fjord near Cape Walsingham, the Eskimo ascend it, so as to avoid the cape, which is always washed by water. If snow and ice are in a suitable condition the passage by way of Ituatukan is always preferred.

From Exeter Sound Kangertlukdjuaq, in Padli Fjord, may be reached by a pass of short extent; but the snow is always so deep here that the passage cannot be effected until June. The peninsulas between Padli Fjord and Exeter Sound, which have no ice foot, can be crossed by narrow isthmuses near the head of the bays.

Before leaving Cumberland Sound and its inhabitants, the Oqomiut, altogether, I wish to add a few remarks on the whale fishery, which the Eskimo formerly carried on in their bulky skin boats. They pursued the monstrous animal in all waters with their imperfect weapons, for a single capture supplied them with food and fuel for a long time. I do not know with certainty whether the natives used to bring their boats to the floe edge in the spring in order to await the arrival of the whales, as the Scotch and American whalers do nowadays, or whether the animals were caught only in summer. On Davis Strait the Padlimiut and the Akudnirmiut used to erect their tents in June near the floe edge, whence they went whaling, sending the meat, blubber, and whalebone to the main settlement. In Cumberland Sound whales were caught in all the fjords, particularly in Kingnait, Issortuqdjuaq; and the narrow channels of the west shore. Therefore the Eskimo could live in the fjords during the winter, as the provisions laid up in the fall lasted until spring. If, therefore, there is a perceptible diminution in the supply of their food it is due to the fact that the whale fishery has been abandoned by them or rather has been yielded up to Europeans and Americans. It is not probable, however, that a sufficient number of whales were ever caught to support the entire population during the whole of the winter. The whaling is still kept up by the Eskimo of Hudson Strait and Hudson Bay, though only to a limited extent, owing to the visits of whaling ships and the establishment of whaling stations.

The Padlimiut and the Akudnirmiut.—The next tribes to be described are the Padlimiut and the Akudnirmiut, but this may be done very briefly, as the nature of this region is similar to that of Saumia. A peculiarity of the Akudnirmiut is their more decided migratory character as compared with the Oqomiut. They do not spend every winter at the same place, as we observed that the Oqomiut do, but are more inclined to visit, in turn, the different winter stations of their country.

In summer the following places are almost always inhabited: Qarmaqdjuin, Eχaloaping in Padli Fjord, Qivitung, and Niaqonaujang. The deer hunting season opens here at the same time as farther south, but it is much facilitated from the fact that the ice breaks up later. The deer visit the numerous islands scattered along the mainland and thus their pasturing ground is easily reached. As the islands of Home Bay constitute a good hunting ground the Eskimo sometimes settle there for a few weeks.

The long, low peninsula Pamiujang, near Nedluqseaq, and the head of Nudlung are the favorite summer settlements of the Padlimiut. Nudlung, Eχalualuin, Ijelirtung, and Inugsuin are visited by the Akudnirmiut. An abundance of deer is found along the southern part of Home Bay, where the plains extend to the sea. It is remarkable that all along this shore there is no island on which birds build their nests. Though fowls do not form an important constituent of the food of the Oqomiut and the more southern tribes, the egg islands are frequently visited. On Davis Strait it is only by chance that ducks &c. are caught, and eggs can scarcely be obtained. The only island which is visited by birds is Avaudjelling, in Home Bay. In July, however, large flocks of eider ducks descend Itirbilung Fjord and many are caught near its head. From this fjord an overland route, which is practicable only in summer, leads to Piling, a district on the shore of Fox Basin, which may be reached in three days. Though the route is well known, it seems to be passing into disuse; at least I do not know any natives who have crossed the land by it. Another interesting road leading overland must be mentioned, namely, the one which leads from Nudlung and Eχalualuin to Majoraridjen and Nettilling. The former region is still visited by the Akudnirmiut, but I know of but one family who went to Nettilling and wintered there.

As a rule, about the beginning of August the Akudnirmiut move to Niaqonaujang in order to have an opportunity of meeting the whalers on their way south. For the same reason the southern families gather at Qivitung.

As soon as the sea is frozen up, part of the natives of Qivitung move southward and settle on Qeqertuqdjuaq, where they stay until February, while in spring some stay here or move farther up the bay, where they establish their huts on Qeqertaq; the rest travel to Padli Fjord and live with the families who had passed the winter there on Padloping. As the floe edge approaches the land here, the country is favorable for bear hunting, which is pursued in March and April. In June the natives move up Padli Fjord to catch salmon, which are found in enormous numbers at Padli. A few visit Agpan, where flocks of loons nest. The natives who intend to return to Qivitung in summer leave about the end of May or the beginning of June.

Those who remain at Qivitung during the winter go sealing in the bay east of the peninsula and subsist upon the product of this occupation, as well as on the walrus meat which was stored up in the summer and autumn. A few leave Qivitung after the consolidation of the floe and settle on Nanuqtaqdjung, an island in Home Bay, near the northern point of Qeqertalukdjuaq.

In the winter the Akudnirmiut of Niaqonaujang generally remove to Ipiutelling, on the southern shore of Koukteling, and in May go farther south, to the island Avaudjelling. In the spring they go bear hunting on Koukteling and the peninsula of Niaqonaujang, where the she bears dig holes in the snow banks, in which they whelp.

Though the isthmuses are of great value in facilitating the intercourse between the separate settlements of Cumberland Sound and Davis Strait, as their headlands are washed by water, they are not indispensable for the tribes of Davis Strait, for the ice is passable at all points. The low peninsulas are crossed by the natives in their travels in preference to rounding their headlands. Thus they not only shorten their journey, but they avoid the rough ice often found off the points.

For example, a pass leads from the western bay of Padli Fjord to Kangertloaping, and another from Tessiujang, near Qivitung, across the narrow and low isthmus into Home Bay. Similar passes are used in crossing Koukteling, the peninsulas of Niaqonaujang, Aqojang, and Aqojartung.

At Niaqonaujang I reached the limit of my travels and have only to add reports which I obtained from other tribes and in other settlements. River Clyde and Aqbirtijung are not always inhabited, but are visited at irregular intervals by the Akudnirmiut, the same who usually stay at Niaqonaujang. It is probable that Aqbirtijung and Kangertlualung are sometimes visited by the Tununirmiut of Pond Bay.

The Aggomiut.—I can say but little about the two subtribes of the Aggomiut (the Tununirmiut and the Tununirusirmiut), as the reports are scanty and the chart of the region is too incorrect to convey any exact information. A few statements may be derived from the Eskimo charts published by Hall (II, pp. 356 and 370). It appears that the natives winter near the entrance of Navy Board Inlet and in the back of Eclipse Sound. Settlements of the Tununirusirmiut at the western entrance of Admiralty Inlet and near its head are mentioned by Hall. Besides seals these natives also pursue the white whales and narwhals which frequent the sound. In summer the Tununirmiut live at the entrance of Pond Bay.

Although I am not informed as to the position of the settlements, and for this reason am unable to judge of the details of the life of the Aggomiut, I can give the more general facts of their relations to the neighboring tribes. Of the greatest importance is their connec-

;ion with the Iglulirmiut, for through them a regular intercourse
.s kept up between the continent of America and the eastern shore of
Baffin Land.   One road leads through Kangertlukdjuaq, a fjord east
of Parry's Murray Maxwell Inlet, to the head of Anaulereëling.   I
received a detailed description of this road from a native whom I met
at Niaqonaujang.   Hall's statement that this way leads to Pond
Bay is very likely erroneous, as the natives probably said that it led
to Tununirn, which comprises the whole district of Eclipse Sound
and the region east of it.   It is possible that another road leads to
Eχaluin, a fjord of Eclipse Sound.   Another route which is often used
leads from Kangertlung, Parry's Gifford River, to Angmang, and
farther west to Tununirusirn.   This route has already been described
by Parry, who attempted to reach the north shore of Baffin Land by
it (II, p. 449).   Parry's description was confirmed in 1869 by Hall
(II, p. 356).   I am somewhat doubtful whether Fury and Hecla Strait,
which is often filled with rough ice, can be passed regularly, and
whether a route leading to Tununirusirn follows the shore of the Gulf
of Boothia, as stated by some of the natives of Davis Strait.   This
uncertainty did not occur to me until after I had read Parry's description.   Communication between Tununirn and Tununirusirn is
by way of the isthmus between Kangertlung and Navy Board Inlet.

The journeys of the Aggomiut are not at all confined to Baffin Land.
In favorable winters they cross Lancaster Sound, passing the small
island Uglirn, and winter on the eastern half of Tudjan (North Devon).
While here they keep up some intercourse with the inhabitants of
Umingman Nuna (Ellesmere Land).

It is said that they cross the ice covered island on sledges.   In four
days they reach the northern shore, whence a long, narrow peninsula,
Nedlung, stretches toward Ellesmere Land.   Through the narrow
passage which separates Tudjan from Nedlung runs a very swift tide
which keeps open a water hole throughout the winter.   All around
this place the ice wastes quickly in the spring and a large basin is
formed which abounds with seals.   Only that part of the peninsula
which lies nearest North Devon is high and steep, presenting a bold
face.   Farther north it is rather low.

Having reached Umingman Nuna, the Eskimo who gave me this
information affirm that they fell in with a small tribe who resided
on this shore.   Here they lived for some time, as there was an abundance of seals during the whole year.   Farther northwest is a large
fjord, Kangertluksiaq, off which an island is found, Qeqertakadlinang by name.   The Eskimo do not visit the land on the other side
of this fjord, as bears are said to be very numerous and large there.
Though these migrations to Jones Sound do not occur very frequently, they have by no means been discontinued.   For instance,
a family which was well known to me has visited Smith Sound, and

the father of some friends of a resident of Cumberland Sound returned about fifteen years ago from a long stay on Tudjan and Nedlung.

The Iglulirmiut.—The last group of natives belonging to Baffin Land are those of Iglulik. Our knowledge of this tribe is due to Parry and Hall. As soon as the sea begins to freeze up, the natives gather on Iglulik, where they hunt the walrus throughout the winter. According to the position of the floe edge, Iglulik, Pingitkalik, or Uglit Islands are the favorite settlements. Later in the winter, when new ice is frequently attached to the floe, part of the families move to the ice northeast of Igluling, where seals are caught with the harpoon. Another winter settlement seems to be near Amitoq. In April young seals are hunted in the bays and fjords, particularly in Hooper Inlet. According to Hall the western coast of Melville Peninsula is sometimes visited during the winter for walrusing and bear hunting (II, p. 343). An overland route leads to this district, crossing the long Grinnell Lake and Brevoort River, thus named by Hall (II, p. 342). As soon as the warm season approaches the natives go deer hunting on Melville Peninsula or more frequently on Baffin Land. From the reports of Parry and Hall and from my own inquiries, there can be no doubt that they visit the eastern shore of Fox Basin.

The Pilingmiut.—Two tribes were settled on the eastern coast of Fox Basin, the Pilingmiut and the Sagdlirmiut, who had but slight intercourse with the Iglulirmiut. I heard both mentioned at times when traveling along Davis Strait. According to my information I should say that Piling is about 74° west and 69° north. From Parry's reports it appears that the intercourse between these tribes and Iglulik was not very active; for, although he had staid two years at Aivillik and Iglulik, the Pilingmiut when visiting the latter tribe did not know anything about this fact, which was one of the greatest importance to all the natives (II, p. 430). Sometimes the Talirpingmiut of Cumberland Sound meet the Pilingmiut, for both tribes go deer hunting northwest of Nettilling. I heard of one such meeting between hunting parties in that district.

The Sagdlirmiut.—The information as to the Sagdlirmiut is yet more scanty than that relating to the inhabitants of Piling. Parry learned that Sagdlirn is about east-northeast of Iglulik (II, p. 549). The description which I received on Davis Strait confirms this opinion, for the direction was denoted as qaningnang, i. e., east-northeast; besides, Sagdlirn was described as a long and narrow island.

WESTERN SHORE OF HUDSON BAY.

A remarkable difference exists between the customs of the western tribes who live on the continent of America and those of the tribes that inhabit Baffin Land and Melville Peninsula. This is chiefly due to the difference in the nature of their territorial surroundings and to the presence of the musk ox, which they frequently hunt. In addition, the tribes of the continent do not hunt the seal in the winter, laying up instead their supply of meat and blubber in the fall. The information in regard to two of these tribes is quite complete, as they have been visited by explorers frequently and at all seasons. The two tribes referred to are the Aivillirmiut, of the northwestern part of Hudson Bay, and the Netchillirmiut of Boothia Felix. Unfortunately the information in respect to the others, the Kinipetu or Agutit, the Sinimiut, Ugjulirmiut, and Ukusiksalirmiut, is less complete.

The Aivillirmiut.—In order to describe the mode of life of the Aivillirmiut I shall give an abstract of Dr. John Rae's observations in 1846–'47 and 1854–'55, of C. F. Hall's life with these natives from 1864 to 1869, and of Lieut. F. Schwatka's residence among them from 1877 to 1879. A pretty correct idea of the migrations and favorite resorts of this tribe at the different seasons may be obtained from the journals of these travelers.

When Rae arrived in Repulse Bay in the latter part of July, 1846, he met with twenty-six natives who were deer hunting among the numerous lakes of Rae Isthmus (I, pp. 35, 40, 48). Another part of the tribe had resorted to Akugdlit, where they hunted the musk ox near Point Hargrave (I, p. 49). Committee Bay (Akugdlit) was filled with a heavy pack about that time, and the natives hunted walrus in their kayaks (I, p. 58). Wherever they killed a deer or musk ox they made deposits of the meat and carefully put up the walrus blubber in sealskin bags for use during the winter. When, about the end of September, the deer were migrating southward and new ice was forming on the lakes, the natives settled in the center of that part of the country which had been their hunting ground during the summer, in order to be near their depots. For this reason they were well scattered all over the country, some establishing their tents on the lakes of the isthmus, others staying on the shore of Repulse Bay, where large deposits of deer meat and blubber had been made. During the winter most of the natives gathered in one settlement east of Fort Hope (near Aivillik), whence they started to bring in their deposits. About the 20th of February they scattered all over the bay (I, p. 91), but it is doubtful whether they did this in order to be nearer their depots or to go sealing. In March the first deer of the season were seen (I, p. 93), but it was not until April that larger herds passed Repulse Bay on their migration northward (I, p. 99). At this time a small supply of trout was procured from Christie Lake, but it was not sufficient for the support of the natives (I, p. 99). Caches of venison were made and frequently visited until late in June (p. 166). The sealing had begun in the beginning of May (p. 135), when the first animals were seen basking on the ice. But

the Eskimo were now almost independent of their old food supply
When the salmon left the lakes and the deer were roaming among
the hills the time of plenty was at hand. The salmon creeks were
visited, deer were caught, and seals pursued on the ice (p. 170). Al
though the first deer were caught in traps in May, the principal sea
son for deer hunting opened after the breaking up of the ice, when
they were easily taken while crossing the lakes.

When Rae wintered the second time in Repulse Bay (1854–'55) he
was much surprised to find no natives there. They had wintered
farther south, and did not come to the bay until May, 1855, when
they could catch seals on the land ice. In 1864, when Hall arrived
at Wager River, Repulse Bay was again deserted. This year of
Hall's stay in Hudson Bay is very instructive, as we learn from his
account the particulars of the migration of the Aivillirmiut from Nu
vung to Repulse Bay. The following facts are taken from his
journal:

In June, 1865, a traveling party arrived in Repulse Bay (Hall II.
p. 177), where numerous deer were met with. Their tents were
erected on Uglariaq, whence seals were pursued, and they began at
once to make blubber deposits (p. 179). They were very eager to
store as much provision as possible, as there was no chance of obtaining a fresh stock at Repulse Bay during the winter. Some of
the party brought their boats to the floe edge in order to follow the
seal and walrus, which were swimming in the water or lying on the
drifting ice in great numbers, while others preferred sledging on the
land floe and shooting the basking seals (p. 181). After the breaking up of the ice, whales were seen, and kayaks and boats were made
ready for their pursuit. In September most of the natives returned
to North Pole Lake to hunt deer at the lower narrows (p. 202), where
the meat was deposited for winter use (p. 204).

On the 19th of October the last deer was killed (p. 205), and most
of the natives returned to the bay. They located at Naujan, the men
in the party numbering 43 (p. 216). During the winter no kind of
hunt was kept up, only a few salmon and trout being caught in the
lakes (p. 210). Towards the latter part of March the settlement was
broken up and its members scattered for the purpose of hunting and
fishing (p. 227). Salmon were caught in North Pole Lake and deer
shot in the narrow passes (p. 227). The sealing did not begin until
the first of April (p. 239). In the summer, deer, seal, walrus, and salmon were caught in great abundance. In the following years the
mode of life was about the same, but it may be remarked that in August the natives lived at Pitiktaujang and afterwards went to Lyon
Inlet (Maluksilaq) to hunt deer (p. 323). Part of them returned to
Repulse Bay, where walrus were caught on the drifting ice during
September. In the ensuing winter (1867–'68) 55 natives had gathered
in a village about twenty miles east of Fort Hope (p. 333), where they

lived on the stores deposited during the preceding summer. After the breaking up of the ice they succeeded in killing several whales, which afforded an ample supply of meat and blubber (p. 363). Subsequently, they hunted deer west of Repulse Bay (p. 364) and near Lyon Inlet, where probably the greater part of the families had staid since the previous year.

In November, Hall found near the head of this inlet a number of natives who came to Repulse Bay towards the end of the year, having heard that a whale had been taken there. By this addition the village of Repulse Bay suddenly increased in population to 120 inhabitants (p. 369). This was the only winter in which the natives began sealing in January (p. 371). In March they built their huts upon the ice and scattered early in the spring for sealing and catching salmon.

From these reports and some more general accounts of these travelers, an idea can be formed of the mode of life of this part of the Aivillirmiut during the different seasons. In the spring, when the seals commence to bask upon the ice, the tents are established on the floe of Repulse Bay, the large winter settlements being broken up into a number of smaller ones. During this season they begin to store away blubber, which is carefully put into sealskin bags. Besides, reindeer are killed in the deer passes. In July a great number of the natives leave the ice and resort to the salmon rivers, where an abundant supply of food is secured, but the sealing is also continued until the breaking up of the ice. At this time of the year (i. e., in August), walrus and seal are taken in large numbers, and thus an ample stock of provisions for winter use is collected. In some seasons a few whales are caught and stored away at once. In September, most of the natives move to the lakes or rivers, particularly North Pole Lake, to hunt deer as well as the musk ox on the hills. Other favorite localities for deer hunting are west of Repulse Bay or near Lyon Inlet. Large deposits of venison are made, and when the deer go south the natives settle in the center of their summer's hunting ground, building their snow houses on the lakes in order to have a supply of water near at hand. About January most of them gather in one settlement, which is established at Uglariaq, Naujan, or Inugsulik. Those who come from Lyon Inlet do not always join the Repulse Bay tribe, but may be identical with Parry's Winter Island Eskimo, who move to the bay south of Lyon Inlet in winter. They go sealing in winter only in case of need, for the hunt seems to be unproductive, and they subsist on the stores deposited during the preceding summer. Towards the latter half of March the settlements are broken up and some of the natives go to the lakes to fish for trout and salmon, while others begin the sealing.

Another winter station of the Aivillirmiut is Akugdlit, which, however, has never been as important as Aivillik itself. Rae found some families here in August, 1846. They hunted the musk ox on the western shore of the bay, and later in the season, upon the pack ice which filled the sea, they hunted the walrus (Rae I, p. 58). They reported that the bay was very unfavorable for any kind of chase, as it is usually filled with closely packed ice, which prevents the visits of animals and endangers the boats of the natives (p. 49). In July the salmon creeks of Akugdlit (Committee Bay) were visited by these families, who extended their hunting ground from Colville Bay to the most northern parts of Melville Peninsula (p. 145). According to Hall a number of families live here at times. They were in the habit of staying at Repulse Bay during the early part of the summer and went to Akugdlit in the autumn to hunt the musk ox and deer. In the winter they transferred their deposits of blubber from Aivillik across the lakes to their settlement. Probably these families returned to Repulse Bay about the first of March, at which time their deposits were always exhausted (Hall II, p. 383). In some seasons the natives journey much farther south, that is, to the country between Cape Fullerton and Wager River. Klutschak's report upon this subject, which is extracted from his observations during Schwatka's search for the Franklin records, will be found tolerably correct (Deutsche Rundschau für Geographie und Statistik, III, 1881, p. 422). The report contains the following statement:

In the spring of every year these Eskimo live on the land floe of Hudson Bay, at some distance from the point where the tides and winds carry the pack ice past the shore. Here is the favorite feeding place of the walrus, and the Eskimo confine themselves to the pursuit of this animal. They settle near one of the numerous islands situated near the shore.

Later in the season they live in tents, and the hunting of seals and walrus is continued as long as the presence of ice permits. The greater part of the Aivillirmiut live near Depot Island (Pikiulaq). Here, on Cape Fullerton, and near the northern entrance of Chesterfield Inlet, the natives deposit their stores for winter use. As soon as the ice is gone they resort to the mainland, where deer, which descend to the shore at this season, are hunted. When the snow begins to cover the country they move inland, where they continue the deer hunt. In October they settle near a deer pass or a lake which is crossed by the herds migrating southward. In December all the deer have left the country and the natives live upon the stores deposited in the fall. Towards the beginning of the new year part of them return to the sea and live upon the deposits of walrus meat or disperse over the land floe, where seals are killed in their breathing holes. Another part take to the hills near Chesterfield Inlet and Wager River, a favorite feeding ground for the musk ox. They only return to the bay in March or April, to hunt seals until the breaking up of the ice. If the supplies of walrus meat are very abundant the Eskimo gather in one large settlement.

It appears from Klutschak's own journal that this report is not quite complete, and I shall therefore add those of his own observations which seem to be important:

The natives who had hunted deer in the fall returned in December to Depot Island, where ten inhabitants lived at that time. They hunted walrus at the edge of the floe during the whole winter, but did not exclusively use their old stores (Klutschak, p. 32). In summer whales were hunted by means of kayaks, the blubber and meat being immediately stored for future use (p. 269). It is interesting to learn that a single family spent a whole year in the interior of the country, about two or three days' journey west of Depot Island, living on the flesh of the musk ox most of the time (p. 196). He does not say what kind of fuel they used.

In Klutschak's chart of Hudson Bay, which is published with his essay, a winter settlement is marked on Wager River, where the natives probably lived on seals caught in the breathing holes.

The mode of life of this tribe, as observed by Hall during his stay among them in 1864, differs in some material points from Klutschak's account. It is particularly important that Hall found them at Wager River.

About forty Eskimo are said to have lived in Nuvung during that year, while others were at Depot Island. Large depots of deer meat were scattered over the country around the settlement (Hall II. p. 76) and were brought in by the natives one by one. In the middle of November, after having finished the work of currying their deerskins, they commenced the walrus hunt, but meantime they frequently fed on deer meat from their depots (Hall II, pp. 102, 128, 132, 133). Towards the end of February they commenced to disperse, at first moving southward in order to be nearer the floe edge (p. 144). In the beginning of March an advance party of natives moved to Wager River, where they intended to catch salmon through the ice and to visit depots in that part of the country (p. 149). In April all the former inhabitants of Nuvung had settled on the ice of Wager River, where salmon in moderate numbers were caught (p. 164), but the main subsistence was the seals, which were at first watched for at the breathing holes, while later on they were killed when basking on the ice.

As a summary of the foregoing statements, we may say that the five principal settlements of the Aivillirmiut are Pikiulaq (Depot Island), Nuvung and Ukusiksalik (Wager River), Aivillik (Repulse Bay), Akugdlit (Committee Bay), and Maluksilaq (Lyon Inlet). They may be divided into two groups, the former comprising the southern settlements, the latter the northern ones. Every one of these settlements has certain well known sites, which are frequented at the proper seasons.

It yet remains to describe the roads which are used in the intercourse between these settlements. From Pikiulaq to Nuvung the natives travel by means of sledges. In the winter of 1864–'65 two journeys were made, the first in December, the latter in January. Besides, boats are used in traveling along the shore in summer. Sledge journeys from Nuvung to Ukusiksalik cannot be accomplished on the ice, as in the entrance of the bay large water holes are formed. The sledges follow a chain of long, narrow lakes beginning near Nuvung and running almost parallel with the coast through a deep gorge. The bay is but a short distance beyond this gorge. I am not acquainted with the sledge road from Nuvung to Aivillik. Rae was visited at Fort Hope by a number of Eskimo, who came by sledges from Nuvung in June (I, p. 169). Hall traveled with the natives in boats, passing the narrows and following the edge of the land ice, while the rest of the families sledged on the shore or on the land ice (II, p. 177). The principal road across Rae Isthmus leads over North Pole Lake and is described by Rae and Hall. The latter accompanied the natives on two sledge roads, the one leading from Sagdlua, in Haviland Bay, to Qariaq, in Lyon Inlet, the other crossing the land farther south. I am not sure whether a road leading from Nebarvik to Committee Bay connects Maluksilaq with Akugdlit. It is doubtful whether the coast between Aivillik and Gore Bay is visited by the natives.

It is remarkable that the Aivillirmiut very rarely go to Southampton Island, though they are sometimes carried across Frozen Strait or Rowe's Welcome by drifting ice. Scarcely ever of their own accord do they visit the island, which they call Sagdlirn. They know that it is inhabited, but have very little intercourse with its people.

The Kinipetu or Agutit.—The reports upon the Kinipetu or Agutit of Chesterfield Inlet are very scanty as compared with those of the beforementioned tribe. All authors agree that they differ materially in their habits from the Aivillirmiut, and it has often been affirmed that they scarcely ever descend to the sea. As there is, however, no other tribe mentioned south of the Aivillirmiut besides this one and as in every voyage to these shores, even far south of Chesterfield Inlet, Eskimo are met with who frequently visit Fort Churchill, the most northern station of the Hudson Bay Company, there can be no doubt that they also visit the shore and the islands and hunt seals. Probably the greater part of the tribe live inland from July to March, hunting deer and the musk ox, and in winter only descend to the sea in order to procure blubber and sealskins during the season in which these are most easily obtained. It may be that another part stay near the head of Chesterfield Inlet all the year round or remain in the hilly country between the deep gulf and Back River hunting the musk ox. According to all reports, they are rather independent of the hunt of sea animals, and they do not even use their skins for garments (Klutschak, Deutsche Rundschau für Geographie und Statistik, III, p. 419). For this reason they would afford interesting material for investigation, and it is unfortunate that no trustworthy accounts of the tribe exist. Back, on his journey to the shores of the Arctic Ocean, found traces of the Eskimo on the lakes of Back River, ample proof that they were in the habit of visiting this region every summer. He found the first traces near 107° west longitude, and farther down, at the mouth of Baillie River. He did not see the natives whom Anderson and Stewart met in the summer of 1855 near McKinley River and later between Pelly and Garry Lakes. Their clothing and even the covers of their kayaks were made of deer and musk ox skins. They observed among these natives such articles of European make as the Hudson Bay Company used for barter and which were traded to the most southern Eskimo tribes of Hudson Bay. Therefore it is likely that these natives belonged to Chesterfield Inlet. This opinion is supported by Klutschak's remark that a native of the mouth of Back River knew an overland route leading from the lakes at its upper course to Chesterfield Inlet.

The Sagdlirmiut of Southampton Island.—Before leaving the subject of the Hudson Bay Eskimo I may mention the inhabitants of Southampton Island, a tribe which is almost unknown and the only record of which was obtained by Captain Lyon during the few hours which he passed among them in 1824 (Attempt to reach Repulse Bay, p. 54). In August he found a few families on the island south of Cape Pembroke, who were living upon salmon which had been deposited in stone caches and who had tents made of sealskins. A winter house was found at the same point. About 1865 an American whaling vessel found some natives on Manico Point living in five tents. Even then they had scarcely any iron, but used the old stone implements; this proves the want of all communication with the natives of the mainland. Parry found traces of Eskimo in York Bay and they have been seen on many other parts of the island. The Hudson Bay tribes call this tribe the Sagdlirmiut, i. e., the inhabitants of Sagdlirn, and their knowledge about them is very scanty, as they meet very rarely and by chance only.

The Sinimiut.—Northwest of Hudson Bay we find a tribe in Pelly Bay. The reports upon it are very scanty and it is difficult to find out the extent of the district which is occupied by it. Ross did not fall in with the tribe, and in the accounts of the Netchillirmiut on their journey to Repulse Bay no mention is made of an intervening tribe (II, p. 263). In April, 1847, Rae found signs of the tribe near Helen Island, in Pelly Bay (I, p. 113). There was an abundance of seals on the ice all around the islands (p. 111), but besides these they had large stocks of dried musk ox and salmon (p. 124). On his second journey he found their winter habitation on Barrow and Cameroon

Lakes (II, p. 938), and on the 20th of April he met with seventeen natives on the mainland west of Augustus Island, among whom were five women. In traveling farther west he fell in with a native who had been hunting the musk ox. On the 17th of May he found twelve natives settled in the same place and living on seal (II, p. 842).

Hall met with this tribe twice, in 1866 and in 1869. On the 28th of April, in his first attempt to reach King William Land, he found the Sinimiut settled near Cape Beaufort, in Committee Bay, where they were probably sealing (II, p. 255). No further account of this meeting is found except the remark that these natives were on their way to Repulse Bay (p. 259). Therefore it is rather doubtful whether the eastern shore of Simpson Peninsula belongs to their customary district. In April, 1869, on his second visit to Pelly Bay, Hall found their deserted winter huts on Cameroon Lake (p. 386). In the early part of the spring they had lived on the ice south of Augustus Island, the only place where seals could be caught, as the rest of the bay was filled with heavy floes which had been carried south by the northerly winds prevailing during the preceding fall. The natives themselves were met with on the mainland west of Augustus Island, where they were hunting the musk ox. When Hall crossed the bay in the first days of June the natives had changed neither their place nor their mode of subsistence.

There is a discrepancy in Nourse's extract from Hall's journal, for he sometimes refers to the Pelly Bay natives as different from the Sinimiut, while in other passages all the inhabitants of the bay are comprised in the latter term. I think this discrepancy is occasioned by the fact that a number of Aivillirmiut had settled in Pelly Bay and some others were related to natives of that locality; the latter Nourse calls the Pelly Bay men, the rest the Sinimiut. The place Sini itself, according to a statement of Hall, is near Cape Behrens, on the northwestern shore of the bay.

As the winter huts of the Sinimiut have been found four times on the lakes of the isthmus of Simpson Peninsula, we may suppose that they generally spend the winter there, living on the stores deposited in the preceding season and occasionally angling for trout and salmon (Rae I, p. 110) or killing a musk ox. In March they leave for the sea in order to hunt seals and to secure a fresh supply of blubber for their lamps. Their chief subsistence is the musk ox; besides, salmon are caught in great numbers, for they live on dried fish until spring (Rae I, p. 124).

BOOTHIA FELIX AND BACK RIVER.

The Netchillirmiut.—Following the shore westward we find the interesting tribes that inhabit Boothia Felix, King William Land, and the mouth of Back River. Among them the Netchillirmiut are the most important. Their favorite hunting grounds seem to have undergone a remarkable change since they were first visited by Ross in 1829. At that period their district occupied the southern part of Boothia Felix, particularly the narrow isthmus and the adjoining parts of both coasts. They were acquainted with Bellot Strait (Ikerasaq), which they described as the way the Victory had to take in order to effect a passage to the western sea. A part of the tribe was in the habit of wintering on Owutta Island; they also probably visited the eastern part of King William Land. The southwestern termination of their district cannot be exactly defined, but from their description of the land south of Lake Willerstedt it appears that they visited Shepherd Bay; besides, I find that in June, 1831, a number of families lived south of Netchillik, i. e., probably in Rae Strait or on Shepherd Bay (Ross II, p. 537).

So far as can be gathered from Ross's account the tribe had three winter settlements, one on the eastern shore of the Isthmus of Boothia, another at Lake Netchillik, and the third on Owutta Island.[1] As to the first meeting of the natives with the Victory two contradictory accounts are found. At first it is related (p. 252) that they came from Akugdlit, having been on the road ten days. Later, and this is more probable, it is said that two natives had descried the ship in September, 1829, when passing near Victoria Harbor (p. 309). Being in great fear, they had immediately traveled to Netchillik to communicate with their countrymen. There they met with a woman who had been on board of Parry's ships, and she had induced all the natives, by her stories, to be on the lookout for the Europeans. At the first meeting, on the 9th of January, 1830, 31 men approached the ship. This would answer to a population of about one hundred and twenty persons, and it is quite unprecedented that such a party should travel for any distance and even beyond the limitations of their own territory and of their customary migrations. Probably a traveling party had joined the Netchillirmiut, who had lived somewhere in Lord Mayor's Bay, and they all went to meet the ship.

From Ross we also learn that during January and February these natives lived on seals, which were killed with harpoons (pp. 250, 255, 259), but, in addition, they had deposits of venison, seal blubber, and fish (pp. 251, 262). Sometimes they went hunting the musk ox on the mainland farther north, and a small party may have staid there throughout the winter (p. 265). In the first days of March they began to scatter all over the ice (p. 290), in order to have a better chance of sealing and of catching young seals in the white coat (pp. 293, 295). The young sealing commenced about the 10th of March. It is worth remarking that this is the only tribe on the continent of

---

[1] From a rather ambiguous statement (p. 355) it would seem that Owutta belongs to the territory of the Ugjulirmiut; but in later passages ample proof is found that it is inhabited by the Netchillirmiut (pp. 423, 427). I myself was formerly misled by the above passage (Zeitschr. Gesell. Erdk., p. 171, Berlin, 1883).

America which pursues the young seal; they are enabled to do this by the extent of the land floe in the large bays. In the last days of March some of the natives started for Sarvaq and Netchillik to fetch their kayaks (p. 315), which they had left there the preceding season. As they intended to hunt deer at the lakes farther north, they were obliged to have their boats at hand at the breaking up of the ice. The further the season advanced the more the settlements were broken up (p. 338), and towards the end of April the first families left for Netchillik to join the other part of the tribe (p. 323). At this season the musk ox and the returning reindeer were frequently hunted (pp. 252, 335, 349). In the first days of May some of the natives went to Netchillik (p. 337), and another party followed a month later (p. 383). They stopped on Middle Lake for a short time to fish for trout (p. 384). A number of families remained near the ship, sealing, catching salmon, and hunting the musk ox (pp. 436, 441, 450, 453) until the beginning of July, when the fishing season ended and they went to the inland lakes to hunt deer and fish for trout in the rapids between the lakes (p. 450). In the summer their principal fishing stations were Lindsay River and Sarvaq.

The other part of the tribe which had lived at Lake Netchillik were even more numerous than that of the coast, as 21 snow houses were found which had been inhabited by them during the winter (p. 389). The number of inhabitants of this village was about one hundred and seventy, and, since there were a few who lived on Owutta Island and yet others who may have been scattered in different parts of the country, it is probable that the whole tribe numbered 350 persons.

As they were seen only a few times by the expedition the reports are rather incomplete. In the winter they lived on a plain, which was called Okavit, on the eastern shore of Lake Netchillik (p. 315). The exact position cannot be learned from Ross's journal. As some mention is made of blubber deposits at Netchillik (p. 388), it is probable that they lived on stores deposited in summer. Toward the end of May and in the beginning of June they were met with at Spence Bay and Josephine Bay. One of their stations was on the island Inugsulik, near Padliaq, the head of Spence Bay. Here their principal food was codfish, which they caught in holes cut through the ice, while the sealing was there a less important interest (pp. 391, 426). The kayaks which were found deposited on the west shore of Boothia as far as Josephine Bay proved that they resorted to this region in the deer hunting season (pp. 406, 407). The families who had been at Owutta during the winter of 1829–'30 were found in June, 1831, in Padliaq, whence they crossed the isthmus and visited Tarionitjoq (p. 431).

In 1830 no natives were seen after the usual time of their departure for the interior of the country, and it was not until April, 1831, that they were found again. They had wintered at Lake Avatutiaq, on the eastern shore of Boothia (p. 511), where they had lived on a large stock of salmon caught in the fall (p. 53!) and on musk oxen which were hunted during the entire year in the hilly country near the lakes. Others had wintered farther south, on Lake Owen (p. 524). A portion of these Eskimo set out for Netchillik in April (p. 522), while the others remained in Tom's Bay and subsisted upon codfish, salmon, and seals (p. 546).

In June another party left for Netchillik, whence some of the natives, who had not seen the ship before, arrived at Victoria Harbor in July, probably having heard of her new station at this place through the returning families (p. 577). In August the last of them left, going west (p. 592).

Though these reports are rather imperfect, they enable us to get a fair idea of the mode of life of this tribe.

In the large bays on the eastern side of the isthmus the natives live just as do the southern tribes of Baffin Land, pursuing the seal at its breathing hole during the winter. Here, as everywhere else, the settlements were broken up early in the spring. The fishing is commenced remarkably early, while in the east scarcely any salmon are caught before the breaking up of the lakes. West of Melville Peninsula the fishing is commenced in March or even earlier. On Boothia the most important means of subsistence for the natives is the codfish, on which they live during the spring and probably during a part of the winter. It is also an important article of food for the other tribes of this region, while farther east it is of no importance. The salmon fisheries of Boothia are very productive, of which Netchillik and Padliaq in Josephine Bay, Stanley and Lord Lindsay Rivers, Qogulortung, Angmalortuq, and Sarvaq may be considered the most important. Deer are hunted while swimming across the numerous lakes of Boothia, and the musk ox in the granite hills of its northern part. Here is also another winter resort of the tribe, from which the island Tukia, north of Lake Avatutiaq, is visited in summer, to collect pyrite or native iron (p. 362), which is used for kindling fire. The life of the western part of the tribe, as far as we are acquainted with it, was described in the foregoing paragraph.

Neither Dease and Simpson, who visited Castor and Pollux River in 1839, nor Rae, on his second voyage to Boothia, met the natives themselves; the latter, however, saw their marks on the islands of Acland Bay (II, p. 840).

The next traveler who fell in with the tribe was M'Clintock, who visited King William Land in search of the Franklin records. In February, 1859, he met several families near Cape Adelaide (p. 230). They traveled during the spring all along the shore and had been near Tasmania Islands in March and April. They were seen by him on their return journey to Netchillik, near Cape Nicholas. They

traveled slowly south, hunting seals. They knew the coast as far as
Bellot Strait and were able to name every cape of this district. A
few families who had wintered in company with this party at Cape
Victoria had returned to Netchillik when the other parties started
north (p. 253). On the 4th of May, twenty deserted snow huts were
found on the southwest point of Matty Island (p. 25;). From the
direction of the sledge tracks, M'Clintock concluded that the natives
who had formerly lived here had gone to Netchillik. On the 7th of
May a settlement of 30 or 40 individuals was found on the eastern
coast of King William Land (p. 260). This party had not communicated with the villages on the mainland of Boothia since the preceding fall (p. 260.)

An interesting change in the territory which is inhabited by this
tribe has occurred since Ross's visit to this country. In order to describe it more fully, I must refer to the relations of the Netchillirmiut to the Ugjulirmiut. At this early period the intercourse between the tribes of Ugjulik and Netchillik was of little consequence.
No European had ever been in their districts, which included Adelaide Peninsula and the southern shore of King William Land
(Ross II, p. 317), but quite a number of persons were known to the
Netchillirmiut (p. 357), who had met them in their trading excursions. In addition to this, a young single man of Ugjulik had been
adopted by a Netchillirmio who lived on the eastern coast of King
William Land and on Owutta Island (p. 355). When the Franklin
expedition perished on King William Land, in 1848, the Netchillirmiut had not yet visited that part of the country. From Schwatka's
inquiries we learn that the tribe that found Crozier and his fellow
sufferers did not extend its migrations beyond Adelaide Peninsula
and the southern shore of King William Land. In the summer of
1848 they attempted in vain to cross Simpson Strait, and were compelled to stay on the island. They traveled all over the country as
far as Peel Inlet, opposite to Matty Island (Gilder, p. 91). Hence
it is obvious that the Netchillirmiut, up to the time of the Franklin
catastrophe, lived in their old territory, as the inhabitants of Boothia
in 1859 had only indirect news of the shipwreck.

When the Ugjulirmiut obtained an enormous stock of metals and
wood by the destruction of Franklin's ships, the Netchillirmiut commenced to visit King William Land, in order to partake also of these
riches. Thus they began, by degrees, to move westward, and became
intermingled with the Ugjulirmiut. Hall mentions quite a number
of Boothians who had met Ross on the eastern shore of the isthmus,
though they were living on King William Land at that time (Hall II,
p. 405). Besides, according to all accounts, the number of women is
much smaller among the Netchillirmiut than that of men, and these
are obliged to look for wives among the neighboring tribes, particularly among the Ugjulirmiut. As these do not differ in the fashion

of their clothing and tattooing from the Netchillirmiut, it is scarcely possible at the present time to separate the tribes. It is worth remarking, however, that Gilder and Klutschak use both terms, and therefore I conclude that the natives themselves are conscious of belonging to different tribes.

Schwatka describes the limits of their territory as he learned them from his observations in the summer of 1879 (Science, December 19, 1884, p. 543). He found them on the mainland opposite King William Land and along the islands in the vicinity of Simpson Strait. They were most numerous along the northern shores of Adelaide Peninsula, their villages being scattered every few miles along the coast from Montreal Island to Smith Point. On the chart accompanying this account the eastern shore of the Back River estuary is included in the district inhabited by the Netchillirmiut.

It is important to compare this description with the observations which were made by Hall in 1869. He found the first traces of natives at the very head of Shepherd Bay, where a sledge track was observed (p. 395). Near Point Acland several snow huts and a number of natives were met with on the 30th of April (p. 396). Farther west he found a village on Point Booth (p. 397), but the most interesting fact is that in May, 1869, the party had fresh salmon from Netchillik (p. 400). This statement is decisive of the question whether the Netchillirmiut still continued their visits to the isthmus from which they take their name.

From Klutschak's journal a few more details may be gathered. From it we learn that in summer the Netchillirmiut scatter, and, while some go sealing near Montreal Island (p. 75), many others go inland to hunt deer in the lakes of the peninsula and farther south (p. 119). A third party resort to King William Land, the southern shore of which they frequent until September, while the more northern parts are seldom visited (p. 79). At this season they leave the island and all return to Adelaide Peninsula (p. 126). I suppose, however, that this report does not refer to the whole tribe, but that another party visited Shepherd Bay in winter. It seems to me very improbable that in the interval between 1869 and 1879 a total change should have occurred. In the spring they catch salmon, which are dried and stored to be used in winter. Their stock of blubber and deer meat is sufficient to last them during the greater part of the winter. At this season they fish only in holes made through the ice. Important winter settlements are at Point Richardson and at the outlet of Qimuqsuq (Sherman Inlet), where all the deer needed are caught in the fall while they are crossing the bay.

Although these statements do not altogether harmonize, it appears, notwithstanding, that King William Land and Adelaide Peninsula, which were not visited by the tribe in the early part of our century, became its favorite hunting ground after the loss of the Franklin expedition. Since that period the more northern parts of Boothia may have been abandoned by the natives, though no certain proof of this can be offered. Netchillik itself and the more southern parts were visited up to 1869, and probably they are yet inhabited by the Eskimo. This cannot be said with positiveness, however, for this part of the country has not been visited since the times of Ross and M'Clintock. The migration of the natives was caused, without doubt and as we have already remarked, by the profusion of metals and wood obtained from the wrecks and the starved traveling parties.

The Ugjulirmiut.—Several important facts regarding the Ugjulirmiut are mentioned above. Dease and Simpson found their first traces on the western shore of Adelaide Peninsula. From Ross's account (I, p. 427) it appears that their territory was the same at that period as it is now, and M'Clintock's meeting with them on the shore of King William Land may be adduced as a proof of this. Their old country is now inhabited by both Ugjulirmiut and Netchillirmiut. Therefore their mode of life is identical and requires no comment. Visits to the northern parts of King William Land have been very rare, but it was on one of these that Franklin's ships were discovered (Klutschak). They rarely went hunting beyond Cape Herschel, but looked for driftwood on the northern shore of the island.

The Ukusiksalirmiut.—The last tribe of the Central Eskimo, the Ukusiksalirmiut, inhabit the estuary of Back River. They were met by Back and by Anderson and Stewart. Recently Schwatka and his party communicated with them on their visit to King William Land. ' Klutschak affirms that they are the remains of a strong tribe which formerly inhabited Adelaide Peninsula but was supplanted by the Netchillirmiut and the Ugjulirmiut. Klutschak calls them Ukusiksalik; Gilder, sometimes Ukusiksalik, sometimes Ugjulik. The latter author relates that a single family living on Hayes River (Kugnuaq) had formerly had its station on Adelaide Peninsula, but had retired to this country when the warlike Netchillirmiut began to visit King William Land and Adelaide Peninsula. Schwatka could identify the same man with one of those whom Back had seen in the estuary of the river in 1833 (Gilder, p. 78). Therefore they must have lived in this district a long time before the Netchillirmiut began to move westward. According to Back the party with which he fell in did not know the land beyond the estuary of Back River, which indicates that they were neither from Ugjulik nor Netchillik. As the Ugjulirmiut lived on Adelaide Peninsula when Ross wintered in Boothia, I do not consider it probable that the Ukusiksalirmiut ever lived in that part of the country, and I cannot agree with Klutschak. I may add Parry's remark, that beyond Ukusiksalik (Wager River) another Ukusiksalik (Back River) was known to the natives of Winter Island.

The reports on their mode of life are very deficient. They were met by Schwatka a little above the great bend of Hayes River in May, 1879; he also met another party in December at the Dangerous Rapids of Back River. Schwatka counted seven families at the former and nine at the latter place. Their principal food consisted of fish, which are caught in abundance in Back River (Klutschak, p. 164). It is said that they have no fuel during the winter. Undoubtedly they use some kind of fuel, and I rather doubt the implication that they do not hunt seals at all. The musk ox and fish, however, are their main food, according to both Klutschak and Gilder. It is very remarkable that all the natives west of Boothia depend much more on fish than do any other tribes of the Central Eskimo.

A word in regard to the roads used in the intercourse between the tribes. From Akugdlit a road leads over the lakes of Simpson Peninsula to Pelly Bay. Rae and Hall traveled over it on their journeys to the northwest and it was used by the Sinimiut when they visited Repulse Bay in 1866. From Pelly Bay two roads lead to Netchillik and the estuary of Back River, the one following the east shore of the Boothia, the other running to Lake Simpson, whence the valley of Murchison River facilitates the access to Inglis Bay. The Isthmus of Boothia is crossed by the two chains of lakes discovered by Ross. In visiting the northeastern part of the peninsula the natives ascend Stanley River and cross the lakes farther north. Between Netchillik and Ugjulik the Eskimo pass by Owutta Island to Peel Inlet, whence they travel overland to the south shore of King William Land and cross Simpson Strait. Another road leads from Cape Colville to Matheson Point, following the south shore of King William Land. In traveling from Ugjulik to Back River they use Sherman Inlet and the adjoining isthmus. It is probable that Back River is visited by natives belonging to Wager River. The existence of a communication between Back River and Chesterfield Inlet is proved by Anderson and Stewart, who found Eskimo at Lake Garry, and by a remark of Klutschak (p. 170), who learned from a native of Back River that Chesterfield Inlet could be reached from the upper part of that river. It is quite probable that thus an immediate though limited intercourse is kept up between the Kinipetu and the Ukusiksalirmiut.

SMITH SOUND.

The natives of Ellesmere Land.— Last of all I have to mention the natives of Ellesmere Land and those of North Greenland. Although the latter are not generally considered as belonging to the central tribes, I find that their habits and their implements resemble those of the Central Eskimo rather than those of the Greenlanders, and therefore a brief mention of them will not be inappropriate. The inhabitants of Umingman Nuna (Ellesmere Land) probably live on the southern shore, near the western part of Jones Sound, and, according to Bessels's and my own inquiries, they travel all around this island, passing by Hayes Sound.

The North Greenlanders.—The North Greenlanders live in the sounds of the peninsula between Melville Bay and Kane Basin, hunting seals on the smooth floes of the bays and pursuing walrus at the floe edges. They make large deposits of the blubber and meat obtained in the fall, on which they live during the winter. They also pursue seals in winter with the harpoon. In summer they hunt reindeer on the mountains adjoining the inland ice.

INFLUENCE OF GEOGRAPHICAL CONDITIONS UPON THE DISTRIBUTION OF THE SETTLEMENTS.

In considering the distribution of the tribes it is evident that they are settled wherever extensive floes afford a good sealing ground during the winter. The Sikosuilarmiut live on the large bay east of King Cape, which is sheltered by numerous islands. The Akuliarmiut are settled near Lesseps and North Bays. I am unable to say whether there is a floe near the winter settlement of the Qaumauangmiut, as there are no reports upon the subject. Probably ice is formed in the sound, which is protected by the Middle Savage Islands, and besides it may be that the natives move to North Bay. The important tribe of Nugumiut lives on Frobisher Bay and the adjoining Grinnell and Field Bays. On the largest floe of this part of the country, in Cumberland Sound, including Lake Nettilling, the largest tribe is settled: the Oqomiut. On Davis Strait ice floes are formed between Cape Mickleham and Cape Mercy, in Exeter Sound, and between Okan and Bylot Island. The tribes are distributed accordingly: the Saumingmiut of Ukiadliving, the inhabitants of Qarmaqdjuin with their winter settlement in Exeter Sound, and the Padlimiut and the Akudnirmiut farther north. The immense land floe of Davis Strait is not so valuable a hunting ground for the Eskimo as Cumberland Sound, the ice being very rough a few miles from the coast and at some places even close inshore. When the sea begins to freeze in the fall the newly formed ice is broken up by severe gales and by the currents and is piled up into high hummocks before it consolidates. The sealing on rough ice during the winter is very difficult and unsuccessful, as it is hard to find the breathing holes and the traveling is very laborious. It is only in the northern parts of Home Bay and in the large fjords that smooth ice is formed. The settlements of the natives are manifestly distributed in accordance with these facts. In every place where smooth ice is formed we find that natives either are settled or have been settled. Aqbirtijung, River Clyde, Ijellirtung, Home Bay, Brodie Bay, Merchant Bay, and Padli are the only places along the shore of Davis Strait where smooth ice occurs. On the long shores between them, which are unsheltered from winds and currents, the ice is always very hummocky, and, therefore, the natives do not settle upon them in the winter. In the far north, extensive floes of smooth ice are formed in Eclipse Sound and Admiralty Inlet.

Concerning the country farther west the reports are rather scanty. The southwest shore of Baffin Land and the eastern entrance of Fury and Hecla Strait are always frozen over and afford a good hunting ground. On the mainland, the large floes of Repulse Bay and Wager River, Chesterfield Inlet and the bights all around it, Pelly Bay and the narrow bays adjoining Boothia Peninsula, and the mouth of Back River are important places for the distribution of the Eskimo.

There are only a few districts where the proximity of open water favors walrus hunting during the winter, and all of these have neighboring floes on which seals may be hunted with the harpoon. These places are Sikosuilaq, Akuliaq, Frobisher Bay, Iglulik, the west shore of Hudson Bay, and Smith Sound. As to the remainder the Eskimo live altogether independent of the open water during the winter.

Generally speaking, two conditions are required for winter settlements, viz, the existence of an extensive floe and smooth ice.

The different mode of hunting in the spring causes a different distribution of the settlements. During this season those regions which had been deserted during the winter are most visited by the hunters. On light dog sledges they travel over the rough ice and along the shores of the fjords and islands. The natives who lived in large settlements during the winter are spread over the whole country, in order that every one may have a better chance of traveling over his own hunting ground. In a few places the young sealing induces the Eskimo to leave the winter settlements; in other places the kayaks are prepared for visiting the floe edge, and bears and the returning birds are hunted.

Though the greater variety of food which is to be obtained and the difference in the methods of hunting in the spring require the dispersion over a wide area of the families which had kept together during the winter, the selection of places for the new settlements remains wholly dependent upon the state of the ice.

After the ice breaks up, the distribution of the deer regulates the location of the summer settlements. While during the winter the state of the ice is of decisive importance, the orography of the land comes now into consideration.

Wherever deep valleys give access to an extensive area, wherever practicable roads enable the natives to ascend the plateaus, summer settlements are established. The heads of the fjords are favorite places, as they abound with salmon. The adjoining valleys and the peninsulas which they form give the best chances for a successful deer hunt. These facts are most apparent on the coast of the steep highland of Nugumiut, over which numerous herds of deer roam.

A great influence is also exerted by the extensive plains of the western part of Baffin Land, which abound in deer. We observe that a number of tribes visit these districts, though their winter stations are at a great distance. The Akuliarmiut of Hudson Strait and the Nugumiut travel to Lake Amaqdjuaq, the Oqomiut stay on Lake Nettilling, and the Akudnirmiut visit Majoraridjen. In the same way all the tribes of Hudson Bay visit the land farther west, which is frequented by herds of the musk ox, and they go even as far as Back River. This important fact shows the attraction which is exerted by a rich country on all the tribes of the neighboring districts.

TRADE AND INTERCOURSE BETWEEN THE TRIBES.

In treating of the single tribes, the routes were mentioned which are followed by the natives as they travel from shore to shore and from settlement to settlement. These routes are established by tradition and the Eskimo never stray from them. In order to obtain a more thorough understanding of the migrations of single individuals and of families, the relations between the tribes and the settlements must be discussed.

By the lively intercourse which is always kept up between the settlements, it cannot fail that marriages between members of different tribes should be of frequent occurrence and that many ties of affinity and consanguinity should thus be created. These relations, however, as distances increase, quickly become less common. For instance, in Cumberland Sound three people are found belonging to Tununirn, about ten belonging to Akudnirn, and quite a number coming from Padli. Also, two Sikosuilarmiut live there, a few natives of Akuliaq and Qaumauang, and very many Nugumiut. Hall's accounts concerning the Nugumiut and the Aivillirmiut prove a similar proportion of strange natives among these tribes. Every tribe may be said to bring together its immediate neighbors, as it is closely related to them, while those which are separated by the tribe itself are strangers to one another. The importance of this mediate position is regulated by the strength of the tribe, by the significance of the country in reference to its produce, and by the routes crossing it.

Thus, the Sikosuilarmiut and the Nuratamiut are closely connected, and may be considered as forming one group with the Akuliarmiut. The Sikosuilarmiut have intercourse with the Igdlumiut, the inhabitants of the northern shore of Labrador. According to Lucien M. Turner, three tribes may be distinguished there as inhabiting the shores of Ungava Bay and the eastern shore of Hudson Bay. This report differs somewhat from the accounts of the Moravian missionaries who have intercourse with the inhabitants of Ungava Bay near Cape Chidleigh. From their reports four tribes may be distinguished: the Kangivamiut of George River, the Kouksoarmiut of Big River, the Ungavamiut of Hope Advance Bay (which is properly named Ungava), and the Itivimiut of Hudson Bay. I am rather undecided whether Ungava is a bay or a large strait separating Cape Wolstenholme and the adjacent land from the continent, as the name Ungava is also reported south of Cape Wolstenholme. The inhabitants of this shore are the Itivimiut of the Labrador Eskimo and the Igdlumiut of the natives of Baffin Land. Probably the intercourse between Sikosuilaq and Cape Wolstenholme is of no great importance. The Sikosuilarmiut visit Trinity Islands (Nannuragassain) in skin boats to hunt walrus and cross by the three islands Tudjaraaq'djung, Akugdlirn, and Tudjaqdjuara'lung to the opposite shore of Hudson Strait. The passage across the strait is considered very dangerous, and therefore is rarely undertaken. The natives do not utter a single word during the long passage; they believe a destructive gale might be conjured up if they did. Only once have natives been met with on Salisbury Island (Lyon, Attempt to reach Repulse Bay, p. 128), but it is doubtful whether they belonged to the northern or to the southern shore of the strait. As for the rest, the passage is only known to me by reports I received in Cumberland Sound, which were confirmed by the whalers visiting the northern shore of Hudson Strait. I do not know whether any intercourse exists between Sikosuilaq and Southampton Island. It is worth remarking that on Mansfield Island numerous ruins of Eskimo habitations have been found (Gordon, Report on the Hudson's Bay Expedition, 1884, p. 38).

The Qaumauangmiut are connected with the Nugumiut in the same manner as with the Akuliarmiut, and many are said to winter near North Bay, which is also visited by the Akuliarmiut. From Hall's reports it would appear that many are settled in Frobisher Bay.

At present the intercourse between the Nugumiut and the Oqomiut is of no significance, as many years may pass without a journey being made from one tribe to the other. Formerly, when many whalers visited Cumberland Sound and Field Bay, a number of Nugumiut immigrated to the sound, and consequently almost half of the Eskimo now settled on the western shore of Cumberland Sound were born in Nugumiut or Ukadliq. At the same time many Oqomiut settled among the Nugumiut. That period was doubtless an exceptional one; at any rate, the long stretch of uninhabited shore between the settlements of the two tribes is not favorable to intimate intercourse. Indeed, even now the Nugumiut are considered strangers in the sound, and, notwithstanding the existence of many intermarriages between the tribes, a number of families are not at all acquainted with one another. It is remarkable that the number of natives born in Nugumiut is much larger on the western shore than on the eastern. They seem to have joined their nearest neighbors, the southern Talirpingmiut, perhaps for the reason that in their district the geographic character of the land is most similar to that of Frobisher Bay. The number of Nugumiut settled among the inhabitants of Nettilling Fjord and among the Kingnaitmiut is far less. Among the Saumingmiut there is no one who has traveled beyond Naujateling, and in Padli or farther north there are very few individuals who have been south of Cumberland Sound. It is only by careful consideration of the birthplace of the different individuals who are members of the settlements of Cumberland Sound that it is possible at the present time to detect the former division of the Oqomiut into subtribes. The inhabitants of the eastern shore are related to the Padlimiut and the Akudnirmiut; those of the western shore, to the Nugumiut. In 1840 a brisk intercourse existed between Padli and the sound (Eenoolooapik, p. 81), and probably sledges crossed the peninsula every winter. Though the intercourse is not so intimate to-day as it is between the settlements of the sound, it is yet active. The Kingnaitmiut form the medium of the regular intercourse between Saumia and Padli, while families removing to Akudnirn travel along the shore of Davis Strait. Among the subtribes of the Oqomiut the Saumingmiut are most nearly related to the Padlimiut and extend their migrations farthest to the north.

The Akudnirmiut, who are closely connected with the Padlimiut, are considered strangers by the Oqomiut. The intercourse between the Akudnirmiut and the Aggomiut is not very frequent, and seems to be maintained as irregularly as that between the Nugumiut and the Oqomiut.

The inhabitants of the northern sounds and of Fury and Hecla Strait frequently visit one another. Parry mentions a number of journeys in each direction (II, p. 436). Hall found natives of Tununirn and Tununirusirn settled in Iglulik (II, p. 356). I myself found two Iglulirmiut among the Akudnirmiut. The intercourse seems to have been always very active, and consequently those tribes may be considered as one group.

The inhabitants of North Devon belong to the Tununirusirmiut, a few families of this tribe sometimes settling on the island and after a few years' absence returning to their former home.

From Parry's, Hall's, and Schwatka's reports it appears that the Aivillirmiut are closely related to the Iglulirmiut, while the Eskimo of Chesterfield Inlet, the Agutit or Kinipetu, form a separate group.

It is remarkable that between the tribes of Hudson Bay and the more western ones a deep distrust exists, which prevents a frequent and unlimited intercourse. The Sinimiut and Netchillirmiut are feared by the Aivillirmiut, though intermarriages and removals from one tribe to the other are not rare. No doubt they are less closely related than are the neighboring tribes hitherto mentioned. Unfortunately, too little is known of the western tribes to admit of a decided opinion whether or not there exists an important difference in customs and habits. The Sinimiut, the Netchiłlirmiut, and the Ugjulirmiut may be comprised in one group, for they all hold frequent intercourse with one another and the last two even inhabit the same region at the present time. The change which the relations between these tribes have undergone since 1833 has already been referred to, as has their intercourse with the Ukusiksalirmiut. Schwatka (Science, Vol. IV, p. 543) states that they occasionally meet the Qidneliq of Coronation Bay, but that both tribes distrust each other. Our knowledge about the migrations from North Devon to Ellesmere Land and North Greenland is very scanty, but it is necessary to mention its existence.

Between tribes that are strangers to one another ceremonies of greeting are customary which are not adapted to facilitate intercourse. The ceremonies will be described further on (see p. 201). For the present it will be sufficient to say that duels, with varying details, are common between a stranger and a man of the tribe, and these sometimes result in the death of the former.

Among neighboring tribes these ceremonies are dispensed with, for instance, between the Padlimiut and Oqomiut, Padlimiut and Akudnirmiut, while a Nugumio or an Akudnirmio unknown in Oqo has there to go through the whole of the performance. The exception in favor of the former tribes is doubtless due to the frequent intermarriages with those tribes, whereby a constant acquaintance is kept up.

Real wars or fights between settlements, I believe, have never happened, but contests have always been confined to single families. The last instance of a feud which has come to my knowledge occurred about seventy years ago. At that time a great number of Eskimo lived at Niutang, in Kingnait Fjord, and many men of this settlement had been murdered by a Qinguamio of Anarnitung. For this reason the men of Niutang united in a sledge journey to Anarnitung to revenge the death of their companions. They hid themselves behind the ground ice and killed the returning hunter with their arrows. All hostilities have probably been of a similar character.

One tradition only refers to a real fight between the tribes. On the steep island Sagdluaqdjung, near Naujateling, ruins of huts are found on the level summit. They are said to have been built by Eskimo who lived by the seashore and were attacked by a hostile tribe of inlanders. The tradition says that they defended themselves with bows and arrows, and with bowlders which they rolled down upon the enemy. The occurrence of huts upon the top of an island is very unusual, and this tradition is the only one referring to any kind of fights or wars. Even the tradition of the expulsion of the Tornit a fabulous tribe said to have lived with the Eskimo on these shores, does not refer to a combat. The details of this tradition will be found in a subsequent chapter.

I wish to state here that my inquiries and my understanding of the facts as they have been reported by other travelers do not agree with the opinions given by Klutschak (Deutsche Rundschau für Geographie und Statistik, III, p. 418), who claims for the Eskimo of the west shore of Hudson Bay reservations which are limited by precise lines of demarkation. In comparing this statement with his own and with Gilder's narratives I am led to believe that the relations between the tribes are the same in these regions as they are farther east. This opinion is strengthened by Dall's remarks on the Alaska tribes (Science, p. 228, 1885).

The reasons for the frequent removals of individual Eskimo to strange tribes are to be looked for in the customs of the natives. I can only mention here that intermarriage, adoption, and the fear of blood vengeance are the principal ones.

It is peculiar to the migratory habits of the Eskimo that almost without exception the old man returns to the country of his youth, and consequently by far the greater part of the old people live in their native districts.

During the last decades the most important inducement to removals has been the presence of the whalers in certain parts of the country. Since the beginning of our century their fleets have visited the west shore of Baffin Bay and Davis Strait, and thus European manufactures have found their way to the inhospitable shores of the Arctic Sea. The most valuable objects which were bartered were metals and wood. The value of the former may be seen in its economical application for knives and harpoon heads. By means of this trade the Akudnirmiut and the Tununirmiut became far superior to the Oqomiut and the Iglulirmiut, with whom they traded extensively in dogs, skins, &c. The Akuliarmiut and the Qaumauangmiut also enjoyed the advantages which accrued from trade with the ships of the Hudson Bay Company.

When the whalers became better acquainted with the natives and the peculiar jargon which is still in use was developed, the traffic became very active, and reached its height after Cumberland Sound was rediscovered by Penny. As soon as the whalers began to winter in the sound and to employ the natives the latter received firearms and European boats in exchange for their wares, and then their modes of living became materially changed. The immense quantity of European manufactured articles which thus came into the possession of the natives induced the removal of many families to the favored region. Particularly did the Nugumiut and the Akudnirmiut migrate during that period. When in the course of time the

Bay of Nugumiut was visited by the whalers removals of members of this tribe became less frequent.

After the Eskimo had become acquainted with the advantages of firearms the natives of Davis Strait also began to trade bearskins for guns and ammunition, having learned how highly they were prized in Cumberland Sound. Besides, they received, in exchange for seals and walrus blubber put up for the whalers, tobacco, pipes, coffee, boxes, &c. In a similar way the Saumingmiut barter with the whalers of Cumberland Sound, whom they visit during the winter, carrying heavy loads of bearskins to the stations.

A brief sketch of the way in which the whaling and the trade with the Eskimo in Cumberland Sound are carried on may be of interest at this point. Two of the whaling stations are still kept up. They are situated on Qeqerten, the settlement of the Kingnaitmiut. When the Eskimo who have spent the summer inland return at the beginning of October they eagerly offer their services at the stations, for they receive in payment for a half year's work a gun, a harmonium or something of that nature, and a ration of provisions for their families, with tobacco every week. Every Saturday the women come into the house of the station, at the blowing of the horn, to receive their bread, coffee, sirup, and the precious tobacco. In return the Eskimo is expected to deliver in the kitchen of the station a piece of every seal he catches.

The time for the fall fishing commences as soon as the ice begins to form. If the weather, which is generally stormy, permits it, the boats leave the harbor to look out for the whales which pass along the east shore of the sound toward the north. During the last few years the catch has been very unprofitable, only a few whales having been seen. As the ice forms quickly the boats must be brought back about the end of October or the beginning of November. Since the whale fishery has become unprofitable the stations have followed the business of collecting seal blubber and skins, which they buy from the Eskimo. (See Appendix, Note 1.)

A lively traffic springs up as soon as the ice becomes strong enough to allow sledges to pass from shore to shore. The sledges of the stations are sent from one settlement to another to exchange tobacco, matches, coffee, bread, &c. for skins and the spare blubber which the Eskimo have carefully saved up. On the other hand, those natives who require useful articles, such as cooking pots, lamps, &c., collect quantities of hides and blubber and go to Qeqerten to supply their wants. The winter passes quickly amid the stir of business, till everything comes to a stop at the end of March, when the young sealing season fairly opens.

When the sun has reached such a height that the snow begins to melt in favored spots, a new life begins at the stations. The skins which have been collected in the winter and become frozen are

brought out of the store room and exposed to the sun's rays. Som
of the women busy themselves, with their crescent shaped knives, ir
cutting the blubber from the skins and putting it away in casks
Others clean and salt the skins, which are likewise packed away. The
men also find enough work to do after the young sealing is over, for
the whale boats must be got ready for the spring fishing. Strangers
whose services have been engaged by the station for the next few
months arrive daily with their families and all their goods to take up
their abode on Qeqerten. The boats are dug out of the deep snow
the oars and sails are looked after, the harpoons are cleaned up and
sharpened, and everything is in busy preparation. The boats are
made as comfortable as possible with awnings and level floors, for
the crews are not to come to the shore for about six weeks.

By the beginning of May, the arrangements having been completed, the boats are put upon the sledges, which, under the direction
of native drivers, are drawn by dog teams, with their crews, to the
floe edge. The sledges being heavily laden and food for the dogs
having to be provided by hunting, each day's stage is rather short.
Arriving at the floe edge the sledges are unloaded and the boats are
launched. Seals and birds of all kinds are now found in profusion
and the chase is opened without delay upon everything that is useful
and can be shot. Sledges are regularly sent back to Qeqerten with
skins and meat for the families of the Eskimo, while the blubber
is packed in casks, which are kept ready on the spot.

The most important object of the expedition is the whale. Harpoons and lines are always in readiness for the contest with the
mighty monster. The boats return to the north with the breaking
up of the ice and the fishing ends in July. The Eskimo are paid
off and dismissed and resume their reindeer hunting, while the whites
are glad to enjoy some rest after the weeks of exhausting labor.

The constant contact between the Eskimo and the whalers has
effected a perfect revolution in the trade between the Eskimo tribes.
As the whale catch in Cumberland Sound has fallen off during the
past fifteen years, a remigration of the population of Davis Strait
has occurred, ships visiting these shores every fall and a regular
traffic being kept up. Therefore many Oqomiut now travel as far
as Qivitung in order to trade there. As Nugumiut is still frequently
visited by whalers, there is no inducement for the inhabitants to leave
their country.

Within a few years the Akuliarmiut also have become amply provided with firearms and European products in general by means of
a new whaling station which has been established in their vicinity.

As to the Iglulirmiut, the importation of European manufactures
at Pond Bay makes the trade with that region even more important
than formerly.

The Aivillirmiut and the Kinipetu have immediate intercourse with the whalers frequenting the western shore of Hudson Bay. Besides, the southern tribes trade with the stations of the Hudson Bay Company.

The more western tribes of Boothia and its environs are dependent on the mediation of the Aivillirmiut for their supply of goods, as they themselves have no chance of communicating with the whites.

Finally, I shall describe the old trading routes which existed between these tribes before matters were totally changed by the influence of the Europeans. Two desiderata formed the principal inducement to long journeys, which sometimes lasted even several years: wood and soapstone. The shores of Davis Strait and Cumberland Sound are almost destitute of driftwood, and consequently the natives were obliged to visit distant regions to obtain that necessary material. Tudjaqdjuaq in particular was the objective point of their expeditions. Their boats took a southerly course, and, as the wood was gathered, a portion of it was immediately manufactured into boat ribs and sledge runners, which were carried back on the return journey; another portion was used for bows, though these were also made of deer's horns ingeniously lashed together. A portion of the trade in wood seems to have been in the hands of the Nugumiut, who collected it on Tudjaqdjuaq and took it north. Another necessary and important article of trade, soapstone, is manufactured into lamps and pots. It is found in a few places only, and very rarely in pieces large enough for the manufacture of the articles named. Among the places visited by the natives for the purpose of obtaining it may be mentioned Kautaq, east of Naujatel- ing; Qeqertelung, near the former place; Qarmaqdjuin (Exeter Bay), and Committee Bay. The visitors come from every part of the country, the soapstone being dug or "traded" from the rocks by depositing some trifles in exchange. In addition to wood and soapstone, metals, which were extremely rare in old times, have formed an important object of trade. They were brought to Baffin Bay either by the Aivillirmiut, who had obtained them from the Hudson Bay Company and the Kinipetu, or by the Akuliarmiut. Even when Frobisher visited the Nugumiut in 1577 he found them in possession of some iron (Frobisher).

The occurrence of flint, which was the material for arrowheads, may have given some importance to places where it occurs. Formerly an important trade existed between the Netchillirmiut and the neighboring tribes. As the district of the former is destitute of driftwood and potstone they are compelled to buy both articles from their neighbors. In Ross's time they got the necessary wood from Ugjulik, the potstone from Aivillik. They exchanged these articles for native iron (or pyrite), which they found on the eastern shore of Boothia and which was used for striking fire. After having collected a sufficient stock of it during several years, they traveled to the neighboring tribes.   For reasons which have been mentioned this trade is now essentially changed.   According to Schwatka there is a mutual distrust between the Ugjulirmiut and the Netchillirmiut on one side and the Qidnelik on the other, for which reason the intercourse between these tribes is very limited.

LIST OF THE CENTRAL ESKIMO TRIBES.

The following list gives the tribes of the Central Eskimo and their geographical distribution:

I. Northern coast of Labrador:
    (1) Kangivamiut (George River).
    (2) Kouksoarmiut (Big River).
    (3) Ungavamiut (Hope Advance Bay).
    (4) Itivimiut (Cape Wolstenholme).
II. Northern shore of Hudson Strait:
    (5) Sikosuilarmiut (King Cape).
    (6) Akuliarmiut (North Bluff).
    (7) Qaumauangmiut (Middle Savage Islands).
III. Davis Strait:
    (8) Nugumiut (Frobisher Bay).
    (9) Oqomiut (Cumberland Sound):
        a. Talirpingmiut (west shore of Cumberland Sound and Nettilling).
        b. Qinguamiut (head of Cumberland Sound).
        c. Kingnaitmiut (Qeqerten and environs).
        d. Saumingmiut (southern part of Cumberland Peninsula).
    (10) Akudnirmiut (Davis Strait).
        a. Padlimiut (Padli Fjord).
        b. Akudnirmiut (Home Bay).
IV. Northern part of Baffin Land, North Devon, and Ellesmere Land:
    (11) Aggomiut.
        a. Tununirmiut (Eclipse Sound).
        b. Tununirusirmiut (Admiralty Inlet and North Devon).
    (12) Inhabitants of Umingman Nuna (Ellesmere Land).
V. Melville Peninsula, Wager River, and Southampton Island:
    (13) *a.* Iglulirmiut (Fury and Hecla Strait).
        b. Amitormiut (eastern coast of Melville Peninsula).
    (14) *a.* Pilingmiut (eastern coast of Fox Basin).
        b. Sagdlirmiut (islands of Fox Basin).
    (15) Aivillirmiut (Repulse Bay and Wager River).
    (16) Sagdlirmiut (Southampton Island):
VI.   (17) Kinipetu (Chesterfield Inlet).
VII. Boothia Felix and King William Land:
    (18) Sinimiut (Pelly Bay).
    (19) Netchillirmiut (Boothia Felix and King William Land).
    (20) Ugjulirmiut (King William Land and Adelaide Peninsula).
    (21) Ukusiksalirmiut (estuary of Back River).
VIII. Qidnelik (coast west of Adelaide Peninsula).
IX. Inhabitants of North Greenland.

HUNTING AND FISHING.[1]

SEAL, WALRUS, AND WHALE HUNTING.

The staple food of the Central Eskimo is the seal, particularly *Pagomys fœtidus*. The methods of hunting this animal differ materially at different seasons, as its mode of life depends on the state of the ice.

In the winter it takes to the smooth parts of the floe a few miles from the coast, where it scratches breathing holes through the ice, in which it rises to blow. It shuns hummocky ice and floes of more than one year's age. Wherever the edge of the ice is at a great distance from the settlements, the only way of procuring seals is by watching for them at these holes. For the pursuit a light harpoon is used, called unang. The shape of this weapon has been somewhat changed since the introduction of rod iron. Formerly it consisted of a shaft having at one end an ivory point firmly attached by thongs and rivets, the point tapering toward the end. The point was slanting on one side so as to form almost an oblique cone. Thus it facilitated the separation of the harpoon head from the unang. On the opposite end of the shaft another piece of ivory was attached, generally forming a knob. The material used in making the shaft was wood, bone, or ivory, according to the region in which it was manufactured. In Iglulik and in Aggo the narwhal's horn was the favorite material for the whole implement, a single horn being sufficient to make a whole shaft. Wherever wood could be procured small pieces were ingeniously lashed together. As the shaft is apt to be broken by the struggles of the animal when struck by the weapon, it was strengthened by a stout thong running along the whole length of the shaft. In all other respects the old design corresponds to the modern one. Unfortunately I have seen no specimen of this description, but a figure may be seen in Ross II, p. 272, in the hand of one of the natives. In Alaska a similar harpoon is in use, a specimen of which is represented in Fig. 1 . It consists of a wooden shaft, with a stout ivory point at the lower end and another at the upper end. Both are fastened to the shaft by whalebone strings. In the upper end a slanting ivory point is inserted, which serves for attaching the harpoon head to it. The whole shaft is strengthened by a seal line, as shown in the figure.

The unang now in use in Baffin Land and on the western shore of Hudson Bay (Fig. 2) consists of a wooden shaft into which an iron rod (unartenga) is sunk. The latter is pointed at the end (see, also, Fig. 3) in about the same way as the old ivory implement. The socket is secured by a small ivory ring (unaqiuta) or a string wound around the end of the shaft. In the socket close to the iron rod

[1] A glossary of the Eskimo words used throughout this paper will be found on p. 251.

a bent nail is inserted, forming a narrow eye (tagusiarbing). Near the center of the whole implement a small piece of ivory (tikagung; see, also, Fig. 28) is fastened to the shaft, forming a support for the hand when throwing the weapon. At the lower end of the shaft a

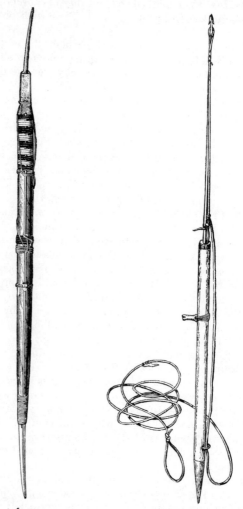

Fig. 1 . harpoon from Alaska. (American Museum of Natural History, New York.)

Fig. 2 . Modern unang or sealing harpoon. (Museum für Völkerkunde, Berlin. IV A 6729.)

string of deer sinews or a thong is fastened, forming a loop (nabiring) which passes through a hole drilled through the shaft. A stout iron point is also attached to the lower end of the shaft (tounga).

The natives carry this implement on all their winter excursions, as it is serviceable for numerous purposes. It is always kept within reach on the sledge, as the strong iron point is useful for cutting down hummocks, should any obstruct the passage of the sledges, or for cutting holes through the ice, or it takes the place of a hatchet in breaking the frozen meat which is carried along for dogs' food. The long iron rod is extremely useful in trying the strength of the ice or the depth of the snow. By taking precautionary measures of this kind the natives pass over extensive floes of weak ice.

FIG. 3 ,. Old style naulang or harpoon head. (Museum für Völkerkunde, Berlin. IV A 6692.) ⅓

The head belonging to the unang is called naulang. Since iron has been introduced in Baffin Land and Hudson Bay, the natives file their harpoon heads out of it, but adhere almost exactly to the old pattern. The old naulang was cut out of bone or more frequently out of ivory (Fig. 3 ¹). It was one inch to two inches long and had a piece of metal inserted into the slit at the top. Through the middle of the instrument a hole was drilled parallel to the plane of the blade. The harpoon line passed through the hole, and as soon as the point struck an animal and a strain was put upon the line it turned at a right angle to the latter, thus acting as a toggle. The effect was increased by two points at the lower end of the naulang, called uming (beard). These pressed into the flesh or the skin of the animal and prevented the harpoon head from slipping back.

The modern naulang (Fig. 4) is about the same length as the old one, but much more slender. While the back of the old pattern was straight, the points of the iron one are bent outward and backward in order to increase its effect.

The naulang is fastened to the harpoon line (iparang). This part of the instrument is much longer than the unang, as it must allow for the struggles of the diving seal. The end of the line passes through the hole of the naulang and a loop is formed and secured by deer sinew or arranged as may be seen in Fig. 4 . At a distance equal to the length of the iron rod of the unang a small thong (taguta) is attached to the line and serves to fasten it to the shaft (see Fig. 2). It is drawn through

FIG. 4 . Modern naulang or harpoon head. (Museum für Völkerkunde, Berlin. IV A 6729.) ⅓

the eye formed by the tagusiar'bing. As soon as a strain is put up
the naulang the line parts from the shaft, as the taguta is only squeeze
into the eye and is easily detached. The harpoon line passes throug
the nabiring or is fastened by a slipping hitch to the shaft of t
unang.

If the unang has a nabiring the line passes through this loop.
few feet below it a small piece of ivory (akparaiktung) is attached
the line, acting as a hook after it has run out. It catches the nabirin
and drags the harpoon along, thus impeding the movements of th
animal (see Fig. 2).

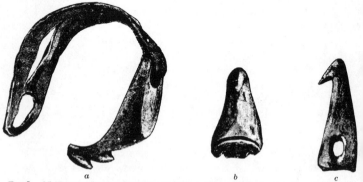

a   b   c

FIG. 5 . Qilertuang or leather strap and clasps for holding coiled up harpoon lines. *a, c* (Nation
Museum, Washington. *a*, 34128 ; *c*, 34132.) *b* (Museum für Völkerkunde, Berlin.) ¼

The rest of the line is coiled up and held by the hunter. The en
is doubled so as to form a loop which serves as a handle when the lin
runs out with the diving seal. Generally, a small piece of leathe
(Fig. 5) with two slits at one end and an ivory clasp (qilertuang
at the other is fastened to this loop; it serves to hold the bights to
gether when the line is detached from the harpoon and rolled up
Some art is bestowed on the manufacture of this clasp (Fig. 5)
Usually it represents a seal, the head of which forms a hook on whic
the slits can be fastened. The clasp is either tied or otherwise se
cured to the leather strap. Some specimens in the British Museum
which are about one hundred and fifty years old, show that these im
plements have not undergone any change during that time.

Parry describes another harpoon head used by the Iglulirmiut fo
the unang. He calls it a siatko (Fig. 6). I myself have not see
any of a similar pattern, but Kumlien gives a sketch of one foun
in a grave at Exeter Sound (Fig. 7). The principal difference be
tween the naulang and the siatko is that the edge of the former i
parallel to the hole through which the line passes, while in the latte
their directions are vertical to each other. The head of the whaling
harpoon (see Fig. 47) acts on the same principle.

When the day begins to dawn the Eskimo prepares for the hunt. The dogs are harnessed to the sledge and the hunting implements are fitted up. The harpoon line and the snow knife are hung over the deer's antlers, which are attached to the hind part of the sledge, a seal or bear skin is lashed upon the bottom, and the spear secured under the lashing. The hunter takes up the whip and the dogs set off for the hunting ground. When near the place where he expects to find seals, the hunter stops the team and takes the implements from the sledge, which is then turned upside down. The points of the runners and the short brow antler are pressed into the snow in order to prevent the dogs from running away. A dog with a good scent is then taken from the team and the Eskimo follows his guidance until a seal's hole is found. In winter it is entirely covered with snow, but generally a very small elevation indicates the situation. The dog is led back to the sledge and the hunter examines the hole to make sure that it is still visited by the seal. Cautiously he cuts a hole through the snow covering and peeps into the excavation. If the water is covered with a new coat of ice the seal has left the hole and it would be in vain to expect its return. The hunter must look for a new hole promising better results.

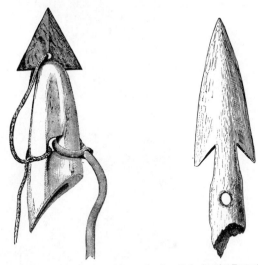

Fig. 6   Siatko or harpoon head of the Iglulir-miut. (From Parry II, p. 550.)   Fig. 7   Siatko found at Exeter Sound. (From a drawing by L. Kumlien.)

If he is sure that the seal has recently visited a hole he marks its exact center on the top of the snow and then fills up his peep hole with small blocks of snow. All these preparations must be made with the utmost precaution, as any change in the appearance of the snow would frighten away the seal. The Eskimo take particular care that no hairs from their clothing fall into the hole or remain sticking in the snow, for they believe that the smell would scare away the animal. The center of the breathing hole must be marked, as the game remains invisible and only a stroke into the center will be likely to hit it. If the snow covering is very thick and strong it is cut down, but is replaced with loose snow, which is heaped around the end of the harpoon, the latter being placed upon the central point.

Fig. 8 . Eskimo in the act of striking a seal. (From a photograph.)

After the harpoon has been extracted a hole remains which forms the mark for the harpooner. If the Eskimo expects the early return of the seal, he spreads a small piece of skin, generally that of a young seal, close to the hole and places his feet upon it, thus keeping them warm. He fastens the naulang to the harpoon shaft, while the lower end of the line is folded up in a coil, which he holds in the left hand. The unang is held in both hands, and thus the hunter sometimes remains for hours, occasionally stooping and listening, until he hears the blowing of the seal. Then, all of a sudden, he stands upright, and, with all his strength, sends the harpoon straight downward into the hole, paying out the line at the same time, but keeping a firm hold of the loop at its end (Fig. 8). Generally the seal is struck near the head. If the line is fastened to the shaft by a slipping hitch it is at once detached and the harpoon either remains sticking in the snow or falls down by the hole. If the line runs through the nabiring, the harpoon is dragged into the water and impedes the movements of the animal. The hunter then begins at once to cut down the snow covering with his knife, which has been left within easy reach, and hauls in the line. As soon as the seal comes to the surface to breathe it is easily dispatched and drawn up on the ice.

The arrangements at the seal hole are more elaborate if the sealer expects to wait a long time. If only a few men go out hunting and famine is impending, he sometimes waits for a whole day or even longer, though it be cold and the wind rage over the icy fields. He builds up a semicircular wall of snow blocks to keep off the piercing wind and makes a seat in the center of it. A skin is spread under his feet and his legs are tied together with a thong, which is fastened by a peculiar kind of buckle (tutareang) with two holes (Fig. 9).

FIG. 9 Tutareang or buckle. (Museum für Völkerkunde, Berlin. IV A 6710.) ⅓

One end of the thong is firmly tied to the buckle, passing through one of the holes, while the opposite end passes tightly through the second hole. The thong may be quickly opened by a strong effort on the part of the hunter, while it helps to keep him quiet. At his right hand (Fig. 10 ; in this drawing it appears on the left) the snow knife is stuck into the snow, while to the left the unang is placed upon two pegs. The coil of the line lies in his lap. His left arm is drawn out of his sleeve, that he may more easily keep warm. Both sleeves are generally held together by a piece of deer's horn with a branch on each side which serves as a hook. Thus the hunter waits until he hears the breathing of the seal. As it usually stays for several minutes he is in no hurry to get ready. Cautiously he places his left arm into the sleeve, having first disengaged it from the hook.

He then takes hold of the coil, picks up his unang, and, having risen, strikes the center of the hole.

Fig. 10 . Eskimo awaiting return of seal to blowhole. (From a photograph.)

Ross (II, p. 268) and Rae (I. p. 123) state that the sealing at the hole is more difficult in daylight than in the dark. I suppose, however, that when the snow is deep there is no difference; at least the Eskimo of Davis Strait never complain about being annoyed by the daylight.

Sometimes a small instrument is used in the hunt to indicate the approach of the seal. It is called qipekutang and consists of a very thin rod with a knob or a knot at one end (Parry II. p. 550, Fig. 20). It is stuck through the snow, the end passing into the water, the knob resting on the snow. As soon as the seal rises to blow, it strikes the rod, which, by its movements, warns the Eskimo. Generally it is

made of whalebone. Sometimes a string is attached to the knob
and fastened by a pin to the snow, as its movements are more easily
detected than those of the knob. The natives are somewhat averse
to using this implement, as it frequently scares the seals.

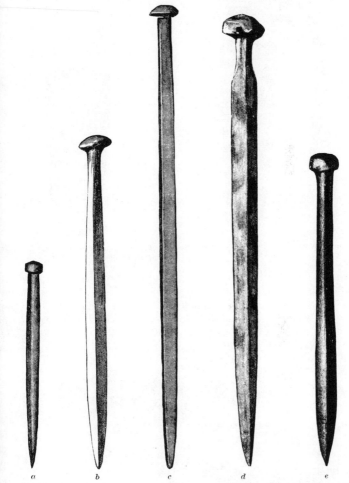

FIG. 11 . Tuputang or ivory plugs for closing wounds. *e* (Museum für Völkerkunde, Berlin. IV A
6706.) *b, c, d* (National Museum, Washington. *b*, 10192; *c*, 10390; *d*, 9836.) ½

After the carcass of the animal has been drawn out of the water,
the wounds are closed with ivory plugs (tuputang) (Fig. 11), which
are carried in a wooden or leathern case (Fig. 12) and are either
triangular or square. The plug is pushed under the skin, which is
closely tied to its head. Another form of plug which, however, is

rarely used, is represented in Fig. 13. The skin is drawn over th
plug and tied over one of the threads of the screw cut into the wood

Fig. 12. Wooden case for plugs. (Museum
für Völkerkunde, Berlin.) ½

Fig. 13. Another form of plug. (Museum
für Völkerkunde, Berlin.) ⅔

After the dead animal's wounds are closed, a hole is cut through th
flesh beneath the lower jaw and a thong is passed through this hol
and the mouth. A small implement called qanging is used for fast
ening it to the seal. It usually forms a toggle and prevents the lin
from slipping through the hole. The patterns represented in Fig
14 are very effective. The hole drilled through the center of th

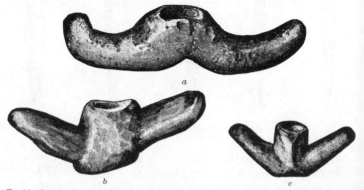

Fig. 14. Qanging for fastening thong to jaw of seal. *a* (Museum für Völkerkunde, Berlin. IV A
6825.) *b*, *c* (National Museum, Washington. *b*, 34126; *c*, 34129.) ¼

strument is wider at the lower end than elsewhere, thus furnishing rest for a knot at the end of the thong. The points are pressed to the flesh of the seal, and thus a firm hold is secured for the whole implement. The Eskimo display some art in the manufacture of this implement, and frequently give it the shape of seals and the like Fig. 15). Fig. 16 represents a small button, which is much less

FIG. 15 . Qanging in form of a seal. (Museum für Völkerkunde, Berlin. IV A 6825.) ¼

ffective than the other patterns. A very few specimens consist merely of rude pieces of ivory with holes drilled through them. Fig. 17 shows one of these attachments serving for both toggle and handle.

FIG. 16 . Qanging in form of a button. (National Museum, Washington. 34130.) ¼

FIG. 17 . Qanging serving for both toggle and handle. (National Museum, Washington. 10400.) ⅔

In order to prevent the line from getting out of order, a whirl (qidjarung) is sometimes used. Fig. 18 represents one brought

FIG. 18 . Qidjarung or whirl for harpoon line. (National Museum, Washington. 34121.) ½

FIG. 19 . Simpler form of whirl. (Museum für Völkerkunde, Berlin.) ¼

from Cumberland Sound by Kumlien, and is described by him (p 38). There was a ball in the hollow body of this instrument, which could not be pulled through any of the openings. One line wa fastened to this ball, passing through the central hole, and anothe one to the top of the whirl. A simpler pattern is represented i Fig. 19.

On its capture, the seal is dragged to the sledge and after bein covered with the bearskin is firmly secured by the lashing. I freezes quickly and the hunter sits down on top of it. If the sea happens to blow soon after the arrival of the hunter, a second on may be procured, but generally the day is far spent when the first sea is killed.

Wherever water holes are found they are frequently visited durin the winter by the Eskimo, especially by those who have firearms They lie in wait at the lower side of the hole, i. e., the side to which the tide sets, and when the seal blows they shoot him, securing hin with the harpoon after he has drifted to the edge of the ice. These holes can only be visited at spring tides, as in the intervals a treach erous floe partly covers the opening and is not destroyed until the next spring tide.

In March, when the seal brings forth its young, the same way o hunting is continued, besides which young seals are eagerly pursued The pregnant females make an excavation from five to ten feet in length under the snow, the diving hole being at one end. They pre fer snowbanks and rough ice or the cracks and cavities of grounded ice for this purpose, and pup in these holes. The Eskimo set out or light sledges dragged by a few dogs, which quickly take up the scent of the seals. The dogs hurry at the utmost speed to the place of the hole, where they stop at once. The hunter jumps from the sledge and breaks down the roof of the excavation as quickly as possible, cutting off the retreat of the seal through its hole if he can. Gener ally the mother escapes, but the awkward pup is taken by surprise, or, if very young, cannot get into the water. The Eskimo draws it out by means of a hook (niksiang) and kills it by firmly stepping on the poor beast's breast. An old pattern of the hook used is rep resented according to Kumlien's drawing in Fig. 20 ; another, made from a bear's claw, in Fig. 21 ; the modern pattern, in Fig. 22 .

Sometimes the natives try to catch the old seal in a most cruel way, by using the love of the dam for her pup to lure her to the surface of the hole. They tie a thong to the hind flipper of the pup and throw it into the hole. It dives at once, crying pitifully. When it comes up to breathe the hunter pushes it back, and frequently the dam returns to her young and attempts to draw it away. As soon as she is seen the harpoon is plunged into her body and she is quickly drawn out of the water and killed.

The young seal is also pursued by foxes, which drag it from the excavation and leave nothing but the skin, which becomes a welcome find for the Eskimo.

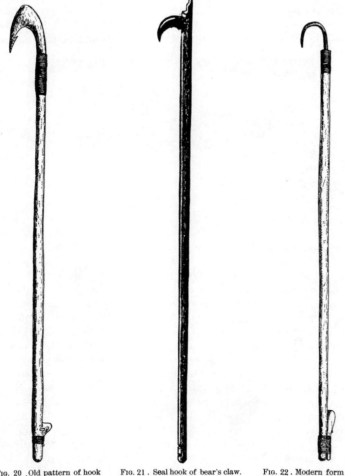

Fig. 20 . Old pattern of hook for drawing out captured seal

Fig. 21 . Seal hook of bear's claw. Actual size, 3 feet. (Museum für Völkerkunde, Berlin. IV A 6728.)

Fig. 22 . Modern form of seal hook. (From a drawing by Kumlien.)

As the season advances and the rays of the sun become warmer the seals break down the snow roofs and are seen basking beside their holes. The young ones remain with their dams until late in June.

At this season a new method of hunting is practiced, by which seals are caught with greater ease than in winter. The hunter approaches the animal from the windward side until he is within seventy or eighty yards of it. He then lies down, after having fastened a piece of skin under his left arm, upon which he reclines. The skin protects him from the melting snow, facilitates speed, and diminishes the noise as he creeps. He moves on toward the seal, resting on his left arm and side and pushing himself forward with his right foot and left arm (Fig. 23). The seal frequently raises his head and gazes around

Fig. 23 . Eskimo approaching seal. (From a photograph.)

to make sure that no danger threatens. As long as the seal is looking around the hunter lies flat and keeps perfectly still, or, if he is somewhat close to the animal, imitates its movements by raising his head and rolling and playing with his hands and feet as a seal does with its flippers. Some natives will utter sounds similar to those of a blowing seal or use a small sledge with a white screen to conceal themselves from view. The sealskin clothing makes man and seal look so extremely alike that it is difficult to distinguish one from the other at some distance. If the hunter succeeds in deceiving the animal it lies down again to sleep and he pushes himself on. As the naps of the seal last but a few moments, the Eskimo approaches very slowly. At last he is near enough. He levels his gun and tries to hit the animal's head, as it must be killed by the first shot, else it jumps into the hole and escapes. If the snow is hard and water has not yet appeared on the top of the ice, a seal may be killed in this way in twenty or thirty minutes. If the snow is very soft and deep it is almost impossible to get near enough, as it is extremely difficult to push one's self along. The approach is rather easy through rough ice, which conceals the hunter, but the seals seldom frequent such places. Sometimes they are found at the edges of rough ice or near the shore and are easily caught when in this position.

Formerly the harpoon was used instead of the gun, and is even now preferred by some hunters. The hunter gets near enough to reach the seal with the harpoon, and having struck his prey has a better chance of securing it, as the weapon prevents its escape.

After the shot has been fired or the harpoon thrown, the Eskimo at once jumps to his feet in order to prevent the escape of the animal to its hole, to which it takes if only wounded. An expert hunter can kill from ten to fifteen seals in one day.

Rae, in describing the method of hunting, states (I, p. 170) that the women at Repulse Bay are very skillful, and when they have no harpoon frequently use a small wooden club, with which they strike the seal on the nose, killing it.

Generally two men go sealing together. They set out early in the morning on one sledge, and while one creeps toward the seals the other keeps the dogs quiet. A single hunter cannot hunt successfully at this season with a sledge, for when he leaves it the dogs will either follow him or, if made fast to the ice, raise such a howling that the seal is put upon its guard. Therefore it is necessary that a continuous watch be kept on the dogs. When the shot is fired and they perceive that the seal is killed, no amount of whipping will restrain them; they rush forward until they have reached the victim, which is then lashed on the sledge.

The hunters go on in search of a second seal, at the sight of which the dogs are again stopped. When the Eskimo intend to remain out only a few hours they leave the dead animals at their holes and load them on the sledge on the return journey. A single hunter cannot leave the settlement for a long distance, but is limited to sealing near the village and killing no more animals than he can drag to it himself. Sometimes it happens that the seals are fast asleep. Then the hunter can go up to them without any precaution and kill them immediately, and even a dog team running at full speed can take them by surprise. In winter a similar method of hunting is followed whenever the edge of the floe is close to the land. In such places all kinds of seals lie on the ice, even in the midst of winter, and are pursued in the way which has been already described.

A strange method of hunting is reported by Ross (II, p. 451) as practiced by the Netchillirmiut. Eight men slowly approached the basking seal until it raised its head, when those in front stopped and shouted as loud as they could ; on which three others ran up with incredible swiftness and the leader struck it with the spear.

Still later in the season, when the snow is all gone, a very successful method of hunting is practiced. All the inhabitants of the settlements set out at once, men, women, and children, and occupy every seal hole over a large area. The men keep their harpoons ready to strike the animal when it comes up to blow, while the women and children are provided with sticks only, with which they frighten away the seals whenever they rise where they are standing. The animals are compelled to rise somewhere, as otherwise they would be drowned, and thus an ample supply is secured in a short time.

After the breaking up of the ice the natives take to their kayaks and the summer hunt is started. As at this season the methods of catching all kinds of seal and walrus are almost identical, I shall describe them together; and, first, the most important part of the hunting gear, the kayak and its belongings.

The kayak (qajaq) is almost exclusively used for hunting by all Eskimo tribes from Greenland to Alaska. According to Bessels the Ita natives do not know its use, though they have retained the word. As a connection exists between this tribe and those of Baffin Land, I have no doubt that they are acquainted with the use of the boat, though it may be of little avail in that ice encumbered region. When I first visited the tribes of Davis Strait no kayak was to be found between Cape Mercy and Cape Raper, nor had there been any for several years. In the summer of 1884, however, two boats were built by these natives.

The general principles of their construction are well known. The kayak of the Nugumiut, Oqomiut, and Akudnirmiut is bulky as compared with that of Greenland and Hudson Bay. It is from twenty-five to twenty-seven feet long and weighs from eighty to one hundred pounds, while the Iglulik boats, according to Lyon (p. 322), range from fifty to sixty pounds in weight. It may be that the Repulse Bay boats are even lighter still. According to Hall they are not heavier than twenty-five pounds (II, p. 216).

FIG. 24   Frame of a kayak or hunting boat.   (Museum für Völkerkunde, Berlin.)

The frame of the kayak (Fig. 24) consists, first, of two flat pieces of wood which form the gunwale (apumang). From ten to twenty beams (ajang) keep this frame on a stretch above. The greatest width between them is a little behind the cock pit (p. 79). A strong piece of wood runs from the cross piece before the hole (masing) to the stem, and another from the cross piece abaft the hole (itirbing) to the stern (tuniqdjung). The proportion of the bow end to the stern end, measured from the center of the hole, is 4 to 3. The former has a projection measuring one-fourth of its whole length. Setting aside the projection, the hole lies in the very center of the body of the kayak. A large number of ribs (tikping), from thirty to sixty, are fastened to the gunwales and kept steady by a keel (kujang), which runs from stem to stern, and by two lateral strips of wood (siadnit), which are fastened between gunwale and keel. The stem projection (usujang), which rises gradually, begins at a strong beam (niutang) and its rib (qaning). The extreme end of the stern (aqojang) is bent upward. The bottom of the boat is partly formed by the keel, partly by the side supports. The stern projection has a keel, but in the body of the boat the side supports are bent down to the depth of the keel, thus forming a flat bottom. Rising again gradually they terminate close to the stern. Between the masing and the itirbing is the hole (pa) of the kayak, the rim of which is formed by a flat piece of wood or whalebone bent into a hoop. It is flattened abaft and sharply bent at the fore part. The masing sometimes rests upon a stud.

FIG. 25. Kayak with covering of skin. (Museum für Völkerkunde, Berlin.)

The whole frame is covered with skins (aming) tightly sewed together and almost waterproof (Fig. 25). Usually the cover consists of three or four skins of *Pagomys fœtidus*. When put upon the frame it is thoroughly wetted and stretched as much as possible so as to fit tightly. It is tied by thongs to the rim of the hole. A small piece of ivory is attached to each side of the niutang and serves to fasten a thong which holds the kayak implements. Two more thongs are sewed to the skin just before the hole, another one behind it, and two smaller ones near the stern.

The differences between this boat and that of the Iglulirmiut may be seen from Lyon's description (page 320). Their kayak has a long peak at the stern, which turns somewhat upward. The rim round the hole is higher in front than at the back, whereas that of the former has the rim of an equal height all around. At Savage Islands Lyon saw the rims very neatly edged with ivory. The bow and the stern of the Iglulik kayaks were equally sharp and they had from sixty to seventy ribs. While the kayaks of the Oqomiut have only in exceptional cases two lateral supports between keel and gunwale, Lyon found in the boats of these natives seven siadnit, but no keel at all. These boats are well represented in Parry's engravings (II, pp. 271 and 508). Instead of the thongs, ivory or wooden holders are fastened abaft to prevent the weapons from slipping down.

If the drawing in Lyon's book (p. 14) be correct, the kayak of the Qaumauangmiut (Savage Islands) has a very long prow ending in a sharp peak, the proportion to the stern being 2 to 1. Its stern is much shorter and steeper than that of the northern boats and carries the same holders as that of the Iglulirmiut.

FIG. 26. Model of a Repulse Bay kayak. (National Museum, Washington. 68126.)

The model of a Repulse Bay kayak is represented in Fig. 26. The rim of the hole is in the same position as in the Iglulik kayak, the fore part resting on a rib bent like a hoop, whereas in the others it rests on a beam. The stern resembles closely that of the Cumberland Sound boats, while the head is less peaked, the keel having a sharper bend at the beginning of the projection, which does not turn upward. Early in the spring and in the autumn, when ice is still forming, a scraper (sirmijaung) (Fig. 27) is always carried in the

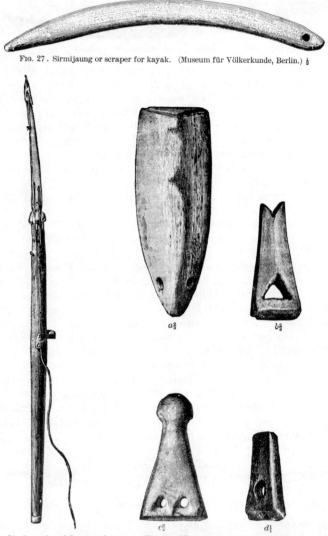

Fig. 27. Sirmijaung or scraper for kayak. (Museum für Völkerkunde, Berlin.) ½

*a*⅔   *b*⅔

*c*⅔   *d*½

Fig. 28. Large kayak harpoon for seal and walrus. Actual length, 6½ feet. (Museum für Völkerkunde, Berlin.)

Fig. 29. Tikagung or support for the hand. *a*, *b*, *c* (National Museum, Washington. *a*, 30000; *b*, 30005; *c*, 30004.) *d* (Museum für Völkerkunde, Berlin.)

kayak for removing the sleet which forms on the skin. When the boat has been pulled on shore, it is turned upside down and the whole bottom is cleaned with this implement. A double bladed paddle (pauting) is used with the boat. It has a narrow handle (akudnang), which fits the hand of the boatman and widens to about four inches at the thin blades (maling), which are edged with ivory. Between each blade and the handle there is a ring (qudluqsiuta).

The kayak gear consists of the large harpoon and its line (to which the sealskin float is attached), the receptacle for this line, the bird spear (with its throwing board), and two lances.

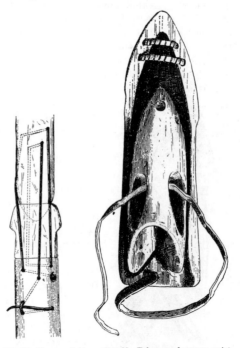

FIG. 30 . Qatirn or ivory head of harpoon shaft. (National Museum, Washington. 34101.) ⅜

FIG. 31 . Manner of attaching the two principal parts of the harpoon.

FIG. 32 . Tokang or harpoon point in sheath. (In the possession of Captain John O. Spicer, Groton, Conn.) ⅜

The large harpoon (Fig. 28) is used for hunting seals and walrus from the kayak. The shaft (qijuqtenga) consists of a stout pole from four and a half to five feet in length, to which an ivory knob is fastened at the lower end. At its center of gravity a small piece of ivory (tikagung) is attached, which serves to support the hand in throwing the weapon. A remarkable pattern of this tikagung, which nicely fits the hand of the hunter, is represented in the first of the series of Fig. 29 , and another one, which differs only in size from that of the unang, in the second.   At right angles to the tikagung a small ivory knob is inserted in the shaft and serves to hold the harpoon line.   At this part the shaft is greatly flattened and the cross section becomes oblong or rhombic.   At the top it is tenoned, to be inserted into the mortice of the ivory head (qatirn).   The latter fits so closely on the tenon that it sticks without being either riveted or tied together.   The qatirn is represented in Fig. 30.   Into the cavity at its top a walrus tusk is inserted and forms with it a ball and socket joint (igimang).

The tusk and the qatirn are fastened to each other in a most ingenious way, which may be readily made out from the engraving (Fig. 31).   The principal effect of this arrangement of the holes and the thong is that the tusk is kept steady by two parallel thongs that prevent it from tipping over and only allow a movement in the plane of the flattening of the shaft as soon as any considerable force is applied to the tusk.

The harpoon head used in connection with this weapon is the to-

Fig. 33 . Tokang or harpoon head taken from a whale in Cumberland Sound. (National Museum, Washington.   34069.) ⅔

kang.   To prevent it from being injured, it is carried in a wooden sheath (Fig. 32).   The iron point is secured by a string of whalebone or sealskin; the lower part is fastened to the sheath as indicated in the figure.   The tokang differs from the naulang in that it is larger and stouter.   In some cases great care is bestowed upon the finishing of this important weapon.

An interesting specimen of this variety of harpoon head was found by Kumlien in Cumberland Sound (Fig. 33).   It was taken from a whale and differs from the device of that country.   The back is bent similar to that of the iron naulang and the barbs have two points each instead of one.   The front part is sharply ridged.   The specimen is very nicely finished.   A few very old harpoon heads of the same pattern are deposited in the British Museum and were of Hudson Strait manufacture; therefore I conclude that Kumlien's specimen is from the same part of the country.

Fig. 34 represents an ancient harpoon head of the same style, the locality of which is unfortunately unknown.   The specimen is of particular interest, as it shows the method of fastening the stone to the ivory part.   A similar specimen is in the collections of the British Museum; it formed part of the Sloane collection.   Both these specimens show perforations at the lower end of the harpoon head which are not found in the modern ones. Probably these served for holding the harpoon head to the shaft by means of a thin line, in order to prevent the head from coming off before the seal or walrus was struck. These holes are similar to the ones shown in Figs. 6 and 47.

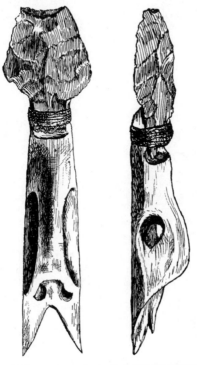

FIG. 34. Ancient tokang or harpoon head. (In A. Sturgis's collection, New York.)

The harpoon line (alirn) is attached to the tokang in the same way as the iparang is to the naulang. When it is fastened to the igimang, the bend of the tusk facilitates the disengagement of the harpoon head, which turns its back to that of the tusk. Attached to the line at the level of the ivory knob which has been mentioned is the teliqbing (Fig. 35), into the hole of which the knob fits closely. As the line from the tokang to the teliqbing is just long enough to allow it to be pulled down far enough to reach the knob, it holds shaft and head firmly together so long as the tusk remains in its position. As soon as a lateral strain is put upon the tusk the distance between the head and the knob is diminished and the teliqbing slips off, thus disengaging the line with the harpoon head from the shaft. Sometimes the teliqbing has two holes, one being used when the line is wet and longer, the other when it is dry and shorter.

In Iglulik the spear is called qatilik (Fig. 36). In pattern it is the same as that of Akudnirn and Oqo, the only difference, accord-

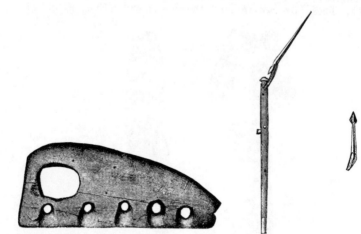

FIG. 35 . Teliqbing, which is fastened to harpoon line. National Museum, Washington. 34123.) ⅓

FIG. 36 . Qatilik or spear from Iglulik (From Parry II, p. 550.)

ing to Parry's description, being that the toung (the tusk) is straight and has a notch near its socket (see Fig. 36), while the harpoon head which belongs to it has only a single point at its lower end.

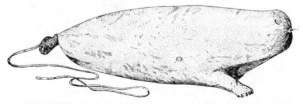

FIG. 37 . Avautang or sealskin float. (National Museum, Washington. 30009.)

This harpoon is placed on the right side of the prow of the kayak, with the point directed towards its head. The harpoon line, with the tokang, lies just before the hunter in a flat receptacle (asedlun), which consists of a wooden ring with a handle, held by thongs before the hole of the kayak. The receptacle rests on the skin cover, having no feet, as has the Greenland one. In Hudson Strait it is secured upon holders. The harpoon line is rolled up in a coil, but its end is fastened to the seal float, which lies behind the hunter and is held in place by a thong. The line passes along the right side of the kayak hole. The float (avautang) (Fig. 37) consists of a whole sealskin which had been removed from the animal dexterously, its entire body being pulled through the mouth, which is enlarged by means of a cut along the throat. The nails of the flippers are frequently extracted and the openings sewed up, the hind flippers and the tail being cut off and firmly tied together by a thong, thus forming a neck (atauta), to which the harpoon line is attached. At the head a pipe for blowing up the skin (poviutang) is inserted (Fig. 38); the skin is firmly tied to the ring of the pipe, on which the stopper is secured as soon as the skin is sufficiently inflated. This device is a very convenient one, for it is difficult to inflate the skin without some kind of mouthpiece. If there are any holes in the float they are closed by a button similar to the one shown in Fig. 38 *a*, which, however, is without a hole.

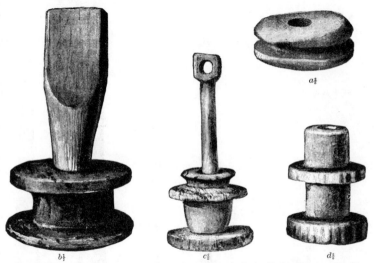

FIG. 38. Different styles of poviutang or pipe for inflating the float. (National Museum, Washington. *a*, 29986; *b*, 34118; *c*, 34119; *d*, 34120.)

If the harpoon is to be used for hunting large animals, such as walrus or whales, a very ingenious contrivance is sometimes inserted between the line and the float in the shape of a wooden hoop with a seal or deer skin stretched over it (niutang) (see Fig. 48). Three or four thongs of equal length are fastened to the hoop at equal distances and bound together. At their point of union they are attached to the line. As soon as a walrus is struck and starts to swim away, the hoop is thrown at right angles to the stretched line and exerts a strong resistance when dragged along, thus diminishing the speed of the animal and quickly exhausting its strength. The float prevents its escape, as it is too buoyant to be drawn under water. The animal cannot dive, and thus the hunter does not lose sight of his prey.

For small seals a similar weapon is used, the agdliaq (Fig. 39), the main difference being that it is much smaller and has a seal bladder for a float attached to the shaft. I have not seen this weapon myself, but Kumlien has brought away parts of it. Fig. 40 shows that its point differs only in size from the large igimang. The head (probably the naulang) is tied to the shaft, which acts as a drag.

The points are fastened to the shaft in almost the same way as the former, the only difference being that they are straight; the drill holes do not cross one another. Fig. 41 represents the heads belonging to this spear; Fig. 42, a large one which is used with the large harpoon. As the lines in all these run as is represented in Fig. 40 b, they cannot act as harpoons. I had no opportunity of seeing any of these weapons myself.

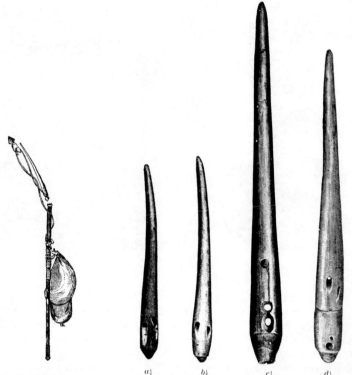

Fig. 39. Agdliaq or spear for small seals. (From Parry II, p. 550.)

Fig. 40. Agdliaq points. (National Museum, Washington. a, 90165; b, 2991; c, 34098; d, 34063.)

In hunting walrus a lance (anguvigang) (Fig. 43) is used which is similar to the igimang. The shaft and the joint are alike in both, only the knob for the teliqbing being absent. The head is made of bone or the straight part of a walrus tusk and has an iron blade on the top. The lance serves to dispatch the animal after it has been harpooned with the igimang.

The joint prevents the shaft from being broken by the struggles of the animal. Its place is behind the hunter on the right side of the kayak, the point being directed toward the stern. Generally a second lance is carried on the left side of the boat parallel with the other. It is either of the same kind or a slender shaft with a long point firmly inserted in it (kapun, ipun). The point is about one and one-third of a foot to one and one-half feet long. This weapon, however, is more particularly in use for hunting deer in the lakes and ponds.

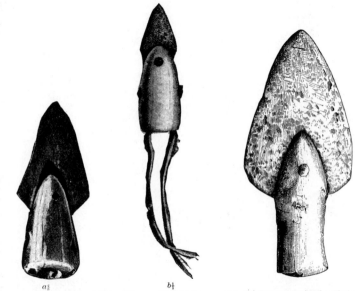

a ⅔   *b* ¼
FIG. 41 Spear heads. (National Museum, Washington.   FIG. 42 ½ Large spear head. (National
a, 34076; *b*, 34068.)   Museum, Washington. 10136.) ¼

The last implement in the kayak gear to be described is the bird spear, nuirn (Fig. 44), with its throwing board, nuqsang (Fig. 45). It has a shaft of about four feet in length, flattened at the lower end. Among the natives on the east and southeast of Baffin Land it has an iron prong at its point, whereas in Iglulik it has two points of unequal length, with double barbs. Three double barbed prongs are attached to the center of the shaft. They have a sharp bend at their lower part, the points running parallel to the shaft. The prongs of the Greenland dart are straight and diverge from the shaft. The lower end of the bird spear fits into the groove of the throwing board. Therefore the end of the shaft is squared. The ivory knob at the end of the spear contains a small hole for the insertion of the spike which is in the end of the groove. When the board is used it is held firmly in the right hand, the first finger passing through the hole by the side of the groove, the thumb clasping the notch on the left side (Fig. 45 *b*), the other fingers those on the right side. The shaft is held by the points of the fingers. When the spear is hurled

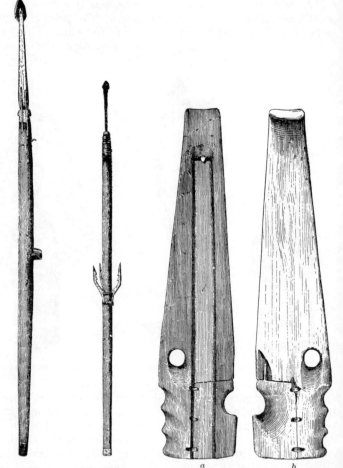

a   *b*

FIG. 43. Anguvigang or lance. Museum für Völkerkunde, Berlin.

FIG. 44. Nuirn or bird spear. (Museum für Völkerkunde, Berlin.)

FIG. 45. Nuqsang or throwing board. (*a* front and *b* back view. (National Museum, Washington. 30013.

the posterior point of the groove describes a wide circle and the fingers let go the shaft, which, remaining in its first position, is driven forward by the spike with great violence, and thus it attains considerable velocity.

I will now give a description of the methods of hunting seals and walrus during the summer. As long as ice cakes are drifting in the bays the natives do not use their seal floats, which would be severed from the line and easily torn to pieces. They paddle to a small cake, on which they lift their kayaks, and cautiously move the cake towards another one on which a seal or walrus is asleep. After they have come within range of their game they shoot it. As an abundance of all kinds of seals and walrus are basking on the ice plenty of food can be obtained.

An ingenious way of walrusing during this season is described by Lyon (p. 330):

When the hunters, in their canoes, perceive a large herd sleeping on the floating ice, as is their custom, they paddle to some other piece near them, which is small enough to be moved. On this they lift their canoes, and then bore several holes, through which they fasten their tough lines, and when everything is ready, they silently paddle the hummock towards their prey, each man sitting by his own line and spear. In this manner they reach the ice on which the walruses are lying snoring; and if they please, each man may strike an animal, though, in general, two persons attack the same beast. The wounded and startled walrus rolls instantly to the water, but the siatko, or harpoon, being well fixed, he cannot escape from the hummock on which the Eskimo have fastened the line. When the animal becomes a little weary, the hunter launches his canoe, and lying out of his reach, spears him to death.

When the ice is gone seals are shot or harpooned with the igimang and the agdliaq. The float prevents their escape and they are killed with the anguvigang or the qapun. Later in summer, when they begin to shed their fur, they lose almost all their blubber and sink when shot; therefore they must be hunted with the harpoon and the float. As the walrus is a dangerous foe should it turn upon the hunters in their light boats, the harpoon is thrown from a great distance, and the animal is not attacked at close quarters until it is well nigh exhausted by dragging the float and the niutang and by loss of blood. A great number of walrus are shot or harpooned while basking on the low islands and rocks.

There are a few shoals and narrow inlets in Frobisher Bay and Cumberland Sound in which great numbers of seals are caught during the summer. In hunting them at those places some of the Eskimo in kayaks occupy the shallow entrance of the inlet, while others scare the seals from its head. As the seals approach its outlet they are speared by those who are lying in wait for them. Since the natives have procured firearms seals are shot from the boats, and in whale boats they even attack the walrus, though they prefer to have drifting ice near at hand in case the fierce animal should turn upon them and tear the boat with its powerful tusks. This method of hunting is very successful in openings which intersect the land floe in spring. To these places an enormous number of seals and walrus resort, and they are shot either when basking at the edge of the water or when blowing.

In the fall, when the small bays are covered with ice and newly formed floes drift to and fro in the open sea, the natives go sealing at the edge of the land ice (Fig. 46). The seals are shot on the drifting ice or in the water and are secured by means of the unang, in the following manner: The hunter jumps upon a small cake, which he pushes on with his spear until he is near the body of the animal, and then drags it upon the land floe with the harpoon line. This method is almost the same as the one used in sealing and walrusing during the winter wherever the open water is close to the shore.

FIG. 46 . Sealing at the edge of the ice. (From a photograph.)

This hunt is described by Gilder in the following words (pp. 182–184):

Usually there are two hunters who approach the walrus, one hiding behind the other, so that the two appear but as one. When the spear is thrown, both hold on to the line, which is wound around their arms so as to cause as much friction as possible, in order to exhaust the animal speedily. * * * When the line is nearly run out the end of the spear shaft is passed through a loop in the end of the line and held firmly by digging a little hole in the ice for the end of the spear to rest in, the foot resting upon the line and against the spear to steady it. This gives the hunter an immense advantage over his powerful game, and if he is fortunate enough to secure this hold there is no escape for the walrus except that the line may cut on the edge of the sharp ice, or the thin ice break off, and hunter, line, and all be precipitated into the water—a not unusual experience in walrus hunting. Another cause of misfortune is for the line to become entangled around the arm of the hunter so that he cannot cast it off, in which case he is most assuredly drawn into the sea, and in nine cases out of ten drowned, for his knife is seldom at hand for an emergency and no amount of experience will ever induce an Inung [Eskimo] to provide against danger.

Sometimes the hunter is alone when he strikes a walrus, and in that case it requires considerable dexterity to secure the spear hold in the ice; or if he fails to get that he may sit down and brace his feet against a small hummock, when it comes to a sheer contest of muscle between the hunter and the walrus. In these contests victory generally perches upon the banner of the walrus, though the Inung [Eskimo] will never give up until the last extremity is reached. Often he is dragged to the very edge of the ice before he finds a protuberance against which to brace his feet, and often he is drawn down under the·ice before he will relinquish his hold. He is very tenacious under such circumstances, for he knows that when he loses the walrus he loses his line and harpoon also.

Hall (I, p. 459) describes the hunt, according to his observations in Frobisher Bay, as follows:

The line is coiled, and hung about the neck of the hunter; thus prepared he hides himself among the broken drifting ice, and awaits the moment for striking his game. The spear is then thrown and the hunter at once slips the coil of line off his head, fastens the end to the ice by driving a spear through a loop in it, and waits till the walrus comes to the surface of the water, into which he has plunged on feeling the stroke of the harpoon; then the animal is quickly despatched by the use of a long lance.

Sometimes the walrus when swimming under an extensive floe of new ice are drowned by being frightened down every time they try to come up to blow.

Formerly whaling was one of the favorite hunts of the Central Eskimo and in some places it is even continued to this day. Whales are either pursued in kayaks or in skin boats. If the kayak is used, they are harpooned in the same way as the walrus, a very large float (avautapāq′) being attached to the harpoon head. The whale is pursued by a great number of kayaks and every boatman endeavors to drive his harpoon into the animal, which, by the loss of blood and the resistance of the niutang and floats, is tired out and killed with lances.

More frequently it is pursued in skin boats (p. 119), which for the purpose are propelled by means of paddles (angun). In this case the crew consists entirely of men, although on other occasions the rowing falls to the women's share; a skillful boatman steers the boat and the harpooner stands in the bow watching his opportunity to strike the whale. The implement used in this pursuit is represented in Fig. 47. I could not procure the weapon itself (sakurpāng′, i. e., the largest weapon), but had a model made by an Akudnirmio, of which the figure is a drawing. The shaft is said to be very long and heavy, measuring from ten to twelve feet. To this shaft a bone point tapering towards the end is firmly attached. The harpoon head consists of two pieces similar to the siatko of the Iglulirmiut (see Fig. 6). The iron edge is inserted into a flat piece of bone, which fits into the slit of a large head. The latter is made from the jawbone of a whale and is extremely heavy. When the whale is struck, both parts, the head and the edge, are disengaged from the shaft and separated from each other, but both enter the flesh of the whale and work in the same way as the tokang.

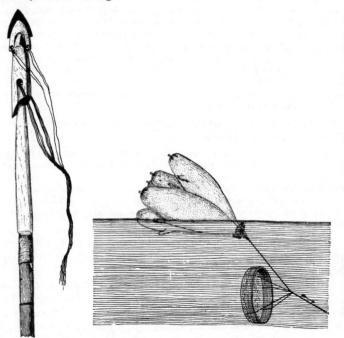

FIG. 47. Model of sakur-
päng' or whaling harpoon.

FIG. 48. Niutang, with floats.

The long harpoon line is coiled up on the first thwart of the boat. On the second one the niutang and five large floats (Fig. 48), which were fastened to the line, are kept ready and heaved overboard as soon as the harpoon is fast to a whale. The buoys and the niutang tire it out quickly and the boat can easily follow it up. It is lanced with the kalugiang whenever it comes up to blow. This lance consists of a heavy handle with a long point of rod iron; formerly bone or narwhal ivory, with an iron edge inserted into its point, was used for this purpose.

The narwhal and the white whale are hunted in the same way as the walrus and the right whale. There are a few shallow bays to which the white whale resorts in the summer. If a shoal of them has entered such a bay, the Eskimo take to their boats and kayaks, and by throwing stones frighten them into the shallowest part, where they are easily harpooned.

DEER, MUSK OX, AND BEAR HUNTING

When the snow has melted and the short summer is at hand the Eskimo start for the deer hunt. The tribes possessed of firearms can easily procure deer all the year round, particularly where uneven land facilitates their approach toward the herd; but in summer the hunt is most important, as it is the only season in which deerskins are fit for clothing.

The favorite method of hunting is to attack the deer in the ponds when swimming from one side to the other. In many places the deer in their migrations are in the habit of crossing the narrow parts of lakes, and here the natives lie in ambush with their kayaks. In other places they are driven into the water by the Eskimo and attacked by the drivers or by hunters stationed on the lake. Favorite places for such a chase are narrow peninsulas, generally called nedlung. The Eskimo deploy into a skirmish line and slowly drive the herd to the point of the peninsula, whence the deer, the retreat being cut off, take to the water.

If the shore be too straight to permit this method of hunting, they drive the deer to a hill stretching to the lake. A line of cairns (inugsung) is erected on the top, intended to deceive the deer, which believe them a new line of hunters approaching from the opposite side. They take to the water, as they see no retreat. If there are no hills a line of cairns is erected in some part of the plain. Such monuments are found all over the country, most of them having the appearance of being very old.

As soon as the deer are in the water the natives pursue them in their kayaks, and as their boats are propelled much more swiftly than the animals can swim they are quickly overtaken and killed with the spear (kapun). Sometimes the wounded deer will turn upon the boat, in which cases the hunter must make his escape with the utmost speed, else he will be capsized or the skin of the boat will be torn to pieces by the animal's antlers.

In some of the narrow valleys with steep faces on both sides the deer are driven toward the hunters. As there is no chance for escape on either side they are killed by the men who lie in ambush. A remarkable tradition referring to the deer hunts of a fabulous tribe in these passes is frequently told by the Eskimo (see p. 227).

Some places are particularly favorable to these methods of hunting. The herds when traveling north in spring and south in autumn take the same course every year, passing rivers, lakes, and valleys at the deer passes. Here the Eskimo stay during the migrations of the deer, as they are sure to fall in with them and to secure plenty of meat and skins during the season. In spring the rivers and lakes are not yet freed from their icy fetters and the pursuit is more difficult; in the autumn, however, they are easily captured in the water. Some important stations of this kind are the island Qeqertome itoq tudlirn, south of Lake Nettilling; the outlet of this lake, Koukdjuaq, particularly the peninsula formed by the river and the south shore of the lake; the country about Qudjitariaq, farther north, and the narrow valley between Piling and Itirbilung : on the continent, the lakes of Rae Isthmus, particularly North Pole Lake; some passes in the hills north of Chesterfield Inlet; the isthmus of Boothia; the entrance of Qimuqsuq, on Adelaide Peninsula; and Simpson Strait.

Referring to the last, Klutschak describes an interesting method of hunting deer which is in vogue in that locality (p. 130). The narrow strait which separates Ita Island from King William Land freezes up early in the season, and the reindeer in trying to cross the strait frequently gather on this island. The Eskimo deploy over the icy bridge and make a terrible noise, frightening the reindeer, which are gradually driven toward a place the ice of which is treacherous at this time of the year. Here they break through and, being able to move only with great difficulty, are easily killed.

Fig. 49 . Wooden bow from Iglulik. (From Parry II, p. 550.)

When the deer have scattered over the country they must be stalked, and, wherever the natives have no firearms, bows and arrows are used.

Fig. 50 . Wooden bow from Cumberland Sound. (National Museum, Washington.)

They have two kinds of bows (pitiqse) : a wooden one (Figs. 49 and 50) and another made of reindeer antlers (Figs. 51 and 52.). Parry gives a very good description of the former (II, p. 510) :

One of the best of their bows was made of a single piece of fir, four feet eight inches in length, flat on the inner side and rounded on the outer, being five inches in girth about the middle where, however, it is strengthened on the concave side, when strung, by a piece of bone ten inches long, firmly secured by tree-nails of the same material. At each end of the bow is a knob of bone, or sometimes of wood covered with leather, with a deep notch for the reception of the string. The only wood which they can procure, not possessing sufficient elasticity combined with strength, they ingeniously remedy the defect by securing to the back of the bow, and to the knobs at each end, a quantity of small lines, each composed of a plat or "sinnet" of three sinews. The number of lines thus reaching from end to end is generally about thirty; but besides these, several others are fastened with hitches round the bow, in pairs, commencing eight inches from one end, and again united at the same distance from the other, making the whole number of strings in the middle of the bow sometimes amount to sixty. These being put on with the bow somewhat bent the contrary way, produce a spring so strong as to require considerable force as well as knack in stringing it, and giving the requisite velocity to the arrow. The bow is completed by a woolding round the middle and a wedge or two here and there, driven in to tighten it.

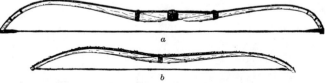

FIG. 51. Bows of reindeer antlers. (National Museum, Washington. *a*, 34053; *b*, 34055.)

The bow represented in Fig. 50 is from Cumberland Sound and resembles the Iglulik pattern. The fastening of the sinew lines is different and the piece of bone giving additional strength to the central part is wanting. In Cumberland Sound and farther south wooden bows each made of a single piece were not very rare; the wood necessary for their manufacture was found in abundance on Tudjan (Resolution Island), whence it was brought to the more northern districts.

FIG. 52. Bow of antlers, with central part cut off straight, from Pelly Bay. (National Museum, Washington. 10270.

The bows which are made of antlers generally consist of three pieces, a stout central one slanted on both sides and two side pieces riveted to it. The central part is either below or above the side ones, as represented in Fig. 51. These bows are strengthened by plaited sinews in the same way as the wooden ones and generally the joints are secured by strong strings wound around them. A remarkable bow made of antlers is represented in Fig. 52. The central part is not slanted, but cut off straight. The joint is effected by two additional pieces on each side, a short stout one outside, a long thin one inside. These are firmly tied together with sinews. The short piece prevents the parts from breaking apart, the long one gives a powerful spring. The specimen here represented was brought home by Hall from the Sinimiut of Pelly Bay, and a similar one was brought by Collinson from Victoria Land and has been deposited in the British Museum. The strings are attached to these bows in the same way as to the wooden ones.

The arrows (qaqdjung) are made of round pieces of wood generally tapering a little towards the lower end, to which two feathers of an owl or some other bird are attached. The bone heads of these

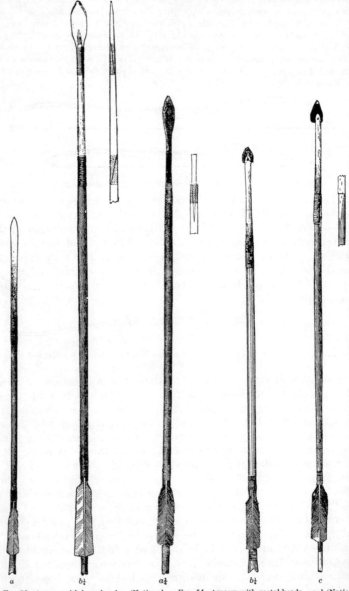

FIG. 53. Arrows with bone heads. (National Museum, Washington. *a*, 34054; *b*, 10270.)

FIG. 54. Arrows with metal heads. *a, b* (National Museum, Washington. *a*, 30056; *b*, 34056.) *c* (Museum für Völkerkunde, Berlin. IV A 6707.)

rrows are joined to the shaft as represented in Fig. 53 , while metal
eads are inserted as shown in Fig. 54 . The difference in the
nethods used by the Mackenzie and the central tribes in fastening

FIG. 55 . Arrowhead from Boothia. (Na-
onal Museum, Washington. 10205.) ½

a   *b*
FIG. 56. Showing attachment of arrowhead vertically
and parallel to shank. (National Museum, Washington.
b, 10137.) ¼

he point to the shaft is very striking.   The arrow point of the for-
ner and of the western tribes is pointed and inserted in the shaft
Fig. 55),[1] while that of the latter is always slanted and lashed to
t (Figs. 53 and 54). The direction of the slant is either parallel
r vertical to the edge (Fig. 56). Other forms of arrows are shown
n Fig. 57 . A similar difference between the fastenings of the
ocket to the spear handle exists in the two localities. The western
ribes give its base the form of a wedge (Fig. 58), which is inserted
n the shaft, while the Central Eskimo use a mortise.

[1] According to the Museum catalogue, the point represented in this figure is from
ictoria Island, Boothia, from Hall's collection ; however, it is a typical western
row.

Formerly slate heads were in general use (Fig. 59); now the heads
are almost everywhere made of iron or tin, riveted or tied to th

FIG. 57. Various forms of arrowhead. National Museum, Washington. a, 29993 ; e, 10213.) $\frac{1}{4}$

FIG. 58. Socket of spear handle from Alaska.
(National Museum, Washington. 36060.) $\frac{1}{4}$

FIG. 59. Slate arrowhead. (National Museum
Washington. 10403.) $\frac{1}{4}$

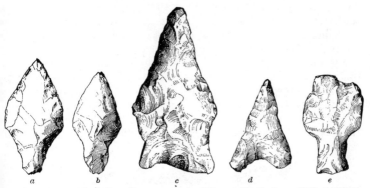

FIG. 60 . Flint arrowheads from old graves. (National Museum, Washington. c, 30109; d, 34138.) ¼

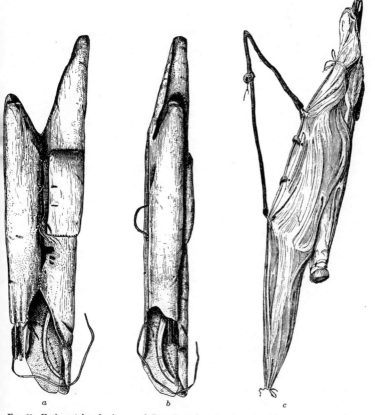

FIG. 61 . Various styles of quiver. a, b Two views of a quiver from Cumberland Sound. (National Museum, Washington. 30015.) c Quiver from Iglulik (from Parry II, p. 550).

point (Fig. 57). In ancient graves flint heads are frequently found some of which are represented in Fig. 60. On Southampton Island stone heads are in use even at the present time. Fig. 34 probably shows how they were attached to the shank.

The quiver (Fig. 61) is made of sealskin, the hair of which is removed. It comprises three divisions, a larger one containing the bow and a smaller one containing four or six arrows, the head directed toward the lower end of the case. When extracted from the quiver they are ready for use. Between the two compartments there is also a small pouch, in which tools and extra arrowheads are carried.

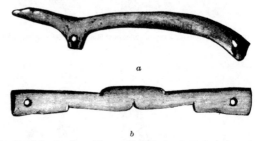

a

b

FIG. 62 . Quiver handles. (Museum für Völkerkunde, Berlin. *a, b,* IV A 6843.)

When traveling the Eskimo carry the quiver by an ivory handle; when in use it is hung over the left shoulder. Fig. 62 represents quiver handles, the first being fashioned in imitation of an ermine.

If the deer cannot be driven into the water the Eskimo either stalk them or shoot them from a stand. In a plain where the hunter can not hide himself it is easier to approach the herd if two men hunt together. They advance, the second man hiding behind the first one by stooping a little. The bows or the guns are carried on the shoulders so as to resemble the antlers of a deer. The men imitate their grunting and approach slowly, now stopping and stooping, now advancing. If the deer look about suspiciously they sit down, the second man lying almost flat on the ground, and both, at some distance off, greatly resemble the animals themselves. Ross (II, p. 252) states that the inhabitants of Boothia imitate the appearance of the deer, the foremost of two men stalking a herd bearing a deer head upon his own.

It is somewhat difficult to approach the deer near enough to get within range, especially if they are hunted with bow and arrow. Generally it is not necessary to get quite near them, for when feeding the herd moves on in the same direction for some time, and the hunter can hide behind a stone lying in that direction and wait until they are within range. After the first shot has been fired they do not take to flight at once, but stand for a few seconds, struck with su

rise, and a clever hunter may kill two or three before they run away.
f the country is very level the Eskimo raise heaps of stones or build
ircular or semicircular walls to conceal themselves and allure the
nimals by grunting. As the deer possess a very fine scent they must
lways be approached from the lee side.

An interesting method of hunting is described by Parry (II, p. 512)
nd confirmed by Hall (II, p. 178). Parry writes:

Two men walk directly from the deer they wish to kill, when the animal almost
ways follows them. As soon as they arrive at a large stone, one of the men hides
hind it with his bow, while the other continuing to walk on soon leads the deer
ithin range of his companion's arrows.

Hall says that one hunter hides himself behind a stone while the
ther utters grunting sounds to attract it.

In winter deer are sometimes caught in traps made by digging
oles in the snow and covering them with slabs of the same material.
ometimes urine is poured upon and around the trap or salt water
e is placed upon it, in order to allure the deer (Klutschak, p. 131).
aving been attracted to the trap they fall through the roof and are
peared in the hole.

Wherever the musk ox is found it is eagerly pursued by the Es-
imo. Though dogs are of no use in the chase of the nimble deer,
ley are of great help in hunting this animal. When a track is
und the dogs are let loose and soon overtake the herd. The latter
rm a circle of defense in which they are kept at bay until the
unter approaches. While the dogs continue attacking and dodg-
g, the musk oxen try to hit them with their horns and do not heed
le Eskimo, who assails them at close quarters with a lance to which
thong is frequently attached. When an ox is wounded it makes
a impetuous attack on the hunter, who dodges to one side. The
gs being at hand again immediately keep it at bay, thus enabling
le hunter to let fly another arrow or throw his lance again. Thus
le struggle continues until the greater part of the herd is killed.
a rare instances an ox dashes out of the circle and escapes from the
ack.

Polar bears are hunted in about the same manner as the musk ox.
he Eskimo pursue them in light sledges, and when they are near
le pursued animal the traces of the most reliable dogs in the team
e cut, when they dash forward and bring the bear to bay. As the
unter gets sufficiently near, the last dogs are let loose and the bear
killed with a spear or with bow and arrow. The best season for
ear hunting is in March and April, when the bears come up the
ords and bays in pursuit of the young seals. At this season the she
ear is accompanied by the cub which was born in February or March.
s skin and flesh are highly prized by the Eskimo. At some places,
r instance at Cape Raper and at Cape Kater on Davis Strait, the
le bears dig holes in the snow banks, in which they sleep during

the winter.   The natives seek these holes and kill the bear before i
awakes.

The chase of the musk ox and that of the bear have become mucl
easier since the introduction of firearms in Arctic America, and th
Eskimo can kill their game without encountering the same danger
as formerly.

HUNTING OF SMALL GAME.

Lastly, I mention the methods used in catching smaller animals
such as wolves, foxes, and hares.   Wolves are only pursued whe
they become too troublesome.   Frequently they linger about th
villages in winter, and when everybody is asleep they attack th
store rooms or the dogs, which have the greatest fear of this voraciou
animal; for, although dogs will brave the bear, they do not ventur
to resist a single wolf.   If a pack of these beasts linger about th
village for weeks preying upon the native stores, traps are finall
built or the Eskimo lie in ambush near a bait to kill them.   Th
wolf trap is similar to the one used to catch deer.   The hole dug i
the snow is about eight or nine feet deep and is covered with
slab of snow, on the center of which a bait is laid.   A wall is buil
around it which compels the wolf to leap across it before he ca
reach the bait.   By so doing he breaks through the roof and, as th
bottom of the pit is too narrow to afford him jumping room, he i
caught and killed there (Rae I, p. 135).

A remarkable method of killing wolves has been described b
Klutschak (p. 192) and confirmed by the Eskimo of Cumberlan
Sound.   A sharp knife is smeared with deer's blood and sunk int
the snow, the edge only protruding.   The wolves lick the knife an
cut their tongues so severely as to bleed to death.   Another metho
is to roll a strip of whalebone, about two feet long, in a coil, whic
is tied up with sinews.   At each end a small metal edge is attached t
the whalebone.   This strip, wrapped in a piece of blubber or meat
is gulped down by the hungry wolf.   As it is digested the sinew
are dissolved and the elastic strap is opened and tears the stomacl
of the animal.   A very ingenious trap is described by Parry (II, p
514):

It consists of a small house built of ice, at one end of which a door, made of th
same plentiful material, is fitted to slide up and down in a groove; to the upper pa
of this a line is attached and, passing over the roof, is led down into the trap at th
inner end, and there held by slipping an eye in the end of it over a peg of ice left fo
the purpose.   Over the peg, however, is previously placed a loose grummet, to whic
the bait is fastened, and a false roof placed over all to hide the line.   The momer
the animal drags at the bait the grummet slips off the peg, bringing with it th
line that held up the door, and this falling down closes the trap and secures him.

Foxes are usually caught in traps.   An ice house about six fee
high is built of hummocks, which are cut down with the point c
the spear.   It is covered with ice slabs, only a hole in the cente

being left. Blocks of snow and slabs of ice are piled up around the building so as to permit easy access to the roof. Some blood is sprinkled round the hole to attract the fox and a larger bait is placed upon the floor of the house. The fox jumps down and, as the only exit is in the center of the roof, cannot escape. Another trap has a slab of ice erected in such a manner as to fall and kill the fox when he touches the bait.

A third trap, similar to the one above mentioned, has been described by Lyon, p. 339:

> It is like a small lime kiln in form, having a hole near the top, within which the bait is placed, and the foxes (for these animals alone are thus taken) are obliged to advance to it over a piece of whalebone, which, bending beneath their weight, lets them into prison, and then resumes its former position: thus a great number of them are sometimes caught in a night. In the summer they are but rarely taken, and it is then by means of a trap of stones, formed like the ice trap, with a falling door.

Hares are either killed with small shot or with arrows or caught in whalebone snares, as are ermines and lemmings.

Waterfowl of all descriptions are caught in abundance in whalebone nooses (Fig. 63) fastened to a long whalebone line or to a thong.

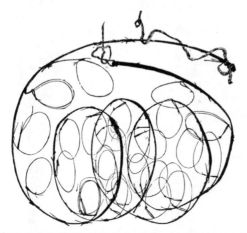

Fig. 63 . Whalebone nooses for catching waterfowl. (In the possession of Captain Spicer, of Groton, Conn.)

The line is set along the edge of a lake, particularly near nesting places. In shallow lakes these lines are placed across the water to catch the diving and swimming birds, which are drawn to the shore with the line. On the low egg islands, which are inhabited by innumerable ducks, snares are set on the nests, and great numbers are caught in a short time. Swans and geese are procured in the same way. Other birds, and particularly partridges, are killed with arrows and with small shot.

Large flocks of ducks and other kinds of birds fly through certain valleys in the fall and in spring when migrating. Great numbers are caught here without any difficulty, as they can be killed with sticks.

A favorite method of catching gulls is by building a flat snow house. One block of the roof is translucent and so thin as to permit the hunter, who is hidden in the house, to push his hand through it. A bait is placed on this block, and as soon as a bird alights to feed it is pulled through the roof into the hut.

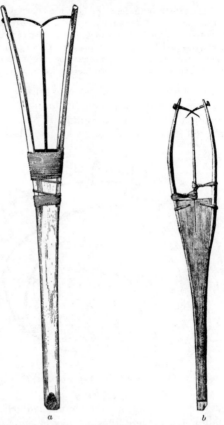

a   *b*

FIG. 64 . Kakivang or salmon spear.   (National Museum, Washington. *a*, 34087; *b*, 34086.) ¼

By far the greater number of birds are caught during the molting season. Partridges can be caught with the hand and waterfowl are pursued with the kayak. The waterfowl dive as soon as the boat comes near them and being frightened down again as soon as they rise they are eventually drowned. One species of goose (kango which frequents the lakes of the country is caught in a remarkable way. A circular wall of stones is raised, with a single entrance. The Eskimo drive a flock of these birds towards the building, one man, whom the stupid creatures follow, leading the way. As soon as they have entered the wall the entrance is shut up and they are slaughtered. If they happen to be met with on the water they are encircled by kayaks and driven towards the shore, one boat leading. Then they are driven within the stone wall as already described.

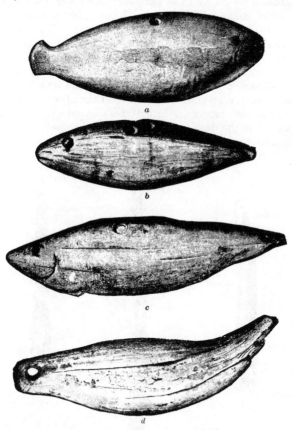

Fig. 65 . Ivory fish used as bait in spearing salmon. *a* From Repulse Bay. *a, c. d* (National Museum, Washington. *a*, 10400 ; *c*, 34109 ; *d*, 34124.) ⅓ *b* (Museum für Völkerkunde, Berlin. IV A 6830.) ⅓

FISHING.

The most important fish is the salmon, which is caught in abundance during the summer. When the lakes begin to break up the salmon descend to the sea, following the narrow lead between the land floe and the water. In some places they are so plentiful as to fill the water completely. Here they are speared with the kakivang (Fig. 64). This instrument consists of a handle which widens towards the end; in the center it has a prong of bone or iron, and two larger ones at the sides, made of deer antlers or musk ox horn. These latter diverge and are furnished with a bone or iron nail on the inner side. The elasticity of these side prongs is increased by thongs or strings holding them tightly together. If the salmon are very plentiful no bait is needed and the natives cannot spear them as quickly as they swim along. When the ice is gone they are caught in the shallow rivers falling from the lakes into the sea. The natives stand on the bank or step into the water. A small ivory fish (Fig. 65) (eχalujang), tied by two or three holes in the back to a plaited string of deer sinews, is used as a bait. Frequently bear's teeth are used for bait. They are attached to a separate line which the hunter continually moves up and down to attract the attention of the fish. When the salmon comes near the bait it is speared with the kakivang. In the left hand the fisherman holds an instrument for stringing the fish (quqartaun), some illustrations of which are given in Fig. 66.

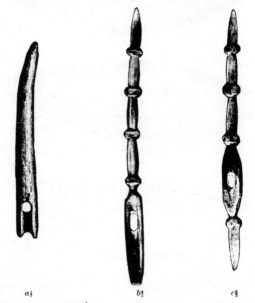

FIG. 66 . Quqartaun for stringing fish. c (Museum für Völkerkunde, Berlin. IV A 6831.)

It is made of ivory. A thong fastened to the hole of the instrument has a thick knot at the opposite end. As soon as a salmon is caught it is taken out of the nippers (kakivang) and the point of th quqartaun is pushed into the gills and brought out again at the mouth; thus the fish remains sticking until it is dead. Sometimes it is killed by pushing the ivory point of the instrument into its neck. When dead it is pushed on the thong.

At some places wears are built, above which the fish are caught. These consist of dikes of stones about one and a half or two feet high, which are piled across a creek some distance below high water mark. The salmon cross the wall at high water, but are cut off from the sea at half tide and are speared while there. In other places the forks of rivers are shut off by dikes, above which the salmon gather.

In autumn salmon are caught when ascending the rivers. Sometimes they linger too long in small ponds and, as the rivers quickly dry up at this season, are prevented from getting out of the pools. Here they are caught until late in the season. Some of these ponds freeze to the bottom in winter, and the natives, when visiting them in the spring, cut holes in the ice and take out the frozen fish.

FIG. 67. Salmon hook. (National Museum, Washington. 10142.) ½

FIG. 68. Salmon hook. (Museum für Völkerkunde, Berlin. 6847.) ½

In the early part of the spring salmon are caught with hooks kakliokia, Iglulik; niksiartaung, Oqo), holes being cut through the ice of the lake. Formerly the hooks were made of deer antlers. Another device consists of a nail, crooked and pointed at one end, the other being let into a piece of ivory or bone (Fig. 67). A third one is represented in Fig. 68.

The fishing line is made of plaited deer sinews and is either held in the hand or tied to a short rod. Along with these hooks baits are used similar to those mentioned in the foregoing description. If the carving represented in Fig. 69 is used, the hook is tied to it by means of two holes on the lower side of the fish, while the line passes through its back.   The fish, in coming near the bait, is generally caught by the hook in the back or side.   In this manner salmon, trout, and all kinds of sea fish are caught.

FIG. 69 . Bait used in fishing with hooks. (National Museum, Washington. 34108.) ⅓

I myself have never seen any nets for fishing, but Klutschak found them in use among the Utkusiksalik tribe, and Petitot (Les grands Esquimaux, p. 278), among the natives of Anderson River. The Labrador Eskimo also use nets.

MANUFACTURES.

MAKING LEATHER AND PREPARING SKINS.

Most of the implements of the Eskimo are made of some part of the animals which they pursue.   The skins are used for clothing, for building purposes, and for covering the frames of boats.   Many implements are made of bone, others of walrus tusks or narwhal horn. As wood is extremely scarce, bone or other parts of animals must make up the deficiency.   I shall here describe the methods of preparing these materials.

FIG. 70 . Butcher's knife with bone handle. (National Museum, Washington. 34090.) ⅓

The skin of the seal (*Pagomys fœtidus*) is dressed in different ways, according to the purpose for which it is intended.   In skinning the animal a longitudinal cut is made across the belly with a common butcher's knife (saving).   Most natives have procured this useful instrument and even in olden times a considerable number had found their way from Hudson Bay territory to their countries.   The large knives of their own manufacture (pilaut) are of similar form, a metal edge being inserted into an ivory blade.   Figure 70 is a more modern knife, an iron blade being fastened to a bone handle.

The skin, with the blubber, is cut from the flesh with the same knife, or still more easily with the pana, the old device of which is represented in Fig. 71 *a* (Parry II, p. 550). This knife is about one foot and a half long (Parry II, p. 503). The use of the small prongs near the blade was not explained by Parry. In Fig. 71 *b* is presented a pana from the eastern coast of Hudson Bay, collected by Dr. R. Bell; the handle is made of bone, the blade of iron. The flippers are cut off at the joints, and thus the whole skin is drawn off in a single piece. In dressing the animal the natives open the belly and first scoop out the blood, then the entrails are taken out, the ribs are separated from the breast bone and from the vertebræ, the fore flippers (with the shoulders and the hind flippers) are taken out, the only part remaining being the head, the spinal column, and the rump bone. Generally these are not eaten, but are used for dogs' food.

a   *b*

Fig. 71 . Pana or knife for dissecting game. *a* (From Parry II, p. 548.) *b* (American Museum of Natural History.)

The knife (ulo) used by the women serves to clean and prepare the skins. This implement, with which almost all the cutting is done, is shaped like a crescent, the handle being attached to the center, and

greatly resembles a mincing knife. Fig. 72 represents the form
which is now in use. Fig. 73 is a very old ulo handle from a stone
circle on Qeqertuqdjuaq (Cape Broughton). It is made of bone and
has a slit for the slate blade. It is worth remarking that this blade
had not been riveted to the handle, but fastened with a kind of glue

FIG. 72. Form of ulo now in use. (Museum
für Völkerkunde, Berlin. IV A 6733.) ⅔

FIG. 73. Old ulo with top of handle broken off
from Cape Broughton, Davis Strait. (Museum für
Völkerkunde, Berlin.) ¼

(see p. 118). There are a few arrow and harpoon heads the blades
of which are inserted in the same manner; the bone is heated and
the blade is inserted while it is hot. As it is cooling the slit becomes
narrower and the blade is firmly squeezed into the bone handle. Part
of a slate blade, which had been riveted to the handle, is shown
in Fig. 74. Fig. 75 represents a handle from a recent grave.

FIG. 74. Fragment of an ulo blade of slate. (Museum für Völkerkunde, Berlin. IV A 6714.) ¼

FIG. 75. Ulo handle from recent grave.
(National Museum, Washington. 34127.)

In preparing the skin the women spread it over a piece of whalebone (asimautang), a small board, or a flat stone, and sit down before
it, resting on their knees, the feet bent under the thighs. They hold
the skin at the nearest edge and, pushing the ulo forward, remove
the blubber from it and deposit the latter in a small tub which stands
near the board. As they proceed to the opposite end of the skin, the
finished part is rolled up and held in the left hand.

If the skin is to be used with the hair on it, the tough membrane (mami) which covers the inner side is removed in the same way as the blubber and, after it has been carefully patched up and holes have been cut all around the edge, is stretched over a gravelly place or on snow by means of long pegs (pauktun), which hold it a few inches above the ground, thus allowing the air to circulate underneath it. The skin itself is washed and rubbed with gravel, snow, or ice and every hole made by the bullet or by the spear or in preparing it is sewed up. It very seldom happens that the women in preparing it damage the skin or even the thin mami. It is particularly difficult to split the skin near a hole. First they finish the work all around it and then carefully sever the membrane at its edge. The skin is dried in the same way as the membrane. In the early part of spring, though it may still be very cold, a few choice young sealskins are dried on snow walls which face to the south.

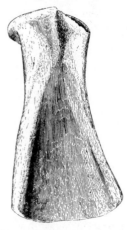

Fig. 76. Modern tesirqun or scraper. (Museum für Völkerkunde, Berlin. IV A 6734.)

Fig. 77. Old style of tesirqun or scraper. (Museum für Völkerkunde, Berlin.)

In order thoroughly to dry a sealskin one fine warm spring day is needed. If the Eskimo are greatly in need of skins they dry them in winter over the lamps. A frame is made of four poles, lashed together, according to the size of the skin. A thong passes through the slits along its edge and around the frame, keeping the skin well stretched. Thus it is placed over the lamps or near the roof of the hut. However, it is disagreeable work to dry the skins inside the huts, and, as they are much inferior to those which are dried on the ground, the Eskimo avoid it if they can. When so prepared the sealskins are only fit for covering tents, making bags, &c.; they are far too hard to be used for clothing, for which purpose the skin of yearlings is almost exclusively used. The young seals, having shed for the first time, have a very handsome coat, the hair being of a fine texture and much longer than in older animals. From the middle of May until late in summer their skins are most suitable for the manufacture of summer clothing, but it is necessary to protect the carcasses of the killed animals from the burning rays of the sun as soon as possible or the skin would be quickly spoiled.

After being dried they are cleaned with the sharp scraper (tesir qun), the modern device of which is represented in Fig. 76. It con sists of a handle having a round back and a flat front, with two grooves for the knuckles of the first and second fingers, while the thumb and the other fingers clasp the handle. The scraper itself consists of a rounded piece of tin riveted to the handle. The old scraper (Fig. 77) was made of a deer's shoulder or of some other bone. I have never seen any that were made of a thigh bone, simi lar to those found by Lucien M. Turner in Ungava Bay.

After being scraped the skin is soaked in salt water and washed again. As soon as it is dry it is softened with the straight scrape (seligoung) (Fig. 78).

Fig. 78. Seligoung or scraper used for softening skins. (Museum für Völkerkunde, Berlin. IV A 6697

Fig. 79 shows some very old stone scrapers found in graves. A the stones are sharpened it is probable that they were used for clean ing the skins. The hole in the right side of the handle is used fo the second finger, the grooves on the back for the third and fourth The bone is fastened to the handle by whalebone straps or thongs

Skins of *Phoca annellata*, *Phoca cristata*, and *Phoca grœnlandic* are prepared in the same way.

Those which are intended for kayak covers, boots, mittens, quivers &c. are prepared in a different way. They are either put into ho water or laid in a brook for a few days until the hair begins t loosen. Then both sides are worked with the ulo, in order to clea and shave them. When the hair is removed they are dried and mad pliable in the same way as has been described. If it is intended t make the skin as soft as possible it is allowed to become putrid be fore it is cleansed. Then the hair and the blubber are removed, an afterwards it is left to hang in the sun for a few days until it acquire a light color.

The large ground seal (*Phoca barbata*) is skinned in a differen manner. Its skin is very thick, thicker even than sole leather, an therefore extremely durable and suitable for all sorts of lines, pa ticularly traces, lashings, and harpoon lines, and for soles, drinkin cups, and boat covers.   This seal is very large, sometimes attaining a length of ten feet.   The skin of the back and of the breast dries unequally, and therefore a piece covering the throat and breast is taken

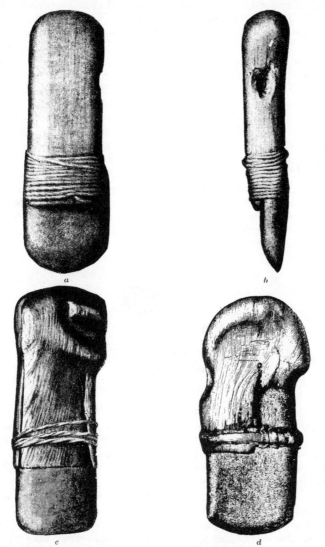

Fig. 79 . Old stone scrapers found in graves. (National Museum, Washington. *a*, *b*, 34083 ; *c*, 34084 ; *d*, 34085.) ⅔

out before the rest is skinned, and the parts are dried separately.   If it is to be used for lines it is cut by making girdles about six inches in width around the body.   The hair and the blubber are removed from these cylindrical rings, from which lines are made by cutting spirally, a strip seventy or eighty feet long being thus obtained. This line is stretched as taut as possible between two rocks, and while drying it undergoes an enormous tension. Before being taken from the rocks the edges are rounded and cleaned with a knife.

Walrus hide is always cut up before being prepared. As soon as the walrus is killed it is cut into as many parts as there are partners in the hunt, every part being rolled up in a piece of skin and carried home in it. Sometimes the skin is used for making boats, but generally it is cut into lines. Both kinds of hide, that of the walrus and that of the ground seal, are as stiff as a board when dried and require much work before being fit for use. They are chewed by the natives until they become thin and pliable. The whole skin must be chewed in this way before it can be used for soles and boat covers. Afterwards it is scraped with the tesirqun and softened with the straight scraper. The new thongs, after being dried between the rocks, must also be chewed until they become sufficiently pliable, after which they are straightened by a stretcher that is held with the feet (Fig. 80'). Frequently they are only pulled over the sole of the boot for this purpose, the man taking hold of the line at two points and pulling the intermediate part by turns to the right and to the left over the sole of the foot.

Fig. 80 . Stretcher for lines. (National Museum, Washington. 9836.) ⅓

Another kind of line is cut from the hide of the white whale, which is skinned in the same way as the ground seal, but, as it must be slit on the spinal column, the single pieces of line are much shorter, and they cannot be used to the same extent as seal lines. Some lines are cut from the skins of *Pagomys fœtidus*, but these are weak and greatly inferior to lines of ground seal hide.

Deerskins are dried in summer and dressed after the ice has formed. Like all other kinds of skins they are not tanned, but curried. They are hung up among the rafters of the hut, and the workers — in Oqo and Akudnirn the women, in Hudson Bay the men — take off their jackets and begin preparing them with the sharp scraper. After being cleaned in this way they are thoroughly dried, either by hanging them near the roof of the hut or, according to Gilder, by wrapping them around the upper part of the body next to the skin, after which they are again scraped with the tesirqun. This done, the flesh side is wetted, the skin is wrapped up for half a day or a day, and afterwards undergoes a new scraping. Then it is chewed, rubbed, and scraped all over, thus acquiring its pliability, softness, and light color.

In the spring the skins of bears and of seals are sometimes dried on large frames which are exposed to the sun, the skins being tied to the frames with thongs. Smaller quadrupeds, as foxes and ermines, are skinned by stripping the entire animal through its mouth without making a single cut in the skin. Birds are opened at the breast and the body is taken out through this small hole, the head, wings, and legs being cut off at the neck and the other joints. Ducks are frequently skinned by cutting the skin around the head and the outer joints of the wings and legs and stripping it off. The skins are cleaned by sucking out the fat and chewing them.

Skins of salmon are used for water proof bags; intestines of seals, particularly those of ground seals, are carefully dried and after being sewed together are used for sails, windows, and kayak jackets.

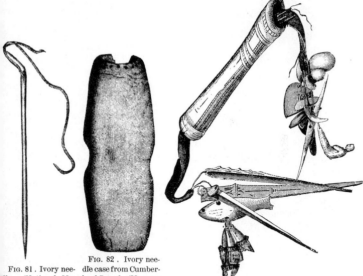

FIG. 81 . Ivory needle. (National Museum, Washington. 34135.) ¼

FIG. 82 . Ivory needle case from Cumberland Sound. (Museum für Völkerkunde, Berlin. 6832.) ¼

FIG. 83 . Common pattern of needle case, Iglulik. (From Parry II, p. 548.)

SUNDRY IMPLEMENTS.

The sewing is done with thread made of deer or white whale sinews. Particularly are those sinews at the back dried and when intended for use they can easily be split as thin as required. At present steel needles are in general use. Wherever they are wanting ivory ones of the same pattern are used (Fig. 81). The thread is fastened to the eyehole by a kind of loop, the short end being twisted around the longer one. Kumlien described a needle of a very different device (p. 25):

This tool was almost exactly like an awl in shape, but had an eye near the point. They must have had to thread this instrument for each stitch. The needle part was apparently of deer horn and the handle of walrus ivory.

Probably it was used like a packing needle for sewing tent covers, &c. The needles (mirqun) are kept in ivory needle cases (umī'ujang). The case represented in Fig. 82 is from a grave in Cumberland Sound. The grooves on both sides are evidently intended for a leather strap which is to be tied around it. This specimen is closed at the bottom and had a stopper for closing the mouth. Fig. 83 is a more common pattern. The ivory piece forms a tube through which a leather strap passes. The needles are stuck into the leather and drawn into the tube. Small ivory implements and ornaments are attached to both ends of the strap.

a   *b*

FIG. 84 . Tikiq or thimble. (National Museum, Washington. 10181.) ½

Thimbles (tikiq) (Fig. 84) are made of an oblong piece of ground sealskin, fitting to the point of the first finger. A rim is cut around half of its circumference and thus it can be drawn over the finger. The women sew by pulling the thread toward them and making an overcast seam.

Whalebone is used for making elastic thongs and in the place of wood; for example, for kayak ribs, for the rim of the kayak hole, boxes, &c. It requires no particular preparation, being easily split and shaped so as to fit any purpose. If wood is to be bent into hoops or deer horn is to be straightened, it is made pliable by being put into boiling water for some time. Bones of whales and other large animals and the penis bone of the walrus are used instead of poles. In olden times, when iron was extremely rare and an effective saw could not be procured, they split the bone by drilling many holes, one close to the other, afterwards breaking the pieces asunder.

Small pieces of bone, used for arrows &c., were straightened, after being steamed, with the implement represented in Fig. 85 .

The drill (Fig. 86) is the most important implement for working in ivory and bone. It consists of three parts : the bow with its string (niuqtung), the drill (qaivun), and the mouthpiece (qingmiaq). The string of the bow is twisted around the shaft of the drill, the mouth-

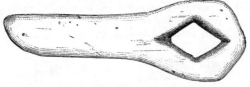

FIG. 85. Instrument for straightening bones.

piece (which is made of wood or of bone) is taken into the mouth, and the rounded end of the drill is placed in its hole. Then the whole implement is put firmly against the place to be perforated and is set in motion by moving the bow. Instead of the latter, a string is sometimes used with a handle at each end. For one man, however, the first device is handier. The string of the second form is usually pulled by one man while the other holds the mouthpiece.

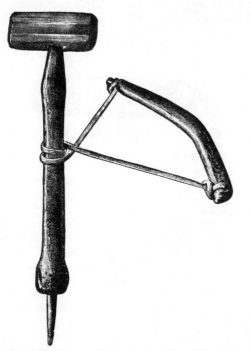

FIG. 86. Drill for working in ivory and bone. (National Museum, Washington. 34114.) ⅔

The same instrument is sometimes used for making fire. Instead of the iron, a piece of hard wood (ground willow) is put into the mouthpiece and placed upon a piece of driftwood cut to the shape represented in Fig. 87. The wooden drill turns rapidly in a hole of the driftwood until it begins to glow. A little moss is applied to the glowing wood and gently blown until it begins to burn. Wherever flint and pyrite are to be had these are used for striking fire. Moss or the wool-like hair of *Eryophorum* serves for tinder.

FIG. 87. Driftwood used in kindling fire from Nugumiut. (National Museum, Washington. 10258.) ¼

Ivory implements are cut out of the tusks with strong knives and are shaped by chipping pieces from the blocks until they acquire the desired forms. In olden times it must have been an extremely troublesome work to cut them out, the old knives being very poor and ineffective. They are finished with the file, which on this account is an important tool for the natives; it is also used for sharpening knives and harpoons. The women's knives are cut, by means of files, from old saw blades; the seal harpoons, from Scotch whale harpoons. If files are not obtainable, whetstones are used for sharpening the iron and stone implements.

FIG. 88. Eskimo graver's tool. (National Museum, Washington. 34105.) ¼

Engravings in bone and ivory are made with the implement represented in Fig. 88. An iron point is inserted in a wooden handle; formerly a quartz point was used. The notch which separates the head from the handle serves as a hold for the points of the fingers. The designs are scratched into the ivory with the iron pin.

Stone implements were made of flint, slate, or soapstone. Flint was worked with a squeezing tool, generally made of bone. Small pieces were thus split off until the stone acquired the desired form. Slate was first roughly formed and then finished with the drill and the whetstone. The soft soapstone is now chiseled out with iron tools. If large blocks of soapstone cannot be obtained, fragments are cemented together by means of a mixture of seal's blood, a kind of clay, and dog's hair. This is applied to the joint, the vessel being heated over a lamp until the cement is dry. According to Lyon (p. 320) it is fancied that the hair of a bitch would spoil the composition and prevent it from sticking.

TRANSPORTATION BY BOATS AND SLEDGES.

THE BOAT (UMIAQ).

The main part of the frame of a boat is a timber which runs from stem to stern (Fig. 89). It is the most solid part and is made of driftwood, which is procured in Hudson Strait, Hudson Bay, and on

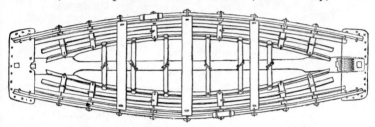

Fig. 89. Framework of Eskimo boat.

the northern shore of King William Land. In Iglulik, and probably in Pond Bay, boats are rarely used and never made, as wood is wanting. The central part of this timber is made a little narrower than the ends, which form stout heads. A mortise is cut into each of the latter, into which posts (kiglo) are tenoned for the bow and for the stern. The shape of this part will best be seen from the engraving (Fig. 90). A strong piece of wood is fitted to the top of these uprights and the gunwales are fastened to them with heavy thongs.

Fig. 90. Kiglo or post.

The gunwales and two curved strips of wood (akuk), which run along each side of the bottom of the boat from stem to stern, determine its form. These strips are steadied by from seven to ten cross pieces, which are firmly tied to them and to the central piece. From this pair of strips to the gunwales run a number of ribs, which stand somewhat close together at the bow and the stern, but are separated by intervals of greater distance in the center of the boat. The cross pieces along the bottom are arranged similarly to the ribs. Between the gunwale and the bottom two or three pairs of strips also run along the sides of the boat and steady its whole frame. The uppermost pair (which is called tuving) lies near the gunwale and serves as a fastening for the cover of the boat. The thwarts, three or four in number, are fastened between the gunwale and these lateral strips. All these pieces are tied together with thongs, rivets not being used at all.

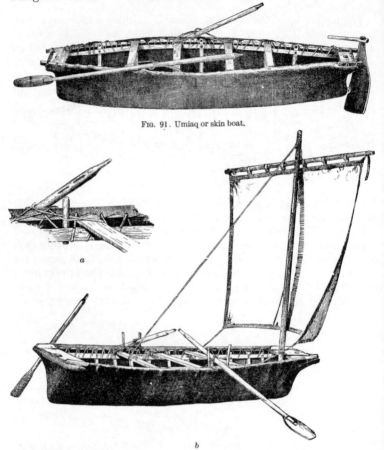

FIG. 91. Umiaq or skin boat.

a

b

FIG. 92. Umiaq or skin boat.

The frame is covered with skins of ground seals (Figs. 91ᵇ, 92). It requires three of these skins to cover a medium sized boat; five to cover a large one. If ground seals cannot be procured, skins of harp or small seals are used, as many as twelve of the latter being required. The cover is drawn tightly over the gunwale and, after being wetted, is secured by thongs to the lateral strip which is close to the gunwale. The wooden pieces at both ends are perforated and the thongs for fastening the cover are pulled through these holes.

The boat is propelled by two large oars. The rowlocks are a very ingenious device. A piece of bone is tied upon the skin in order to protect it from the friction of the oar, which would quickly wear it through (Fig. 92 *a*). On each side of the bone a thong is fastened to the tuving, forming a loop. Both loops cross each other like two rings of a chain. The oar is drawn through both loops, which are twisted by toggles until they become tight. Then the toggles are secured between the gunwale and the tuving.

The oar (ipun) consists of a long shaft and an oval or round blade fastened to the shaft by thongs. Two grooves and the tapering end serve for handles in pulling. Generally three or four women work at each oar.

For steering, a paddle is used of the same kind as that used in whaling (see p. 91). A rudder is rarely found (Fig. 91.), and when used most probably is made in imitation of European devices.

If the wind permits, a sail is set; but the bulky vessel can only run with the wind. The mast is set in the stem, a mortise being cut in the forehead of the main timber, with a notch in the wooden piece above it to steady it. A stout thong, which passes through two holes on each side of the notch, secures the mast to the wooden head piece. The sail, which is made of seal intestines carefully sewed together, is squared and fastened by loops to a yard (sadniriaq) which is trimmed with straps of deerskin. It is hoisted by a rope made of sealskin and passing over a sheave in the top of the mast. This rope is tied to the thwart farthest abaft, while the sheets are fastened to the foremost one.

THE SLEDGE AND DOGS.

During the greater part of the year the only passable road is that afforded by the ice and snow; therefore sledges (qamuting) of different constructions are used in traveling.

Fig. 93 . Qamuting or sledge.

The best model is made by the tribes of Hudson Strait and Davis Strait, for the driftwood which they can obtain in abundance admits the use of long wooden runners. Their sledges (Fig. 93) have two runners, from five to fifteen feet long and from twenty inches to two and a half feet apart. They are connected by cross bars of wood or bone and the back is formed by deer's antlers with the skull attached. The bottom of the runners (qamun) is curved at the head (uinirn) and cut off at right angles behind. It is shod with whalebone, ivory, or the jawbones of a whale. In long sledges the shoeing (pirqang) is broadest near the head and narrowest behind. This device is very well adapted for sledging in soft snow; for, while the weight of the load is distributed over the entire length of the sledge, the fore part, which is most apt to break through, has a broad face, which presses down the snow and enables the hind part to glide over it without sinking in too deeply.

FIG. 94 . Sledge shoe.   (National Museum, Washington.   34096.) ¼

The shoe (Fig. 94) is either tied or riveted to the runner. If tied, the lashing passes through sunken drill holes to avoid any friction in moving over the snow. The right and left sides of a whale's jaw are frequently used for shoes, as they are of the proper size and permit the shoe to be of a single piece. Ivory is cut into flat pieces and riveted to the runner with long treenails. The points are frequently covered with bone on both the lower and upper sides, as they are easily injured by striking hard against hummocks or snowdrifts. Sometimes whalebone is used for the shoes.

The cross bars (napun) project over the runners on each side and have notches which form a kind of neck. These necks serve to fasten the thongs when a load is lashed on the sledge. The bars are fastened to the runners by thongs which pass through two pairs of holes in the bars and through corresponding ones in the runners. If these fastenings should become loose, they are tightened by winding a small thong round them and thus drawing the opposite parts of the thong tightly together. If this proves insufficient, a small wedge is driven between the thong and the runner.

The antlers attached to the back of the sledge have the branches removed and the points slanted so as to fit to the runners. Only the brow antlers are left, the right one being cut down to about three inches in length, the left one to one and a half inches. This back forms a very convenient handle for steering the sledge past hummocks or rocks, for drawing it back when the points have struck a snowdrift, &c. Besides, the lashing for holding the load is tied to the right brow antler and the snow knife and the harpoon line are hung upon it.

Under the foremost cross bar a hole is drilled through each runner. A very stout thong (pitu) consisting of two separate parts passes through the holes and serves to fasten the dogs' traces to the sledge.

A button at each end of this thong prevents it from slipping through the hole of the runner. The thong consists of two parts, the one ending in a loop, the other in a peculiar kind of clasp (partirang).

FIG. 95. Clasp for fastening traces to sledge. (National Museum, Washington. 34110.) ½

Fig 95 represents the form commonly used. The end of one part of the thong is fastened to the hole of the clasp, which, when closed, is stuck through the loop of the opposite end (see Fig. 93). A more artistic design is shown in Fig. 96. One end of the line is tied to the hole in the under side of this implement. When it is in use the loop of the other end is stuck through another hole in the center and hung over the nozzle. The whole represents the head of an animal with a gaping mouth. The dogs' traces are strung upon this line by means of the uqsirn, an ivory implement with a large and a small eyelet (Fig. 97). The trace is tied to the former, while the latter is strung upon the pitu.

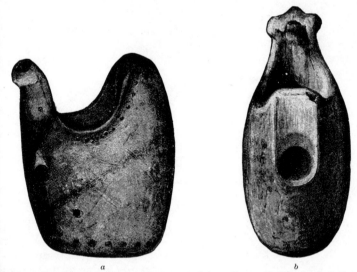

a   b

FIG. 96. Artistic form of clasp for fastening traces to sledge. (Museum für Völkerkunde, Berlin.) ½

The dogs have harnesses (ano) made of sealskin (Fig. 98') or sometimes of deerskin, consisting of two bights passing under the fore legs. They are joined by two straps, one passing over the breast, the other over the neck. The ends are tied together on the back, whence the trace runs to the sledge. According to Parry (II, p. 517), the Iglulik harnesses consisted of three bights, one passing over the breast and shoulder and two under the fore legs.

FIG. 97. Uqsirn, for fastening traces to pitu. *a* (National Museum, Washington. 34122.) ½ *b* (Museum für Völkerkunde, Berlin.) ½

It was mentioned at another place (p. 67) that in sealing a dog is taken out of the sledge to lead the hunter to the breathing hole.

FIG. 98. Ano or dog harness. (Museum für Völkerkunde, Berlin. IV A 6730.)

For this purpose the traces of some harnesses are made of two pieces, which are united by the sadniriaq, a clasp similar to that of the pitu (Figs. 98 , 99). If the dog is to be taken from the sledge the fore part of the trace is unbuttoned.

FIG. 99. Sadniriaq or clasp. (National Museum, Washington.) ⅘

Besides this form of sledge a great number of others are in use. Whenever whales are caught their bone is sawed or cut into large pieces, which are shod with the same material. If large bones are not to be had, a substitute is found in walrus skins or rolls of sealskins, which are wetted and sewed up in a bag. This bag is given the desired form and after being frozen to a solid mass is as serviceable as the best plank. In Boothia frozen salmon are used in the same way and after having served this purpose in winter are eaten in the spring. Other sledges are made of slabs of fresh water ice, which are cut and allowed to freeze together, or of a large ice block hollowed out in the center. All these are clumsy and heavy and much inferior to the large sledge just described.

Parry (II, p. 515) states that at Iglulik the antlers are detached from the sledge in winter when the natives go sealing. The tribes of Davis Strait do not practice this custom, but use scarcely any sledge without a pair of antlers.

As to the appearance of the dogs I would refer to Parry (II, p. 515) and other writers and confine my remarks to a description of their use by the Eskimo.

As the traces are strung upon a thong, as just described, the dogs all pull at one point ; for that reason they may seem, at first sight, to be harnessed together without order or regularity ; but they are arranged with great care. The strongest and most spirited dog has the longest trace and is allowed to run a few feet in advance of the rest as a leader; its sex is indifferent, the choice being made chiefly with regard to strength. Next to the leader follow two or three strong dogs with traces of equal length, and the weaker and less manageable the dogs the nearer they run to the sledge. A team is almost unmanageable if the dogs are not accustomed to one another. They must know their leader, who brings them to terms whenever there is a quarrel. In a good team the leader must be the acknowledged chief, else the rest will fall into disorder and refuse to follow him. His authority is almost unlimited. When the dogs are fed, he takes the choice morsels; when two of them quarrel, he bites both and thus brings them to terms.

Generally there is a second dog which is inferior only to the leader, but is feared by all the others. Though the authority of the leader is not disputed by his own team, dogs of another team will not submit to him. But when two teams are accustomed to travel in company the dogs in each will have some regard for the leader of the other, though continuous rivalry and quarrels go on between the two leaders. Almost any dog which is harnessed into a strange team will at first be unwilling to draw, and it is only when he is thoroughly accustomed to all his neighbors and has found out his friends and his enemies that he will do his work satisfactorily. Some dogs when put into a strange team will throw themselves down and struggle and

howl. They will endure the severest lashing and allow themselve
to be dragged along over rough ice without being induced to rise and
run along with the others. Particularly if their own team is in sigh
will they turn back and try to get to it. Others, again, are quite will
ing to work with strange dogs.

Partly on this account and partly from attachment to their masters
dogs sold out of one team frequently return to their old homes, and
I know of instances in which they even ran from thirty to sixty mile
to reach it. Sometimes they do so when a sledge is traveling for a
few days from one settlement to another, the dogs not having lef
home for a long time before. In such cases when the Eskimo go to
harness their team in the morning they find that some of them have
run away, particularly those which were lent from another team for
the journey. In order to prevent this the left fore leg is sometime
tied up by a loop which passes over the neck. When one is on a
journey it is well to do so every night, as some of the dogs are rather
unwilling to be harnessed in the morning, thus causing a great loss
of time before they are caught. In fact such animals are custom
arily tied up at night, while the others are allowed to run loose.

Sometimes the harnesses are not taken off at night. As some dogs
are in the habit of stripping off their harness, it is fastened by tying
the trace around the body. Though all these peculiarities of the dogs
give a great deal of trouble to the driver, he must take care not to
punish them too severely, as they will then become frightened and
for fear of the whip will not work at all.

Before putting the dogs to the sledge it must be prepared and
loaded. In winter the shoes of the runners are covered with a thick
coat of ice, which diminishes the friction on the snow. If the shoes
are of good bone, ivory, or whalebone, the icing is done with water
only, the driver taking a mouthful and carefully letting it run over
the shoe until a smooth cover of about one third of an inch in thick
ness is produced. The icicles made by the water which runs down
the side of the runner are carefully removed with the snow knife,
and the bottom is smoothed with the same implement and afterward
somewhat polished with the mitten. Skin runners and others which
have poor shoes are first covered with a mixture of moss and water
or clay and water. This being frozen, the whole is iced, as has been
described. Instead of pure water, a mixture of blood and water or
of urine and water is frequently used, as this sticks better to the bone
shoe than the former.

This done, the sledge is turned right side up and loaded. In winter,
when the snow is hard, small sledges with narrow shoes are the best.
In loading, the bulk of the weight is placed behind. When the snow
is soft or there are wide cracks in the floe, long sledges with broad
shoes are by far the best. In such cases the heaviest part of the
load is placed on the middle of the sledge or even nearer the head.

Particularly in crossing cracks the weight must be as near the head as possible, for if the jump should be unsuccessful a heavy weight at the hind part would draw the sledge and the dogs into the water.

The load is fastened to the sledge by a long lashing (naqetarun). This is tied to the first cross bar and after passing over the load is drawn over the notch of the next bar, and so on from one notch, over the load, to a notch on the opposite side. After having been fastened in this way it is tightened. Two men are required for the work, one pulling the lashing over the notch, the other pressing down the load and lifting and lowering the thong in order to diminish the friction, thus making the pulling of the other man more effective. The end is fastened to the brow antler. Implements which are used in traveling are hung upon the antlers at the back of the sledge. In spring, when the snow is melting and water is found under it, the travelers frequently carry in their pouch a tube for drinking (Fig. 100).

FIG. 100. Tube for drinking. (National Museum, Washington. 10383.) ⅓

When the sledge has been loaded the dogs are hitched to it and the driver takes up the whip and is ready for starting. The handle of the whip is about a foot or a foot and a half in length. It is made of wood, bone, or whalebone and has a lash of from twenty to twenty-five feet in length. The lash is made of walrus or ground seal hide, the lower end being broad and stiff, thus giving it greater weight and a slight springiness near the handle, which facilitates its use. A broad piece of skin clasps the handle, to which it is tied with seal thongs. Another way of making the lower part heavy is by plaiting ground seal lines for a length of a foot or a foot and a half.

When starting the driver utters a whistling guttural sound which sounds like h! h!, but cannot exactly be expressed by letters, as there is no vowel in it, and yet on account of the whistling noise in the throat it is audible at a considerable distance. The dogs, if well rested and strong, jump to their feet and start at once. If they are lazy it requires a great deal of stimulating and lashing before they make a start. If the load is heavy it is difficult to start it and the Eskimo must use some strategy to get them all to pull at once. The sledge is moved backward and forward for about a foot, so as to make a short track in which it moves easily. Then the driver sings out to the dogs, at the same time drawing the traces tight with his hands and pulling at the sledge. The dogs, feeling a weight at the traces, begin to draw, and when the driver suddenly lets go the traces the sledge receives a sudden pull and begins to move. If assistance is at hand the sledge may be pushed forward until it gets under way.

It is extremely hard work to travel with a heavy load, particularly in rough ice or on soft snow. The dogs require constant stimulating; for this purpose a great number of exclamations are in use and almost every Eskimo has his own favorite words for driving. The general exclamation used for stimulating is the above mentioned h! h! or aq! aq! which is pressed out from the depths of the breast and the palate, the vowel being very indistinct. Others are: djua! the a being drawn very long and almost sung in a high key, or ah! pronounced in the same way; ıatit! or jauksa koksa! and smacking with the tongue. If a seal is seen basking on the ice or if the sledge happens to pass a deserted snow hut, the driver says, Ha! Do you see the seal? Ai! A seal! a seal! (Ha! Takuviuk? Ai! Uto! uto!) and Ai! There is a house; a small house! (Ai! Iglu; igluaqdjung!) or, Now we go home! (Sarpoq! Sarpoq!) The latter, however, are only used when the dogs are going at a good rate.

For directing the sledge the following words are used: Aua, aua! Aua! ja aua! for turning to the right; χoiaχoi! ja χoia! for turning to the left. In addition the whip lash is thrown to the opposite side of the dogs. The leader is the first to obey the order, but a turn is made very slowly and by a long curve. If the driver wants to make a sharper turn he must jump up and run to the opposite side of the sledge, throwing the whip lash at the same time toward the team. For stopping the dogs the word Ohoha! pronounced in a deep key, is used.

If the traveling is difficult the driver must walk along at the right side of the sledge and wherever hummocks obstruct the passage he must direct it around them either by pushing its head aside or by pulling at the deer's skull at the back. But notwithstanding all this stimulating and all the pulling the sledge is frequently stopped by striking a piece of ice or by sinking into soft snow. As soon as it sinks down to the cross bars it must be lifted out, and when the load is heavy the only means of getting on is by unloading and afterwards reloading. In the same way it must be lifted across hummocks through which a road is cut with the end of the spear, which, for this purpose, is always lashed in a place where it is handy for use, generally on the right side of the bottom of the sledge. The difficulties of traveling across heavy ice which has been subjected to heavy pressures have frequently been described. When the sledge stops the dogs immediately lie down, and if they cannot start again, though pulling with all their strength, the leader frequently looks around pitifully, as if to say, We cannot do more!

Traveling with a light sledge and strong dogs is quite different. Then the team is almost unmanageable and as soon as it is hitched up it is off at full speed. The driver sits down on the fore part and lets the whip trail along, always ready for use. Now the dogs have time enough for playing and quarreling with one another. Though they generally keep their proper place in the team, some will occasionally jump over the traces of their neighbors or crawl underneath them; thus the lines become quickly entangled, and it is necessary to clear them almost every hour.

If any dog of the team is lazy the driver calls out his name and he is lashed, but it is necessary to hit the dog called, for if another is struck he feels wronged and will turn upon the dog whose name has been called; the leader enters into the quarrel, and soon the whole pack is huddled up in one howling and biting mass, and no amount of lashing and beating will separate the fighting team. The only thing one can do is to wait until their wrath has abated and to clear the traces. It is necessary, however, to lay the mittens and the whip carefully upon the sledge, for the leader, being on the lookout for the traces to be strung, may give a start when the driver is scarcely ready, and off the team will go again before the driver can fairly get hold of the sledge. If anything has dropped from it he must drive in a wide circle to the same place before he can stop the team and pick it up. On an old track it is very difficult to stop them at all. When attempting to do so the driver digs his heels into the snow to obstruct their progress and eventually comes to a stop. Then he stands in front of the sled and makes the dogs lie down by lashing their heads gently. Should the dogs start off he would be thrown upon the sledge instead of being left behind, which might easily happen should he stand alongside.

The sledge is steered with the legs, usually with the right foot of the driver, or, if it must be pulled aside from a large hummock, by pulling the head aside or by means of the deer's antlers. If two persons are on the sledge — and usually two join for a long drive — they must not speak to each other, for as soon as the dogs hear them they will stop, turn around, sit down, and listen to the conversation. It has frequently been said that the method of harnessing is inconvenient, as the dogs cannot use their strength to the best advantage; but whoever has driven a sledge himself will understand that any other method would be even more troublesome and less effective. On smooth ice and hard snow any method of harnessing could be used; but, on rough ice, by any other method every cross piece would quickly break on attempting to cross the hummocks. Frequently the traces catch a projecting point and the dogs are then pulled back and thrown against the ice or under the sledge if the trace does not break. If for any reason a dog should hang back and the trace should trail over the snow the driver must lift it up to prevent it from being caught by the sledge runner, else the dog will be dragged in the same way as if the trace were caught by a hummock. Many dogs are able in such cases to strip off their harnesses and thus escape being dragged along, as the team cannot be stopped quickly enough to prevent this. Besides the driver must see to it that the dogs do not step across their traces, which in such cases would run between their hind legs, for should this happen the skin might be severely chafed. If the driver sees a trace in this position he runs forward and puts it back without stopping the team. Particular attention must be paid to this matter when the dogs rise just before starting.

The sledges are not used until the ice is well covered with snow, as the salt crystals formed on the top of the ice in the autumn hurt the dogs' feet and cause sores that heal slowly. Late in the spring, when the snow has melted and sharp ice needles project everywhere, the feet of the dogs are covered with small pieces of leather, with holes for the nails, which are tied to the leg. As they are frequently lost and the putting on of these shoes takes a long time, their use is very inconvenient.

At this season numerous cracks run through the floe. They are either crossed on narrow snow bridges which join the edges at convenient places or on a drifting piece of ice by floating across.

A few more words in conclusion concerning the training of the dogs. The Eskimo rarely brings up more than three or four dogs at the same time. If the litter is larger than this number the rest are sold or given away. The young dogs are carefully nursed and in winter they are even allowed to lie on the couch or are hung up over the lamp in a piece of skin. When about four months old they are first put to the sledge and gradually become accustomed to pull along with the others. They undergo a good deal of lashing and whipping before they are as useful as the old ones.

If food is plentiful the dogs are fed every other day, and then their share is by no means a large one. In winter they are fed with the heads, entrails, bones, and skins of seals, and they are so voracious at this time of the year that nothing is secure from their appetite. Any kind of leather, particularly boots, harnesses, and thongs, is eaten whenever they can get at it. In the spring they are better fed and in the early part of summer they grow quite fat. In traveling, however, it sometimes happens at this time of the year, as well as in winter, that they have no food for five or six days. In Cumberland Sound, Hudson Strait, and Hudson Bay, where the rise and fall of the tide are considerable, they are carried in summer to small islands where they live upon what they can find upon the beach, clams, codfish, &c. If at liberty they are entirely able to provide for themselves. I remember two runaway dogs which had lived on their own account from April until August and then returned quite fat.

The Eskimo of all these regions are very much troubled with the well known dog's disease of the Arctic regions. The only places where it seems to be unknown are Davis Strait and Aggo. Here every man has a team of from six to twelve dogs, while in Cumberland Sound, in some winters, scarcely any have been left. (See Appendix, Note 2.)

HABITATIONS AND DRESS.

THE HOUSE.

The houses of the Eskimo differ according to the season. All the tribes from Smith Sound to Labrador and from Davis Strait to Victoria Land are in the habit of building snow houses in winter. Though they erect another more durable kind of winter house, these are more frequently in use. The principles of construction are the same everywhere. A level place is selected for erecting the snow house.

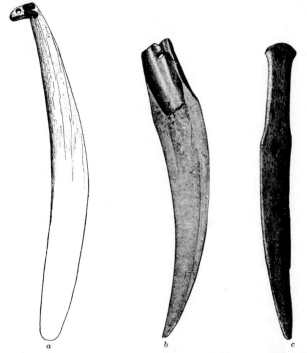

Fig. 101. Various styles of snow knife. (National Museum, Washington. *a*, 10386 ; *b*, 10385.)

To be suitable for cutting into blocks the snowbank must have been formed by a single storm, for blocks which are cut from drifts composed of several layers break when cut. It must be very fine grained, but not so hard that it cannot be readily cut with the saw or the snow knife. The whole building is constructed of blocks of about three feet or four feet in length, two feet in height, and from six inches to eight inches in thickness. They are cut with snow knives or dovetail saws, which for this reason are much in demand. The old snow knife (sulung) was made of ivory and had a slight curve (Fig. 101).

The blocks are cut either vertically or horizontally, the former way being more convenient if the snowdrift is deep. Two parallel cuts of the breadth and the depth of the blocks are made through the drift, and after having removed a small block the Eskimo go on cutting or sawing parallel to the surface. A cross cut is then made and the block is loosened with the point of the foot and lifted out of the bank. Vertical blocks are more easily detached from the snowdrift than horizontal ones.

Two men unite in building a house, the one cutting the blocks, the other building. At first a row of blocks is put up in a circle, the single pieces being slanted so as to fit closely together. Then the first block is cut down to the ground and the top of the row is slanted so as to form one thread of a spiral line. The builder places the first block of the second row with its narrow side upon the first block and pushes it with his left hand to the right so that it touches the last block of the first row. Thus the snow block, which is inclined a little inward, has a support on two sides. The vertical joint is slanted with the snow knife and tightly pressed together, the new block resting on the oblique side of the former. In building on in this way the blocks receive the shape of almost regular trapezoids. Every block is inclined a little more inward than the previous one, and as the angle to the vertical becomes greater the blocks are only kept in their places by the neighboring ones. In order to give them a good support the edges are the more slanted as their angle is greater.

This method of building is very ingenious, as it affords the possibility of building a vault without a scaffold. If the blocks were placed in parallel rows, the first block of a new row would have no support, while by this method each reclines on the previous one. When the house has reached a considerable height the man who cuts the blocks outside must place them upon the last row. The builder supports them with his head and pushes them to their proper places. The key block and those which are next to it are either cut inside or pushed into the house through a small door cut for the purpose. The key block is generally shaped irregularly, as it is fitted into the hole which remains; usually the last two blocks are triangular. When the vault is finished the joints between the blocks are closed up by cutting down the edges and pressing the scraps into the joints. Larger openings are closed with snow blocks and filled up with loose snow pressed into the fissures. Thus the whole building becomes a tight vault, without any holes through which the warm air inside may escape. Such a snow house, about five feet high and seven feet in diameter, is used as a camp in winter journeys. It takes about two hours for two skilled men to build and finish it. For winter quarters the vaults are built from ten to twelve feet high and twelve to fifteen feet in diameter. In order to reach this height the builder makes a bench on which he steps while finishing the upper part of the building.

The plan of a snow house of the Davis Strait tribes is a little different from that of the Hudson Bay and the Iglulik tribes.

I shall first describe the former according to my own observations (Figs. 102 and 103).

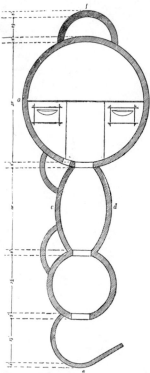

The entrance to the main building is formed by two, or less frequently by three, small vaults. The first one (uadling) is a small dome about six feet in height, with a door two and a half feet in height; the second one is a long passage of equal height formed by an elliptical vault (igdluling). Its roof is generally arched, but sometimes the top is cut off evenly and covered with slabs of snow. Both vaults together form the entrance and are called toqsung. A door about three feet high leads into the main room, the floor of which is about nine inches above that of the former. Two very small vaults are always attached to the whole building (Fig. 102). One is situated alongside of the uadling and the igdluling, and serves as a storeroom for clothing and harness (sirdloang). It is not connected with the interior of the hut, but one of the blocks of the vault can be taken out and is made to serve as a lid. On the left side of the entrance of the main building is another small vault (igdluarn), which is accessible from

Fig. 102. Ground plan of snow house of Davis Strait tribes.

the main building. It serves for keeping spare meat and blubber. Frequently there is a second igdluarn on the opposite side, and sometimes even a third one in the igdluling. Another appendix of the main building is frequently used, the audlitiving (Fig. 102 and Fig. 103 c). It is a vault similar to the sirdloang and is attached to the back of the main room. It serves for storing up meat for future use.

Directly over the entrance a window is cut through the wall, either square or more frequently forming an arch, which is generally covered with the intestines of ground seals, neatly sewed together, the seams standing vertically (Fig. 104). In the center there is a hole (qingang) through which one can look out. In some instances a piece of fresh water ice is inserted in the hole. According to Ross it is always used by the Netchillirmiut (II, p. 250), who make the slab by letting water freeze in a sealskin.

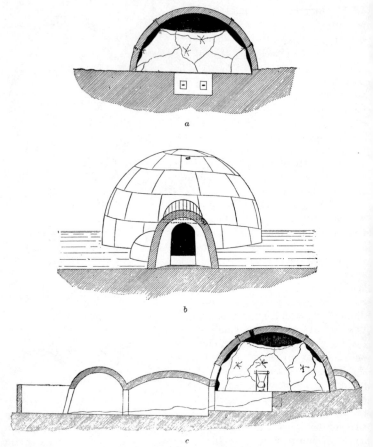

a

b

c

FIG. 103. Snow house of Davis Strait, sections.

In the rear half and on both sides of the door a bank of snow two and a half feet high is raised and cut off straight, a passage trench five feet wide and six feet long remaining. The rear half forms the bed, the adjoining parts of the side benches are the place for the lamps, while on both sides of the entrance meat and refuse are heaped up. Frequently the snowbank on which the hut is built is deep nough so that the bed needs very little raising, and the passage is ut into the bank. As this is much more convenient in building, he huts are generally erected on a sloping face, the entrance lying n the lower part, which faces the beach.

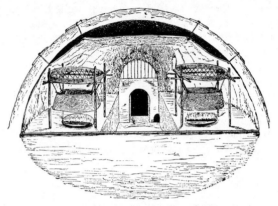

FIG. 104. Section and interior of snow house.

Before the bed is arranged and the hut furnished the vault is lined vith skins, frequently with the cover of the summer hut. The lining ilupiqang) is fastened to the roof by small ropes (nirtsun), which re fastened by a toggle on the outside of the wall (Fig.'104). In he lower part of the building the lining lies close to the wall; in he upper part it forms a flat roof about two or three feet below the op of the vault. The effect of this arrangement is to prevent the varm air inside from melting the snow roof, as above the skins there s always a layer of colder air. Close to the top of the building a mall hole (qangirn) is cut through the wall for ventilation. The amps require a good draught, which is secured by this hole. The old air enters through the door, slowly filling the passage, and after eing warmed rises to the lamps and escapes through the skin cover nd the hole. The moisture of the air forms long ice needles on the nside of the roof. Sometimes they fall down upon the skins, and nust be immediately removed by shaking it until they glide down the sides, else they melt and wet the room thoroughly. Frequently high ice funnel forms around the hole from the freezing moisture f the escaping air.

The southern and western tribes rarely line the snow house. he continuous dropping from the roof, however, causes great incon-enience, and, besides, the temperature cannot be raised higher than wo or three degrees centigrade above the freezing point, while in he lined houses it is frequently from ten to twenty degrees centi-

grade, so that the latter are much more comfortable. To avoid th
dropping the natives apply a cold piece of snow to the roof before th
drop falls down, which at once freezes to it, the roof acquiring b
this repeated process a stalactitic appearance. The eastern tribes us
the lining in their permanent houses without any exception. Th
western and southern tribes, who leave the walls bare, heap a thic
layer of loose snow over the whole building, almost covering i
up, the window and the ventilating hole alone excepted. For th
purpose snow shovels are used.

The edge of the bed is formed by a long pole. The surface of th
snowbank which forms the foundation for the bed is covered wit
pieces of wood, oars, paddles, tent poles, &c. These are covere
with a thick layer of shrubs, particularly *Andromeda tetragon*
Over these numerous heavy deerskins are spread, and thus a ver
comfortable bed is made.

According to Parry the arrangement in Iglulik is as follows (I.
p. 501):

> The beds are arranged by first covering the snow with a quantity of small stone
> over which are laid their paddles, tent poles, and some blades of whalebon
> above these they place a number of little pieces of network made of thin slips
> whalebone, and lastly a quantity of twigs of birch and of the *Andromeda tetragon*
> * * * The birch, they say, had been procured from the southward by wa
> of Nuvuk. * * * There deerskins, which are very numerous, can now b
> spread without risk of their touching the snow.

At night, when the Eskimo go to bed, they put their clothing, the
boots excepted, on the edge of the platform under the deerskins, thu
forming a pillow, and lie down with the head toward the entranc
The blankets (qipiq) for their beds are made of heavy deerskin
which are sewed together, one blanket serving for a whole family
The edge of the blanket is trimmed with leather straps.

On the side benches in front of the bed is the fireplace, which consis
of a stone lamp and a framework from which the pots are suspende
(see Fig. 104). The lamp (qudlirn), which is made of soapstone, is
shallow vessel in the shape of a small segment of a circle. Sometime
a small space is divided off at the back for gathering in the scraps
blubber. The wick consists of hair of *Eryophorum* or of dried mos
rubbed down with a little blubber so as to be inflammable. It
always carried by the women in a small bag. The whole vessel
filled with blubber as high as the wick, which is spread along th
straight side of the vessel. It requires constant attention to keep th
desired length burning without smoking, the length kindled bein
in accordance with the heat or light required. The trimming of th
wick is done with a bit of bone, asbestus, or wood, with which th
burning moss is spread along the edge of the lamp and extinguishe
or pressed down if the fire is not wanted or if it smokes. At the sam
time this stick serves to light other lamps (or pipes), the burnt poin

eing put into the blubber and then kindled. Sometimes a long, arrow vessel stands below the lamp, in which the oil that drops om the edge is collected.

In winter the blubber before being used is frozen, after which it is noroughly beaten. This bursts the vesicles of fat and the oil comes ut as soon as it is melted. The pieces of blubber are either put nto the lamp or placed over a piece of bone or wood, which hangs om the framework a little behind the wick. In summer the oil nust be chewed out. It is a disgusting sight to see the women and nildren sitting around a large vessel all chewing blubber and spiting the oil into it.

The frame of the fireplace consists of four poles stuck in the snow n a square around the lamp and four crossbars connecting the poles t the top. From those which run from the front to the back the ettle (ukusik) is suspended by two pairs of strings or thongs. It s made of soapstone and has a hole in each corner for the string. The kettle which is in use among the eastern tribes has a narrow im and a wide bottom (Fig. 105), while that of the western ones is ust the opposite. Parry, however, found one of this description in River Clyde (I, p. 286). When not in use it is shoved back by means f the strings. Since whalers began to visit the country a great umber of tin pots have been introduced, which are much more erviceable, the process of cooking being quickened.

FIG. 105. Ukusik or soapstone kettle.

On the top of the frame there is always a wood or bone hoop with net of thongs stretched across it (inetang). It serves to dry clothng, particularly boots, stockings, and mittens, over the fire. In the assage near the entrance to the hut there is frequently a small lamp adlirn), which is very effective for warming the cold air entering hrough the door, and in the remotest corner in the back of the hut here is sometimes another (kidlulirn). When all the lamps are ighted the house becomes warm and comfortable.

Two small holes are frequently cut in the snowbank which forms he ledge, at about the middle of its height (see Fig. 103 a). They re closed with small snow blocks, each of which has a groove for a andle, and serve to store away anything that must be kept dry.

At night the entrance of the inner room is closed with a large sno
block, which stands in the passage during the day.

These huts are always occupied by two families, each woman hav
ing her own lamp and sitting on the ledge in front of it, the one o
the right side, the other on the left side of the house.   If more fam
ilies join in building a common snow house, they make two mai
rooms with one entrance.   The plan of such a building is seen i
Fig. 106.

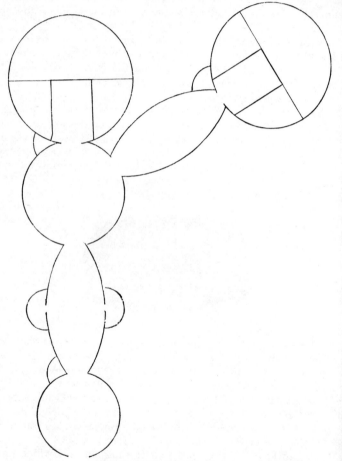

FIG. 106. Plan of double snow house.

The plans of the Iglulik and Hudson Bay houses are different fron
the one described here.   The difference will best be seen by compar
ing the plans represented in Fig. 107 and Fig. 108, which have beer

reprinted from Hall and Parry, respectively, with the former ones. Among the eastern tribes I have never seen the beds on the side of the passage, but always at the rear of the house.

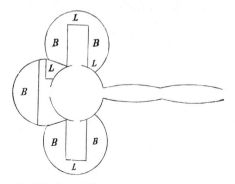

FIG. 107. Plan of Iglulik house. (From Parry II, p. 500.)

Besides these snow houses a more solid building is in use, called qarmang. On the islands of the American Archipelago and in the neighboring parts of the mainland numerous old stone foundations are found, which prove that all these islands were once inhabited by the Eskimo. It has often been said that the central tribes have forgotten the art of building stone houses and always live in snow huts.

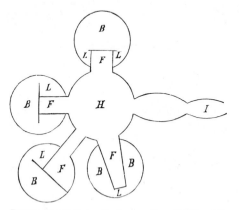

FIG. 108. Plan of Hudson Bay house. (From Hall II, p. 128.)

At the present time they do not build houses, but cover the walls of an old hut with a new roof whenever they take possession of it. There is no need of any new buildings, as the Eskimo always locate the old settlements and the old buildings are quite sufficient to satisfy all their wants.

Those in good condition have a long stone entrance (ka′teng) (Fig. 109), sometimes from fifteen to twenty feet long. This is made by cutting an excavation into the slope of a hill. Its walls are covered with large slabs of stone about two and a half feet high and three feet wide, the space between the stone and the sides of the excava-

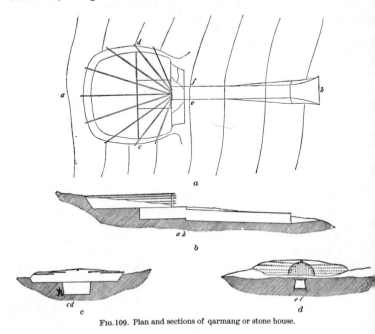

Fig. 109. Plan and sections of qarmang or stone house.

tion being afterwards filled up with earth. The floor of the passage slopes upward toward the hut. The last four feet of the entrance are covered with a very large slab and are a little higher than the other parts of the roof of the passageway. The slab is at the same height as the benches of the dwelling room, which is also dug out, the walls being formed of stones and whale ribs. The plan of the interior is the same as that of the snow house, the bed being in the rear end of the room and the lamps on both sides of the entrance. The floor of the hut is about eight inches higher than that of the passage. The roof and the window, however, differ from those of the snow house. In the front part of the hut the rib of whale is put up, forming an arch. A great number of poles are lashed to it and run toward the back of the house, where they rest on the top of the wall, forming, as it were, the rafters. The whole curve formed by the rib is covered with a window of seal intestines while the poles are covered with sealskins, which are fastened in front to the whale rib. At the other end they are either fastened to the ribs in the wall or, more frequently, are steadied by stones The roof is covered with a thick layer of *Andromeda*, and another skin, which is fastened in the same way, is spread over both covers. This kind of hut is very warm, light, and comfortable. The stone banks forming the bed are covered as already described.

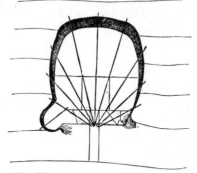

FIG. 110. Plan of large qarmang or stone house for three families.

If three families occupy one house the whale's rib which forms the window is placed a few feet farther forward than in the previous case, at the end of the large slab which forms the roof of the last part of the passage.

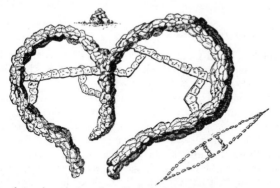

FIG. 111. Plan of stone house in Anarnitung, Cumberland Sound. (From a drawing by L. Kumlien.

By means of poles and bones a small side room is built (qareang), the ceiling of which is sewed to that of the main room (Fig. 110). The large slab which is in front of the window (at the end of the passage) is utilized as a storeroom for both families living on that side of the house; a place being left open only in the middle, where the spy hole is. In some instances this side room is inclosed in the stone walls of the hut.

Fig. 111 and Fig. 112 present sketches of plans of some of these houses. From such sketches it appears that several houses might have a common entrance.

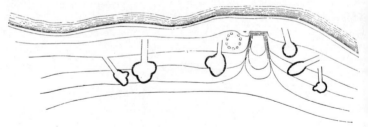

Fig. 112. Plan of group of stone houses in Pangnirtung, Cumberland Sound.

In Anarnitung I observed no passage at all for the houses, the walls being entirely above the ground and piled up with bowlders and sod. They are, however, covered in the same way as the others and the entrance is made of snow.

Fig. 113. Plan and sections of qarmang or house made of whale ribs.

A winter house built on the same plan is represented in Fig. 113. The wall is made entirely of whale ribs, placed so that their ends cross one another. The poles are tied over the top of the ribs and the whole frame is covered with the double roof described above. A few narrow snow vaults form the entrance. The front rib forms the door, and thus the hut becomes quite dark. Huts of this kind are also called qarmang or qarmaujang, i. e., similar to a qarmang.

In Ukiadliving I found, along with a great number of fine qarmat, some very remarkable storehouses, such as are represented in Fig. 114. Structures of this kind (ikan') consist of heavy granite pillars, on the top of which flat slabs are piled to a height of from nine to ten feet. In winter, blubber and meat are put away upon these pillars, which are sufficiently high to keep them from the dogs. Sometimes two pillars, about ten feet apart, are found near the huts. In winter the kayak is placed upon them in order to prevent it from being covered by snowdrifts or from being torn and destroyed by the dogs. In snow villages these pillars are made of snow.

The purpose of the long, kayak-like building figured by Kumlien (see Fig. 111) is unknown to me. I found a similar one, consisting of two rows of stones, scarcely one foot high but twenty feet long, in Pangnirtung, Cumberland Sound, but nobody could explain its use.

FIG. 114. Storehouse in Ukiadliving. (From a sketch by the author.)

In the spring, when the rays of the sun become warmer, the roofs of the snow houses fall down. At this season the natives build only the lower half of a snow vault, which is covered with skins.

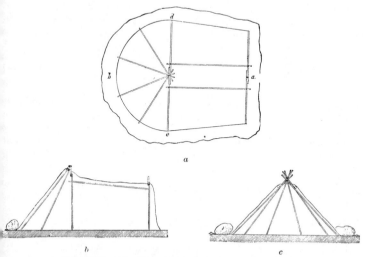

FIG. 115. Plan and sections of tupiq or tent of Cumberland Sound.

Still later they live in their tents (tupiq) (Fig. 115). The framework consists of poles, which are frequently made of many pieces of wood ingeniously lashed together. The plan (Fig. 115 *a*) is the same as that of the winter houses. At the edge of the bed and at the entrance two pairs of converging poles are erected. A little below the crossing points two cross strips are firmly attached, forming the ridge. Behind the poles, at the edge of the bed, six or eight others are arranged in a semicircle resting on the ground and on the crossing point of those poles. The frame is covered with a large skin roof fitting tightly. The back part, covering the bed, is made of sealskins; the fore part, between the two pairs of poles, of the thin membrane which is split from the skins (see p. 111), and admits the light. The door is formed by the front part of the cover, the left side (in entering) ending in the middle of the entrance, the right one overlapping it, so as to prevent the wind from blowing into the hut. The cover is steadied with heavy stones (Fig. 115 c). In Cumberland Sound and the more southern parts of Baffin Land the back of the hut is inclined at an angle of 45°; in Davis Strait it is as steep as 60°, or even more. In the summer tent the bed and the side platforms are not raised, but only separated from the passage by means of poles.

Farther north and west, in Pond Bay, Admiralty Inlet, and Iglulik, where wood is scarce, the Eskimo have a different plan of construction (Fig. 116). A strong pole is set up vertically at the end of the passage, a small cross piece being lashed to its top. The entrance is formed by an oblique pole, the end of which lies in the ridge of the roof. The latter is formed by a stout thong which runs over the top of both poles and is fastened to heavy stones on both sides. If wood is wanting, then poles are made from the penis bones of the walrus. Parry found one of these tents at River Clyde, on his first expedition, and describes it as follows (I, p. 283):

> The tents which compose their summer habitations, are principally supported by a long pole of whalebone, 14 feet high, standing perpendicularly, with 4 or 5 feet of it projecting above the skins which form the roof and sides. The length of the tent is 17, and its breadth from 7 to 9 feet, the narrowest part being next the door and widening towards the inner part, where the bed, composed of a quantity of the small shrubby plant, the *Andromeda tetragona*, occupies about one-third of the whole apartment. The pole of the tent is fixed where the bed commences, and the latter is kept separate by some pieces of bone laid across the tent from side to side. The door which faces the southwest, is also formed of two pieces of bone, with the upper ends fastened together, and the skins are made to overlap in that part of the tent, which is much lower than the inner end. The covering is fastened to the ground by curved pieces of bone, being generally parts of the whale.

This kind of tent differs from the one described by me only in the construction of its door.

I could not find a description of the tent of the Hudson Bay Eskimo. There is only one illustration in Klutschak (p. 137) and one in Ross (II, p. 581) representing tents of the Netchillirmiut. In the former there are a few conical tents, such as are used by the eastern tribes before a sufficient number of skins for a large tent can be procured. The same kind is represented in Ross's book. The other tent drawn by Klutschak is similar to the Iglulik one, but the arrangement of the poles in the back part is invisible. The entrance is formed by two converging poles and a rope runs over the ridge and is tied to a rock.

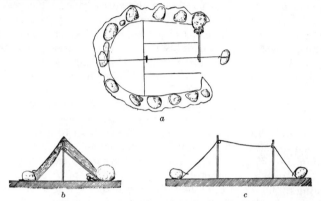

Fig. 116. Plan and sections of tupiq or tent of Pond Bay.

The small tents which are used in the spring are made of a few converging poles forming a cone. They are covered with a skin roof.

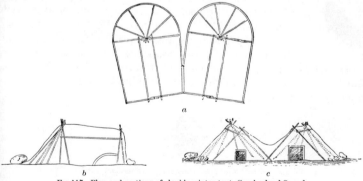

Fig. 117. Plan and sections of double winter tent, Cumberland Sound.

Some families, instead of building snow houses or stone houses in winter, cover the summer tent with shrubs and spread over them a second skin cover. In front of the tent snow vaults are built to protect the interior from the cold. In some instances several families join their tents (Fig. 117). In the front part where the tents adjoin each other the covers are taken away and replaced by a whale rib which affords a passage from one room to the other.

The plans of the feasting houses will be found in another place (p. 192).

CLOTHING, DRESSING OF THE HAIR, AND TATTOOING.

The styles of clothing differ among the tribes of the Central Eskimo. In summer the outer garment is always made of sealskins, though the women wear deerskins almost the entire year. The sealskin clothing is made from the skins of *Pagomys fœtidus*, yearlings being used, and also from those of *Callocephalus*, if they can be obtained. The latter particularly are highly valued by the natives. The inner garment is made either of the skin of the young seal in the white coat or of a light deerskin. It is cut entirely with the woman's knife and is sewed with deer sinews.

The prettiest clothing is made by the tribes of Davis Strait. Both men and women wear boots, trousers, and jackets. The style of the men's clothing may be seen from Figs. 8 and 10, which represent men in the winter clothing, and 24 and 46, which show them in summer clothing. The summer boots are made from the hairless skin of *Pagomys fœtidus*, the soles from that of *Phoca*, the sole reaching to the top of the foot. The leg of the boot is kept up by a string passing through its rim and firmly tied around the leg. At the ankle a string passes over the instep and around the foot to prevent the heel from slipping down. On the top of the foot a knob (qaturang) is sometimes attached to the string as an ornament (Fig. 118). The stocking is made of light deerskin. It reaches above the knee, where it has a trimming made from the white parts of a deerskin, whereas the boot ends below the knee. Next to the stocking is a slipper, which is made of birdskin, the feathers being worn next to the foot. This is covered with a slipper of sealskin, the hair side worn outward and the hair pointing toward the heel. The boot finishes the footgear. In the huts the birdskin slippers are frequently laid aside.

Fig. 118. Qaturang or boot ornament. (Museum für Völkerkunde, Berlin. IV A 6850.

The breeches of the men consist of an outside and an inside pair, the former being worn with the hair outside; the latter, which are made of the skins of young seals or of deer, with the hair inside. They are fastened round the body by means of a string and reach a little below the knee. Their make will best be seen from the figures. Only the southern tribes trim the lower end of the trousers by sewing a piece to them, the hair of which runs around the leg, while above it runs downward. This pattern looks very pretty.

The jacket does not open in front, but is drawn over the head. It has a hood fitting closely to the head. The back and the front are made of a sealskin each. The hood of the Oqomiut is sharply pointed, while that of the Akudnirmiut is more rounded. The jackets are cut straight and have a slit in front. Some have a short tail behind, particularly the winter jackets. The cut of the winter clothing, which

FIG. 119. Woman's jacket. (National Museum, Washington.)

is made of deerskin, is the same as the former, and it is frequently trimmed with straps of deerskin. The jacket is rarely worn with the hood down, as it is only used while hunting and traveling. It is

a   *b*   *c*

FIG. 120. Ivory beads for women's jackets. *a* (Museum für Völkerkunde, Berlin. IV A 6841.) *b, c* National Museum, Washington. 34134.) ⅓

ever brought into the huts, but after being cleaned from the adhering snow with the snowbeater (tiluqtung, as named by the eastern tribes; arautaq, as called by Hudson Bay tribes) is kept in the store-room outside the house.

The women's trousers are composed of two pieces. The upper one fits tightly and covers the upper half of the thigh. It is made of the skin of a deer's belly. The other parts are, as it were, leggings, which reach from a little below the knee to the middle of the thigh and are kept in place by a string running to the upper part of the trousers. The women's jacket (Fig. 119) is much more neatly trimmed than that of the men. It is frequently adorned with ivory or brass beads running round the edge (Fig. 120). It has a wide and large hood reaching down almost to the middle of the body. In front the jacket has a short appendage; behind, a very long tail which trails along the ground (see Fig. 119). If a child is carried in the hood, a leather girdle fastened with a buckle (Fig. 121) is tied around the waist and serves to prevent the child from slipping down. The first specimen given in Fig. 121 is remarkable for its artistic design.

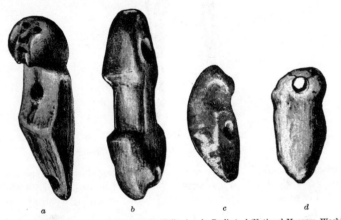

Fig. 121. Girdle buckles. *a, c, d* (Museum für Völkerkunde, Berlin.) *b* (National Museum, Washington. 34125.) ⅓

Among the Akudnirmiut of Davis Strait another fashion is more frequently in use much resembling that of Iglulik. The women have a wider jacket with a broader hood, enormous boots with a flap reaching up to the hip, and breeches consisting of one piece and reaching to the knees. Unfortunately I have no drawing of this clothing and must therefore refer to Parry's engravings, which however, are not very well executed, and to the figures representing dolls in this costume (see Fig. 139).

When children are about a month old they are put into a jacket made from the skin of a deer fawn and a cap of the same material their legs remaining bare, as they are always carried in their mother' hood. In some places, where large boots are in use, they are said to be carried in these. The cap is separate and is always made of the head of a fawn, the ears standing upright on each side of the head. The jacket is either quite open in front or has a short slit. Children of more than two years of age wear the same clothing, with trousers and boots (Fig. 122). When they are about eight years old they are clothed like men (Fig. 123.). Girls frequently wear the same kind of dress for some time, until they are from nine to ten years old, when they assume the clothing of the women.

Fig. 122 Infant's clothing. (Museum für Völkerkunde, Berlin.)

Fig. 123 Child's clothing.

As to the mode of clothing of the other tribes I give the descriptions of the authors.

Parry describes the dress of the Iglulirmiut as follows (II, p. 495):

In the jacket of the women, the tail or flap behind is very broad, and so long as almost to touch the ground; while a shorter and narrower one before reaches halfway down the thigh. The men have also a tail in the hind part of their jacket, but of smaller dimensions; but before, it is generally straight or ornamented by a single collop. The hood of the jacket * * * is much the largest in that of the women, for the purpose of holding a child. The back of the jacket also bulges out in he middle to give the child a footing, and a strap or girdle below this, and secured ound the waist by two large wooden buttons in front, prevents the infant from alling through when, the hood being in use, it is necessary thus to deposit it. * * * The upper (winter) garment of the females, besides being cut according to a regular and uniform pattern, and sewed with exceeding neatness, which is the case with all the dresses of these people, has also the flaps ornamented in a very becoming manner by a neat border of deerskin, so arranged as to display alternate breadths of white and dark fur. This is, moreover, usually beautified by a handsome fringe, consisting of innumerable long, narrow threads of leather hanging down from it. This ornament is not uncommon also in the outer jackets of the men. When seal hunting, they fasten up the tails of their jackets with a button behind.

The breeches and the foot gear of the men are described as being much the same as those of the Akudnirmiut. Parry remarks (loc. cit.) that several serpentine pieces of hide are sewed across the soles to prevent them from wearing out:

The inner boot of the women, unlike that of the men, is loose around the leg, coming as high as the knee joint behind, and in front carried up by a long, pointed flap nearly to the waist and there fastened to the breeches. The upper boot, with the hair as usual outside, corresponds with the other in shape, except that it is much more full, especially on the outer side, where it bulges out so preposterously as to give the women the most awkward, bow-legged appearance imaginable. * * * Here, also, as in the jacket, considerable taste is displayed in the selection of different parts of the deerskin, alternate strips of dark and white being placed up and down the sides and front by way of ornament. The women also wear a moccasin (itigega) overall in the winter-time.

The dress of the Aivillirmiut is similar to that of the Iglulirmiut (Gilder, p. 139).

Traces of clothing found in old graves of Cumberland Sound and Frobisher's description of the dress of the Nugumiut show that the style of clothing now used by the Iglulirmiut formerly obtained in all parts of Baffin Land.

All the Eskimo wear mittens. Those used in winter are made of the skin of young seals or of deerskin. In summer they use hairless sealskin, and sometimes make them with two thumbs, so as to turn the mitten round if one side should become wet.

The manner of dressing the hair practiced by the tribes of Northeastern Baffin Land differs from that of other tribes. On Davis Strait and in Hudson Bay the men allow it to grow to a considerable length, but frequently cut it short on the forehead. If all the hair is long it is kept back by a band made of the skin of deer antlers taken in the velvet. Sometimes these ties are very neatly finished. Frobisher states that the Nugumiut shaved part of their heads. The Kinipetu shave the top of the head; the Netchillirmiut wear their hair short.

The women have two styles of dressing their hair. They always part it on the top of the head. The back hair is wound into a bunch protruding from the back of the head or nicely arranged in a knot. The hair at the sides is plaited and folded over the ears, joining the knot behind. The other way is to arrange these parts in small pig tails reaching a little below the ears. They are kept in order by an ivory or brass ring (see Fig. 126).

The manner in which the Iglulirmiut dress their hair is thus described by Parry (II, p. 493):

They separate their locks into two equal parts, one of which hangs on each side of their heads and in front of their shoulders. To stiffen and bind these they use a narrow strap of deerskin, attached at one end to a round piece of bone, fourteen inches long, tapered to a point, and covered over with leather. This looks like a little whip, the handle of which is placed up and down the hair and the strap wound round it in a number of spiral turns, making the tail, thus equipped, very much resemble one of those formerly worn by our seamen. The strap of this article of dress, which is altogether called a tugliga, is so made from the deerskin as to show when bound round the hair, alternate turns of white and dark fur, which give it a very neat and ornamental appearance. * * * Those who are less nice dispose * * * their hair into a loose plait on each side or have one tugliga and one plait.

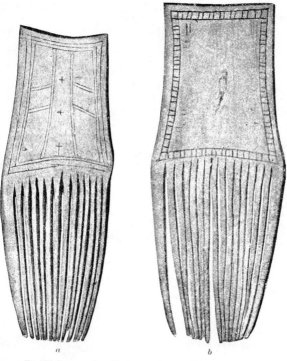

FIG. 124. Ivory combs. (National Museum, Washington. 10195.) ½

The natives of Southampton Island arrange their hair in a bunch protruding from the forehead (sulubaut). The same dress is worn at certain feasts on Davis Strait (p. 200).

For dressing the hair ivory combs are in use, two specimens of which are represented in Fig. 124.

The clothing is frequently trimmed with straps of white deerskin, giving it a pleasing appearance. The edge of the women's jacket is adorned with ivory beads. Instead of these, teeth, deer's ears, foxes' noses, or brass bells are sometimes used.

FIG. 125. Buckles. *c* (From Tununirnusirn.) (National Museum, Washington. *a*, 10196 ; *b*, 10400 *c*, 10177; *d*, 10196; *e*, 10195; *f*, 10207.) ⅓

The inner jackets of the men are sometimes trimmed with beads feathers, or leather straps, forming a collar and figures of differen kinds on the back and on the breast. An amulet is worn in th middle of the back (p. 184). These ornaments and the amulet ar only visible when the outer garment is taken off in the hut.

Fig. 125 represents a number of buckles serving to carry needle-cases or similar implements at the girdle, to which the eye is tied, the button being fastened to the implement. Head ornaments are in frequent use and are sometimes beautifully finished.

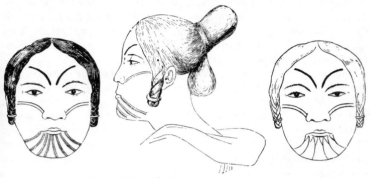

FIG. 126 Manner of tattooing face and wearing hair.

The women are in the habit of adorning their faces by tattooing. It is done, when they are about twelve years of age, by passing needle and thread covered with soot under the skin, or by puncture, the points of the tattooing instruments being rubbed with the same substance in both cases, which is a mixture of the juice of *Fucus* and soot, or with gunpowder, by which process they obtain a blue color. The face, arms, hands, thighs, and breasts are the parts of the body which are generally tattooed. The patterns will be seen in Figs. 126 and 127.

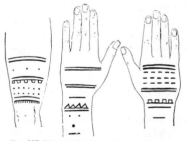

FIG. 127 Manner of tattooing legs and hands.

SOCIAL AND RELIGIOUS LIFE.

DOMESTIC OCCUPATIONS AND AMUSEMENTS.

It is winter and the natives are established in their warm snow houses. At this time of the year it is necessary to make use of the short daylight and twilight for hunting. Long before the day begins to dawn the Eskimo prepares for hunting. He rouses his house-mates; his wife supplies the lamp with a new wick and fresh blubber and the dim light which has been kept burning during the night quickly brightens up and warms the hut. While the woman is busy preparing breakfast the man fits up his sledge for hunting. He takes the snow block which closes the entrance of the dwelling room during the night out of the doorway and passes through the low passages. Within the passage the dogs are sleeping, tired by the fatigues of the day before. Though their long, heavy hair protects them from the severe cold of the Arctic winter, they like to seek shelter from the piercing winds in the entrance of the hut.

The sledge is iced, the harnesses are taken out of the storeroom by the door, and the dogs are harnessed to the sledge. Breakfast is now ready and after having taken a hearty meal of seal soup and frozen and cooked seal meat the hunter lashes the spear that stands outside of the hut upon the sledge, hangs the harpoon line, some toggles, and his knife over the antlers, and starts for the hunting ground. Here he waits patiently for the blowing seal, sometimes until late in the evening.

Meanwhile the women, who stay at home, are engaged in their domestic occupations, mending boots and making new clothing, or they visit one another, taking some work with them, or pass their time with games or in playing with the children. While sitting at their sewing and at the same time watching their lamps and cooking the meat, they incessantly hum their favorite tunes. About noon they cook their dinner and usually prepare at the same time the meal for the returning hunters. As soon as the first sledge is heard approaching, the pots, which have been pushed back during the afternoon, are placed over the fire, and when the hungry men enter the hut their dinner is ready. While hunting they usually open the seals caught early in the morning, to take out a piece of the flesh or liver, which they eat raw, for lunch. The cut is then temporarily fastened until the final dressing of the animal at home.

In the western regions particularly the hunters frequently visit the depots of venison made in the fall, and the return is always followed by a great feast.

After the hunters reach home they first unharness their dogs and unstring the traces, which are carefully arranged, coiled up, and put away in the storeroom. Then the sledge is unloaded and the spoils are dragged through the entrance into the hut. A religious custom commands the women to leave off working, and not until the seal is cut up are they allowed to resume their sewing and the preparing of skins. This custom is founded on the tradition that all kinds of sea animals have risen from the fingers of their supreme goddess who must be propitiated after being offended by the murder of her offspring (see p. 175). The spear is stuck into the snow at the entrance of the house, the sledge is turned upside down, and the ice coating is removed from the runners. Then it is leaned against th wall of the house, and at last the hunter is ready to enter. He strips off his deerskin jacket and slips into his sealskin coat. The former is carefully cleaned of the adhering ice and snow with the snowbeater and put into the storeroom outside the house.

This done, the men are ready for their dinner, of which the women do not partake. In winter the staple food of the Eskimo is boiled seal and walrus meat, though in some parts of the western districts it is musk ox and venison, a rich and nourishing soup being obtained by cooking the meat. The natives are particularly fond of seal and walrus soup, which is made by mixing and boiling water, blood, and blubber with large pieces of meat.

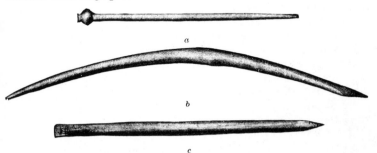

FIG. 128 Forks. a, b (From Iglulik.) (National Museum, Washington. a, 10395; b, 10393.)

The food is not always salted, but sometimes melted sea water ice, which contains a sufficient quantity of salt, is used for cooking. Liver is generally eaten raw and is considered a tidbit. I have seen the intestines eaten only when there was no meat.

FIG. 129. Ladle of musk ox horn. (National Museum, Washington. 10682.) ¼

Forks (Fig. 128)[1] are used to take the meat out of the kettle and the soup is generally poured out into a large cup. Before the introduction of European manufactures these vessels and dishes generally consisted of whalebone. One of these has been described by Parry (I, p. 286). It was circular in form, one piece of whalebone being bent into the proper shape for the sides and another flat piece of the same material sewed to it for a bottom, so closely as to make it perfectly watertight. A ladle or spoon (Fig. 129) is sometimes used in drinking it, but usually the cup is passed around, each taking a sip in turn. In the same way large pieces of meat are passed round, each taking as large a mouthful as possible and then cutting

[1] The fork first represented in this figure is evidently broken, a series of knobs having originally formed the handle.

off the bit close to the lips. They all smack their lips in eating. The Eskimo drink a great deal of water, which is generally kept in vessels standing near the lamps. When the men have finished their meal the women take their share, and then all attack the frozen meat which is kept in the storerooms. The women are allowed to participate in this part of the meal. An enormous quantity of meat is devoured every night, and sometimes they only suspend eating when they go to bed, keeping a piece of meat within reach in case they awake.

After dinner the seals, which have been placed behind the lamps to thaw, are thrown upon the floor, cut up, and the spare meat and skins are taken into the storerooms. If a scarcity of food prevails in the village and a hunter has caught a few seals, every inhabitant of the settlement receives a piece of meat and blubber, which he takes to his hut, and the successful hunter invites all hands to a feast.

The dogs are fed every second day after dinner. For this purpose two men go to a place at a short distance from the hut, taking the frozen food with them, which they split with a hatchet or the point of the spear. While one is breaking the solid mass the other keeps the dogs off by means of the whip, but as soon as the food is ready they make a rush at it, and in less than half a minute have swallowed their meal. No dog of a strange team is allowed to steal anything, but is kept at a distance by the dogs themselves and by the whip. If the dogs are very hungry they are harnessed to the sledge in order to prevent an attack before the men are ready. They are unharnessed after the food is prepared, the weakest first, in order to give him the best chance of picking out some good pieces. Sometimes they are fed in the house; in such a case, the food being first prepared, they are led into the hut singly; thus each receives his share.

All the work being finished, boots and stockings are changed, as they must be dried and mended. The men visit one another and spend the night in talking, singing, gambling, and telling stories. The events of the day are talked over, success in hunting is compared, the hunting tools requiring mending are set in order, and the lines are dried and softened. Some busy themselves in cutting new ivory implements and seal lines or in carving. They never spend the nights quite alone, but meet for social entertainment. During these visits the host places a large lump of frozen meat and a knife on the side bench behind the lamp and every one is welcome to help himself to as much as he likes.

The first comers sit down on the ledge, while those entering later stand or squat in the passage. When any one addresses the whole assembly he always turns his face to the wall and avoids facing the listeners. Most of the men take off their outer jacket in the house and they sit chatting until very late. Even the young children do not go to bed early.

The women sit on the bed in front of their lamps, with their legs under them, working continually on their own clothing or on that of the men, drying the wet footgear and mittens, and softening the leather by chewing and rubbing. If a bitch has a litter of pups it is their business to look after them, to keep them warm, and to feed

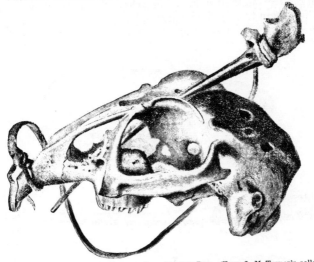

Fig. 130 Skull used in the game ajegaung, from Ungava Bay. (From L. M. Turner's collection.) (National Museum, Washington. 90227.) ⅓

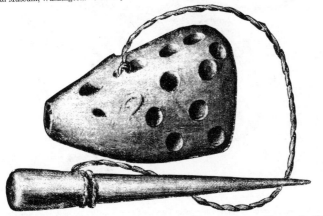

Fig. 131 Ivory carving representing head of fox, used in the game ajegaung. (Museum für Völkerkunde, Berlin. IV A 6820.) ⅓

them regularly. Generally the pups are put into a small harness and are allowed to crawl about the side of the bed, where they are tied to the wall by a trace. Young children are always carried in their mothers' hoods, but when about a year and a half old they are allowed to play on the bed, and are only carried by their mothers when they get too mischievous. When the mother is engaged in any hard work they are carried by the young girls. They are weaned when about two years old, but women suckle them occasionally until they are three or four years of age. During this time they are frequently fed from their mothers' mouths. When about twelve years old they begin to help their parents, the girls sewing and preparing skins, the boys accompanying their fathers in hunting expeditions.

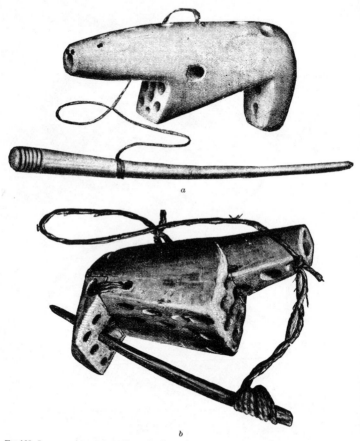

Fig. 132. Ivory carvings representing polar bear, used in the game ajegaung. *a* (Museum für Völkerkunde, Berlin. IV A 6819.) *b* (National Museum Washington. 34078.) ⅔

The parents are very fond of their children and treat them kindly. They are never beaten and rarely scolded, and in turn they are very dutiful, obeying the wishes of their parents and taking care of them in their old age.

In winter gambling is one of the favorite amusements of the Eskimo. Figs. 130–132 represent the ajegaung, used in a game somewhat similar to our cup and ball. The most primitive device is Fig. 130, a hare's skull with a number of holes drilled through it. A specimen was kindly lent to me by Lucien M. Turner, who brought it from Ungava Bay; but in Baffin Land exactly the same device is in use. Fig. 131 represents the head of a fox, in ivory; Fig. 132, a polar bear. The specimen shown in Fig. 132 b was brought from Cumberland Sound by Kumlien. The neck of the bear is more elaborate than the one shown in a. The attachment of the part representing the hind legs is of some interest. The game is played as follows: First, the skull or the piece of ivory must be thrown up and caught ten times upon the stick in any one of the holes. Then, beginning with the hole in front (the mouth), those of the middle line must be caught. The three holes on the neck of the bear are double, one crossing vertically, the other slanting backward, but both ending in one hole on the neck. After the mouth has been caught upon the stick the vertical hole in the neck is the next, then the oblique one, and so on down the middle line of the animal's body. If, in the first part of the game, the player misses twice he must give up the pieces to his neighbor, who then takes his turn. In the second part he is allowed to play on as long as he catches in any hole, even if it be not the right one, but as soon as he misses he must give it up. After having caught one hole he proceeds to the next, and the player who first finishes all the holes has won the game.

FIG. 133 Figures used in playing tingmiujang, a game similar to dice. (Museum für Völkerkunde, Berlin. IV A 6823.) ¼

A game similar to dice, called tingmiujang, i. e., images of birds, is frequently played. A set of about fifteen figures like those represented in Fig. 133 belong to this game, some representing birds, others men or women. The players sit around a board or a piece of leather and the figures are shaken in the hand and thrown upward. On falling, some stand upright, others lie flat on the back or on the side. Those standing upright belong to that player whom they face; sometimes they are so thrown that they all belong to the one who tosses them up. The players throw by turns until the last figure is taken up, the one getting the greatest number of the figures being the winner.

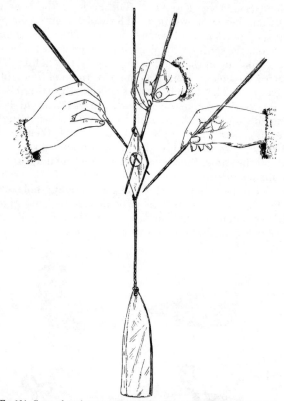

Fig. 134. Game of nuglutang. (Museum für Völkerkunde, Berlin. IV A 6821.)

A favorite game is the nuglutang (Fig. 134). A small, rhomboidal plate of ivory with a hole in the center is hung from the roof and steadied by a heavy stone or a piece of ivory hanging from its lower end. The Eskimo stand around it and when the winner of the last game gives a signal every one tries to hit the hole with a stick. The one who succeeds has won. This game is always played amid great excitement.

The säketän resembles a roulette. A leather cup with a rounded bottom and a nozzle is placed on a board and turned round. When it stops the nozzle points to the winner. At present a tin cup fastened with a nail to a board is used for the same purpose (Fig. 135).

FIG. 135. The säketän or roulette. (Museum für Völkerkunde, Berlin. IV A 6854)

Their way of managing the gain and loss is very curious. The first winner in the game must go to his hut and fetch anything he likes as a stake for the next winner, who in turn receives it, but has to bring a new stake, in place of this, from his hut. Thus the only one who loses anything is the first winner of the game, while the only one who wins anything is the last winner.

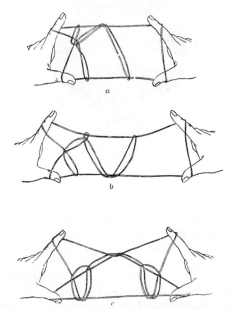

FIG. 136. The ajarorpoq or cat's cradle. *a* representing deer ; *b*, hare ; *c*, hill and ponds.

The women are particularly fond of making figures out of a loop, a game similar to our cat's cradle (ajarorpoq). They are, however, much more clever than we in handling the thong and have a great variety of forms, some of which are represented in Fig. 136.

As an example I shall describe the method of making the device representing a deer (Fig. 136*a*): Wind the loop over both hands, passing it over the back of the thumbs inside the palms and outside the fourth fingers. Take the string from the palm of the right hand with the first finger of the left and vice versa. The first finger of the right hand moves over all the parts of the thong lying on the first and fourth fingers of the right hand and passes through the loop formed by the thongs on the thumb of the right hand; then it moves back over the foremost thong and takes it up, while the thumb lets go the loop. The first finger moves downward before the thongs lying on the fourth finger and comes up in front of all the thongs. The thumb is placed into the loops hanging on the first finger and the loop hanging on the first finger of the left hand is drawn through both and hung again over the same finger. The thumb and first finger of the right and the thumb of the left hand let go their loops. The whole is then drawn tight. A few other devices from Hudson Bay are represented by Klutschak (p. 139).

FIG. 137. Ball. (Museum für Völkerkunde, Berlin.. IV A 6822.)

The ball (Fig. 137) is most frequently used in summer. It is made of sealskin stuffed with moss and neatly trimmed with skin straps. One man throws the ball among the players, whose object it is to keep it always in motion without allowing it to touch the ground. Another game of ball I have seen played by men only. A leather ball filled with hard clay is propelled with a whip, the lash of which is tied up in a coil. Every man has his whip and is to hit the ball and so prevent his fellow players from getting at it.

A third game at ball called igdlukitaqtung is played with small balls tossed up alternately from the right to the left, one always being in the air. Songs used in the game will be found in the last pages of this paper.

An amusement of women and children is to point successively on
the forehead, the cheek, and the chin and to pronounce as rapidly as
possible sulubautiχu′tika, tudliχu′tika, tadliχu′tika, tudliχú′tika,
i. e., the forehead, the cheek, the chin, the cheek.

a   b
Fig. 138. Dolls in dress of the Oqomiut. (Museum für Völkerkunde, Berlin. IV A 6702.) ⅔

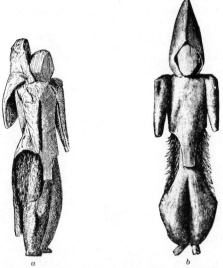

a   b
Fig. 139. Dolls in dress of the Akudnirmiut. (Museum für Völkerkunde, Berlin. IV A 6702.) ⅔

Young children play with toy sledges, kayaks, boats, bows and
arrows, and dolls. The last are made in the same way by all the
tribes, a wooden body being clothed with scraps of deerskin cut in
the same way as the clothing of men. Fig. 138 shows dolls in the
dress of the Oqomiut; Fig. 139, in that of the Akudnirmiut.

In summer children and grown up people exercise by sitting down on their knees in a large circle and simultaneously jumping up and down, by kneeling and holding their toes in their hands and trying to outdo one another in running in this position, &c.

A favorite amusement during the long winter nights is telling tales and composing songs. Old traditions are always related in a highly ceremonious manner. The narrator takes off his outer jacket pulls the hood over his head, and sits down in the rear part of the hut, turning his face toward the wall, and then tells the story slowly and solemnly. All the stories are related in a very abridged form the substance being supposed to be known. The form is always the same, and should the narrator happen to say one word otherwise than is customary he will be corrected by the listeners.

Children tell one another fables and sing short songs. Comic songs making fun of any person are great favorites. Details on the poetry and music of the Eskimo will be found further on.

Parry's description of the games and sports practiced by the Iglulirmiut is so interesting that I insert it here (II, p. 538):

On an occasion when most of the men were absent from the huts on a sealing excursion, the women joined in playing, one of them being the chief performer. Being requested to amuse the rest, she suddenly unbound her hair, platted it, tied both ends together to keep it out of her way, and then stepping out into the middle of the hut, began to make the most hideous faces that can be conceived, by drawing both lips into her mouth, poking forward her chin, squinting frightfully, occasionally shutting one eye, and moving her head from side to side as if her neck had been dislocated. This exhibition, which they call ajokitarpoq, and which is evidently considered an accomplishment that few of them possess in perfection, distorts every feature in the most horrible manner imaginable, and would, I think, put our most skillful horse-collar grinners quite out of countenance.

This performance is identical with one described later (p. 170) as practiced during the meals in summer.

The next performance consists in looking steadfastly and gravely forward and repeating the words tăbā'-tăbā'; kjaibo, kjaibo; kebang inutovik, kebang inutovik; amatama, amatama, in the order in which they are here placed, but each at least four times, and always by a peculiar modulation of the voice speaking them in pairs as they are coupled above. The sound is made to proceed from the throat in a way much resembling ventriloquism, to which art it is indeed an approach. After the last amatama she always pointed with her finger toward her body, and pronounced the word angakoq, steadily retaining her gravity for five or six seconds, and then bursting into a loud laugh, in which she was joined by all the rest. The women sometimes produce a much more guttural and unnatural sound, repeating principally the word ikeri-ikeri, coupling them as before, and staring in such a manner as to make their eyes appear ready to burst out of their sockets with the exertion. Two or more of them will sometimes stand up face to face, and with great quickness and regularity respond to each other, keeping such exact time that the sound appears to come from one throat instead of several. Very few of the females are possessed of this accomplishment, which is called pitkusiraqpoq, and it is not uncommon to see several of the younger females practising it. A third part of the game, distinguished by the word kaitikpoq, consists only in falling on each knee alternately, a

iece of agility which they perform with tolerable quickness, considering the bulky
and awkward nature of their dress. * * * Then the same woman came forward, and letting her arms hang down loosely and bending her body very much forward, shook herself with extreme violence, as if her whole frame had been strongly
convulsed, uttering at the same time, in a wild tone of voice, some of the unnatural
sounds before mentioned.

This being at an end, a new exhibition was commenced in which ten or twelve
women took a part, and which our gentlemen compared to blind man's buff. A circle
being formed, and a boy dispatched to look out at the door of the hut, a woman
placed herself in the center, and, after making a variety of guttural noises for about
half a minute, shut her eyes, and ran about till she had taken hold of one of the
others, whose business it then became to take her station in the center, so that almost
every woman in her turn occupied this post, and in her own peculiar way, either
by distortion of countenance or other gestures, performed her part in the game.
This continued three-quarters of an hour, and, from the precaution of placing a
lookout who was withdrawn when it was over, as well as from some very expressive
signs which need not here be mentioned, there is reason to believe that it is usually
followed by certain indecencies, with which their husbands are not to be acquainted. * * *

The most common amusement however, and to which their husbands made no
objection, they performed at Winter Island expressly for our gratification. The
females, being collected to the number of ten or twelve, stood in as large a circle as
the hut would admit, with a man in the center. He began by a sort of half howling, half singing noise, which appeared as if designed to call the attention of the
women, the latter soon commencing the Amna Aya song. This they continued without variety, remaining quite still while the man walked round within the circle; his
body was rather bent forward, his eyes sometimes closed, his arms constantly moving up and down, and now and then hoarsely vociferating a word or two as if to
increase the animation of the singers, who, whenever he did this, quitted the chorus
and rose into the words of the song. At the end of ten minutes they all left off at
once, and after one minute's interval commenced a second act precisely similar and
of equal duration, the man continuing to invoke their muse as before. A third act
which followed this, varied frequently towards the close only in his throwing his feet
up before and clapping his hands together, by which exertion he was thrown into a
violent perspiration. He then retired, desiring a young man (who as we were informed was the only individual of several then present thus qualified) to take his
place in the center as master of the ceremonies, when the same antics as before were
again gone through. After this description it will scarcely be necessary to remark
that nothing can be poorer in its way than this tedious singing recreation, which, as
well as in everything in which dancing is concerned, they express by the word mumipoq. They seem, however, to take great delight in it; and even a number of the men
as well as all the children crept into the hut by degrees to peep at the performance.

The Eskimo women and children often amuse themselves with a game not unlike
our "skip-rope." This is performed by two women holding the ends of a line and
whirling it regularly round and round, while a third jumps over it in the middle according to the following order. She commences by jumping twice on both feet, then
alternately with the right and left, and next four times with the feet slipped one behind the other, the rope passing once round at each jump. After this she performs
a circle on the ground, jumping about half a dozen times in the course of it, which
bringing her to her original position, the same thing is repeated as often as it can
be done without entangling the line. One or two of the women performed this
with considerable agility and adroitness, considering the clumsiness of their boots
and jackets, and seemed to pride themselves in some degree on the qualification. A

second kind of this game consists in two women holding a long rope by its ends and whirling it round in such a manner over the heads of two others standing close together near the middle of the bight, that each of these shall jump over it alternately. The art therefore, which is indeed considerable, depends more on those whirling the rope than on the jumpers, who are, however, obliged to keep exact time in order to be ready for the rope passing under their feet.

Of all these games I observed only the one called pitkusiraqpoq by Parry, which I saw played several times at Cumberland Sound. (See Appendix, Note 3.)

While in times of plenty the home life is quite cheerful, the house presents a sad and gloomy appearance if stormy weather prevents the men from hunting. The stores are quickly consumed, one lamp after another is extinguished, and everybody sits motionless in the dark hut. Nevertheless the women and men do not stop humming their monotonous amna aya and their stoicism in enduring the pangs of hunger is really wonderful. At last, when starvation is menacing the sufferers, the most daring of the men resolves to try his luck. Though the storm may rage over the icy plain he sets out to go sealing. For hours he braves the cold and stands waiting and watching at the breathing hole until he hears the blowing of the seal and succeeds in killing it.

When those who have remained at home hear the sound of the returning sledge, they rush out of the houses to meet it. Quickly they help the bold hunter to get on shore. The sledge is unloaded, the seal dragged into the house, and every one joyfully awaits his share. The animal is cut up, every household receiving a piece of meat and blubber. The gloomy huts are again lighted up and the pots, which had been out of use for some days, are again hung up over the lamps.

If the hunter, however, has tried in vain to procure food, if the storm does not subside, the terrors of famine visit the settlement. The dogs are the first to fall victims to the pressing hunger, and if the worst comes cannibalism is resorted to. But all these occurrences are spoken of with the utmost horror. In such cases children particularly are killed and eaten. Fortunately, however, such occurrences are very rare.

VISITING.

As soon as the ice has consolidated in winter a lively intercourse springs up between the settlements. Friends visit one another, trading excursions are undertaken, and almost every few days visitors arrive at the village. They are welcomed with great hospitality. The sledge is unloaded and the dogs are fed by the host. The visitor is led into the hut, served with the choicest pieces of meat, and the hostess puts his clothing in order. In the winter these visits are generally short, rarely lasting more than a few days.

Longer journeys are postponed until spring, when food can be procured more easily. These journeys are planned a long time before they are made. While the families generally leave what they can spare of their household goods in winter at their summer settlement, they bring away everything they possess to the winter village if they intend to visit a neighboring tribe in the spring. In April or May they leave their snow houses; the tent poles and the whole of their goods are loaded upon the sledge, only the boats being left behind in charge of some friend, and then they start upon their long, lonely journey. On the first day they do not travel far, but make the first halt after about a twelve-mile journey. As the load is heavy the men and women sit on the top of the sledges only to rest. The driver walks alongside and the women lead the way, the dogs pulling more willingly if they see somebody ahead of the sledge. At night it is not unloaded, only those things being taken out which are necessary for building a small tent and for cooking. In order to protect the sledge from the attacks of the dogs, the pitu (see p.122) is taken out and fastened to an eye cut into the ice with the end of the spear. After having traveled about three days a longer halt is made ; the sledge is unloaded, the dogs are unharnessed, and the men go out hunting in order to procure food for the dogs and for themselves. Thus they slowly proceed until they at last reach the end of their journey. Here they settle down with the friends whom they have come to visit, establish a hut of their own, and spend a whole year with them. In the following spring they retrace their journey to their own homes. Journeys of four to five hundred miles in one spring are not of rare occurrence; longer journeys, however, frequently last for years.

A journey c. two hundred miles, going and coming, is sometimes accomplished in one season. For such a journey they would set out in March or April, leaving all their goods behind, and live with the friends whom they visit for a month or two, returning about June. While on the visit the visitors help their friends to provide for their families.

In traveling in the spring the Eskimo always use snow goggles to protect themselves from snow blindness. The modern ones (Fig. 140), which are made of wood and have a shade and a narrow slit for each eye, are very effective. The old design is represented in Fig. 141, the specimen being made of ivory.

Long journeys are sometimes made in summer, several families traveling together in their boats. As, however, the open season is very short in many parts of Northeastern America, spring journeys are more frequently made.

When traveling by boat the tent poles, skin covers, and all the household goods are stowed away in the bottom. The women do the pulling, three or four working at each oar, while a man sits on the stern board steering with a paddle. They move on at their leisure, stopping whenever they are tired or when a seal is seen blowing near the boat. The kayaks are tied to the stern and towed along. Children and dogs lie about in the bottom of the boat. In the center there is a tub containing all kinds of provisions, and every now and then they take some refreshment from it. During the nights the

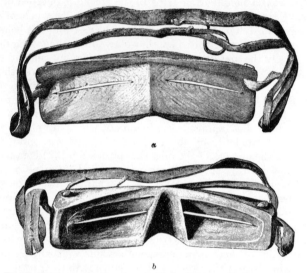

FIG. 140. Modern snow goggles, of wood. (National Museum, Washington. 29978.) ½

tents are erected at suitable points. The natives are well acquainted with these, and, if they are not compelled by severe weather to seek shelter at the nearest point, always visit the same places. These have a smooth, sloping beach, fresh water, and dry, gravelly places in which the tents are built.

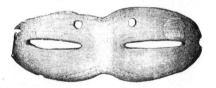

FIG. 141. Old form of snow goggles, of ivory, found in Idjorituaqtuin, Cumberland Sound. (Museum für Völkerkunde, Berlin. IV A 6833.)

SOCIAL CUSTOMS IN SUMMER.

When the rays of the sun begin to be warmer and the roofs of the snow houses tumble down the natives live in a very uncomfortable way until a sufficient number of sealskins are procured to build a tent. Sometimes a family live under a roof too small to cover them

all, though they sit as close as possible, and too low to permit them
to sit upright ; but, as seals are basking everywhere on the ice, this
state of affairs does not last long. The women split a number of large
skins and dry them on the snow, and by the middle of May they can
build a pretty large tent; but it is not until they settle permanently
at the place of the summer village that the large tent is sewed and
put up.

At this season salmon and venison form the staple food of the
Eskimo. The old men, women, and children, who stay at the lakes
or at the salmon rivers, depend almost entirely upon this food. They
fish and eat the salmon in a raw as well as in a cooked state. Birds
are caught and eaten raw. The surplus salmon are split and dried
on poles erected for the purpose. Deer shoulders, legs, and backs
are also cut into thin pieces and dried. Sometimes the dried fish and
venison are deposited in stone caches for later use, but most of it is
eaten in summer, especially when the Eskimo go traveling. When
the men go deer hunting they take a supply of dried salmon with
them, and thus can stay out for a week or even longer. When a
deer is killed it is skinned at once, the legs being slit and the belly
opened. The paunch is carefully tied up, as the contents are a favorite dish of the Eskimo. The head, the legs, and the ribs are cut off
and after being piled up the whole is covered with heavy stones, only
the horns protruding from the top of the depot. The hams and the
skin are generally carried to the hut at once, and, if the distance is
not too great or the carcass can be reached with sledges or boats, the
whole animal is brought home. Large depots are only made in the
fall, when there is no danger of the meat spoiling.

At this season the natives visit deer passes and lakes, near which
they establish their huts. The tents and all the household goods are
packed up in heavy bundles, some of which are carried by the dogs,
the load hanging on both sides of the back; others, by men and
women, being secured by one strap which passes over the forehead
and by another which passes over the breast. Their strength and
their perseverance in carrying heavy loads over long distances are
remarkable.

The social life in the summer settlements is rather different from
that in winter. At this season the families do not cook their own
meals, but a single one provides for the whole settlement. The day
before it is her turn to cook, the woman goes to the hills to fetch
shrubs for the fire. Three stones are put up near the hut as a fireplace, the opening facing the wind. The kettle is placed on the top
of it and the fire is fed with shrubs and blubber. When the meal is
ready the master of the house stands beside it, crying Ujo! Ujo!
(boiled meat) and everybody comes out of the hut provided with a
knife. The dish is carried to a level place and the men sit down
around it in one circle, while the women form another. Then large

lumps of meat are passed around, everybody cutting off a piece and taking a swallow of the soup, which is passed around in a large leather cup. These dinners, which are held in the evening after the return from the hunt, are almost always enlivened by a mimic performance. A man or an old woman sits down in the center of the circle and amuses the assembly by singing and dancing or by making faces. A favorite performance is one in which a man, with blackened face and with a thong tied around his head, writhes and makes odd grimaces.

After dinner the men sit chatting or gambling before the huts, while the women and children amuse themselves by running about, playing at ball, or dancing.

A strict religious custom forbids the Eskimo to work on the deerskins which are obtained in summer before the ice has formed; they are only dried and tied up in large bundles. In the fall, when on their way to the winter settlements, the Eskimo travel rather quickly. The boats are piled up with the spoils of the summer hunt and the place of destination is generally reached before the stormy weather sets in.

When it gets colder short excursions are made by boat in order to collect shrubs for covering the tents. Several families join in building a common hut, and on a fine day the old tents are torn down and the tent poles are converted into a strong frame, which is covered with a double roof. The bed and the platforms for the lamps are raised and henceforth all the cooking is done inside.

As soon as the first seals are caught with the harpoon the deer skins are prepared. If they were deposited under stones in summer, sledges set out to bring them to the settlements, and then they are distributed for winter clothing. According to Hall the western tribes are in the habit of spreading all the skins on one place and distributing them among the inhabitants of the settlement. I did not observe the same custom among the eastern tribes. Then they devote themselves to dressing the skins. On Davis Strait this work falls to the share of the women, while among the Hudson Bay tribes it is done by the men. At this season the great religious feasts of the natives are celebrated, which announce, as it were, the commencement of winter.

SOCIAL ORDER AND LAWS.

The social order of the Eskimo is entirely founded on the family and on the ties of consanguinity and affinity between the individual families. Generally children are betrothed when very young, but these engagements, not being strictly binding, may be broken off at any time. When the children reach maturity the girl learns the duties of a woman and the boy those of a man. As soon as he is able to provide for a family and she can do the work falling to her share, they are allowed to marry. It happens frequently that the young man's parents are unwilling to allow him to provide for his parents-in-law, and then *he* may be rejected at any moment. Usually the young couple must begin housekeeping with the young wife's family and the young man, if belonging to a strange tribe, must join that of his wife. It is not until after his parents-in-law are dead that he is entirely master of his own actions. Though the betrothal be entered into in the days of childhood the bride must be bought from the parents by some present. In other instances the men choose their wives when grown up and sometimes a long wooing precedes the marriage. The consent of the bride's parents, or, if they are dead, that of her brothers, is always necessary. Marriages between relatives are forbidden: cousins, nephew and niece, aunt and uncle, are not allowed to intermarry. There is, however, no law to prevent a man from marrying two sisters. It is remarkable that Lyon states just the reverse (p. 353). I am sure, however, that my statements are correct in reference to the Davis Strait tribes.

Should the newly married couple join the wife's family this would serve as a check to polygamy, which, however, is quite allowable. It is only when the new family settles on its own account that a man is at full liberty to take additional wives, among whom one is always considered the chief wife. Monogamy is everywhere more frequent than polygamy, only a very few men having two or more wives. According to Ross polyandry occurs with the Netchillirmiut (II, pp. 356, 373). As long as the mother-in-law lives with the young family the wives are subordinate to her, while the mothers of both parties are independent of each other. No example came to my notice of both parents living with the newly married couple. Sometimes the man and wife do not set up a new household at once, but each remains at home. The property necessary for establishing a new family is the hunting gear of the man and the knife, scraper, lamp, and cooking pot of the women.

A strange custom permits a man to lend his wife to a friend for a whole season or even longer and to exchange wives as a sign of friendship. On certain occasions it is even commanded by a religious law (see p. 197). Nevertheless I know of some instances of quarrels rising from jealousy. Lyon states, however, that this passion is unknown among the Iglulirmiut (p. 355). The husband is not allowed to maltreat or punish his wife; if he does she may leave him at any time, and the wife's mother can always command a divorce. Both are allowed to remarry as soon as they like, even the slightest pretext being sufficient for a separation.

I may be allowed to refer once more to the division of labor between the man and woman. The principal part of the man's work is to provide for his family by hunting, i. e., for his wife and children and for his relatives who have no provider. He must drive the sledge in traveling, feed the dogs, build the house, and make and keep in order his hunting implements, the boat cover and seal floats excepted. The woman has to do the household work, the sewing, and the cooking. She must look after the lamps, make and mend the tent and boat covers, prepare the skins, and bring up young dogs. It falls to her share to make the inner outfit of the hut, to smooth the platforms, line the snow house, &c. On Davis Strait the men cut up all kinds of animals which they have caught; on Hudson Bay, however, the women cut up the seals. There the men prepare the deerskins, which is done by the women among the eastern tribes. Everywhere the women have to do the rowing in the large boats while the man steers. Cripples who are unable to hunt do the same kind of work as women.

Children are treated very kindly and are not scolded, whipped, or subjected to any corporal punishment. Among all the tribes infanticide has been practiced to some extent, but probably only females or children of widows or widowers have been murdered in this way, the latter on account of the difficulty of providing for them. It is very remarkable that this practice seems to be quite allowable among them, while in Greenland it is believed that the spirit of the murdered child is turned into an evil spirit, called angiaq, and revenges the crime (Rink, p. 45).

Besides the children properly belonging to the family, adopted children, widows, and old people are considered part of it. Adoption is carried on among this people to a great extent.

If for any reason a man is unable to provide for his family or if a woman cannot do her household work, the children are adopted by a relative or a friend, who considers them as his own children. In the same way widows with their children are adopted by their nearest relative or by a friend and belong to the family, though the woman retains her own fireplace.

It is difficult to decide which relative is considered the nearest, but the ties of consanguinity appear to be much closer than those of affinity. If a woman dies the husband leaves his children with his parents-in-law and returns to his own family, and if a man dies his wife returns to her parents or her brothers, who are the nearest relatives next to parents or children. When a woman dies, however, after the children are grown up the widower will stay with them. In case of a divorce the children generally remain with the mother.

As a great part of the personal property of a man is destroyed at his death or placed by his grave, the objects which may be acquired by inheritance are few. These are the gun, harpoon, sledge, dogs, kayak, boat, and tent poles of the man and the lamp and pots of the woman. The first inheritor of these articles is the eldest son living with the parents. Sons and daughters having households of their own do not participate in the inheritance. An elder adopted son has a preference over a younger son born of the marriage. Details of the laws which relate to inheritance are unknown to me.

Sometimes men are adopted who may almost be considered servants. Particularly bachelors without any relations, cripples who are not able to provide for themselves, or men who have lost their sledges and dogs are found in this position. They fulfill minor occupations, mend the hunting implements, fit out the sledges, feed the dogs, &c.; sometimes, however, they join the hunters. They follow the master of the house when he removes from one place to another, make journeys in order to do his commissions, and so on. The position, however, is a voluntary one, and therefore these men are not less esteemed than the self dependent providers.

Strangers visiting their friends for a season are generally in a similar position, though they receive a wife if the host happens to have more than one; if the friend has hunting gear, a sledge, and dogs of his own, he can arrange a separate fireplace in the hut.

In summer most families have each their own tent, but in the fall from two to four join in building a house. Frequently the parents live on one side, the family of the son-in-law on the other, and a friend or relative in a small recess. Sometimes two houses have a common entrance or the passages communicate with one another. The inhabitants of both parts usually live quite independently of one another, while the oldest man of every house has some influence over his housemates.

If the distance between the winter and the summer settlement is very great or when any particular knowledge is required to find out the haunts of game, there is a kind of chief in the settlement, whose acknowledged authority is, however, very limited. He is called the pimain (i. e., he who knows everything best) or the issumautang. His authority is virtually limited to the right of deciding on the proper time to shift the huts from one place to the other, but the families are not obliged to follow him. At some places it seems to be considered proper to ask the pimain before moving to another settlement and leaving the rest of the tribe. He may ask some men to go deer hunting, others to go sealing, but there is not the slightest obligation to obey his orders.

Every family is allowed to settle wherever it likes, visiting a strange tribe being the only exception. In such a case the newcomer has to undergo a ceremony which consists chiefly in a duel between a native of the place and himself. If he is defeated he runs the risk of being killed by those among whom he has come (see pp. 57, 201).

There are numerous regulations governing hunting, determining to whom the game belongs, the obligations of the successful hunter towards the inhabitants of the village, &c.

When a seal is brought to the huts everybody is entitled to a share of the meat and blubber, which is distributed by the hunter himself or carried to the individual huts by his wife. This custom is only practiced when food is scarce. In time of plenty only the housemates receive a share of the animal.

A ground seal belongs to all the men who take part in the hunt, the skin especially being divided among them. A walrus is cut up at once into as many parts as there are hunters, the one who first struck it having the choice of the parts and receiving the head. A whale belongs to the whole settlement and its capture is celebrated by a feast (p. 193).

A bear or a young seal belongs to the man who first saw it, no matter who kills it.

Lost objects must be restored to the owner if he is known, game, however, excepted; for example, if a harpoon line breaks and the animal escapes, but is found later by another man, the game belongs to the latter. In Hudson Bay he is also allowed to keep the harpoon and line.

There is no way of enforcing these unwritten laws and no punishment for transgressors except the blood vengeance. It is not a rare occurrence that a man who is offended by another man takes revenge by killing the offender. It is then the right and the duty of the nearest relative of the victim to kill the murderer. In certain quarrels between the Netchillirmiut and the Aivillirmiut, in which the murderer himself could not be apprehended, the family of the murdered man has killed one of the murderer's relations in his stead. Such a feud sometimes lasts for a long time and is even handed down to a succeeding generation. It is sometimes settled by mutual agreement. As a sign of reconciliation both parties touch each other's breasts, saying, Ilaga (my friend) (Klutschak, p. 70).

If a man has committed a murder or made himself odious by other outrages he may be killed by any one simply as a matter of justice. The man who intends to take revenge on him must ask his countrymen singly if each agrees in the opinion that the offender is a bad man deserving death. If all answer in the affirmative he may kill the man thus condemned and no one is allowed to revenge the murder. (See Appendix, Note 4.)

Their method of carrying on such a feud is quite foreign to our feelings. Strange as it may seem, a murderer will come to visit the relatives of his victim (though he knows that they are allowed to kill him in revenge) and will settle with them. He is kindly welcomed and sometimes lives quietly for weeks and months. Then he is suddenly challenged to a wrestling match (see p. 201), and if defeated is killed, or if victorious he may kill one of the opposite party, or when hunting he is suddenly attacked by his companions and slain.

RELIGIOUS IDEAS AND THE ANGAKUNIRN (PRIESTHOOD).

Although the principal religious ideas of the Central Eskimo and those of the Greenlanders are identical, their mythologies differ in many material points. I will only mention here that they believe in the Tornait of the old Greenlanders, while the Tornarsuk (i. e., the great Tornaq of the latter) is unknown to them. Their Supreme Being is a woman whose name is Sedna.

The first report on this tradition is found in Warmow's journal of his visit to Cumberland Sound (Missionsblatt aus der Brüdergemeinde, 1859, No. I, p. 19). The editor says:

The name of the good spirit is Sanaq or Sana, and he seems to be worshiped as the unknown deity. Nobody could give a definite answer to Brother Warmow's frequent questions as to what they believed he was. They only said they invoked his help if they were in need. "Then we ask him," one of the men said, "and Takaq (the moon) gives us what we want, seals and deer." Another one said that Sanaq had lived on the earth and afterwards ascended to the moon.

In Hall's account of his explorations in Frobisher Bay it is mentioned that the tribes of that country, the Nugumiut, believe in a Supreme Being, and the following statement is given (Hall I, p. 524):

There is one Supreme Being, called by them Anguta, who created the earth, sea, and heavenly bodies. There is also a secondary divinity, a woman, the daughter of Anguta, who is called Sidne. She is supposed to have created all things laving life, animal and vegetable. She is regarded also as the protecting divinity of the Inuit people. To her their supplications are addressed; to her their offerings are made; while most of their religious rites and superstitious observances have reference to her.

It is of great importance that in the journals of Hall's second journey Sedna is mentioned a few times (spelled Sydney), this being the only proof that she is known among the tribes of Hudson Bay.

The statements of the whalers visiting the Sikosuilarmiut and the Akuliarmiut of Hudson Strait correspond with my own observations. Before entering into a comparison of this tradition with similar ones belonging to other tribes, I will give the particulars of the myth as I received it from the Oqomiut and the Akudnirmiut.

SEDNA AND THE FULMAR.

Once upon a time there lived on a solitary shore an Inung with his daughter Sedna. His wife had been dead for some time and the two led a quiet life. Sedna grew up to be a handsome girl and the youths came from all around to sue for her hand, but none of them could touch her proud heart. Finally, at the breaking up of the ice in the spring a fulmar flew from over the ice and wooed Sedna with enticing song. "Come to me," it said; "come into the land of the birds, where there is never hunger, where my tent is made of the most beautiful skins. You shall rest on soft bearskins. My fellows, the fulmars, shall bring you all your heart may desire; their feathers shall clothe you; your lamp shall always be filled with oil, your pot with meat." Sedna could not long resist such wooing and they went together over the vast sea. When at last they reached the country of the fulmar, after a long and hard journey, Sedna discovered that her spouse had shamefully deceived her. Her new home was not built of beautiful pelts, but was covered with wretched fishskins, full of holes, that gave free entrance to wind and snow. Instead of soft reindeer skins her bed was made of hard walrus hides and she had to live on miserable fish, which the birds brought her. Too soon she discovered that she had thrown away her opportunities when in her foolish pride she had rejected the Inuit youth. In her woe she sang: "Aja. O father, if you knew how wretched I am you would come to me and we would hurry away in your boat over the waters. The birds look unkindly upon me the stranger; cold winds roar about my bed; they give me but miserable food. O come and take me back home. Aja."

When a year had passed and the sea was again stirred by warmer winds, the father left his country to visit Sedna. His daughter greeted him joyfully and besought him to take her back home. The father hearing of the outrages wrought upon his daughter determined upon revenge. He killed the fulmar, took Sedna into his boat, and they quickly left the country which had brought so much sorrow to Sedna. When the other fulmars came home and found their companion dead and his wife gone, they all flew away in search of the fugitives. They were very sad over the death of their poor murdered comrade and continue to mourn and cry until this day.

Having flown a short distance they discerned the boat and stirred up a heavy storm. The sea rose in immense waves that threatened the pair with destruction. In this mortal peril the father determined to offer Sedna to the birds and flung her overboard. She clung to the edge of the boat with a death grip. The cruel father then took a knife and cut off the first joints of her fingers. Falling into the sea they were transformed into whales, the nails turning into whalebone. Sedna holding on to the boat more tightly, the second finger joints fell under the sharp knife and swam away as seals (*Pagomys fœtidus*); when the father cut off the stumps of the fingers they became ground seals (*Phoca barbata*). Meantime the storm subsided, for the fulmars thought Sedna was drowned. The father then allowed her to come into the boat again. But from that time she cherished a deadly hatred against him and swore bitter revenge. After they got ashore, she called her dogs and let them gnaw off the feet and hands of her father while he was asleep. Upon this he cursed himself, his daughter, and the dogs which had maimed him whereupon the earth opened and swallowed the hut, the father, the daughter, and the dogs. They have since lived in the land of Adlivun, of which Sedna is the mistress.

This tradition is handed down in an old song. I shall give the substance of it here, as it differs in some points from the above myth.

The story begins when the fulmar carries Sedna to his home and she discovers that he has brought her to a very wretched tent. The next year the father and a brother, whom I find mentioned nowhere else, came to visit her and take her home. The fulmar follows their boat and causes a heavy gale to rise which almost upsets it. The father cuts off her fingers, which are transformed into whales, seals, and ground seals. Besides, he pierces her eye and thus kills her. Then he takes the body into the boat and carries it to the shore. There he lays it on the beach and covers it with a dogskin. When the flood comes in it covers Sedna.

Sedna and her father are described by the angakut (see p. 183), who sometimes visit her house or see them when both dwell among the natives, as follows: She is very large and much taller than the Inuit. In accordance with the second form of the tradition she has only one eye and is scarcely able to move. Her father is also a cripple and appears to the dying, whom he grasps with his right hand, which has only three fingers.

There is a remarkable resemblance between this tradition and one related by Lyon (p. 362), who describes the religious ideas of the Iglulirmiut, more particularly the genii of one of their angakut. He says that the principal spirits are Aiviliajoq (Ay-willi-ay-oo) or Nuliajoq (Noo-le-ay-oo), a female spirit, and her father, Napajoq (Nappayok) or Anautalik (An-now-ta-lig). Then he continues:

The former is in the first place the mother, protectress, and not unfrequently the monopolist of sea animals, which she sometimes very wantonly confines below, and by that means causes a general scarcity in the upper world. When this is the case, the angakok is persuaded to pay her a visit, and attempt the release of the animals on which his tribe subsist. I know not what ceremonies he performs at the first part of the interview; but as the spell by which the animals are held lies in the hand of the enchantress, the conjuror makes some bold attempts to cut it off, and, according to his success, plenty, more or less, is obtained. If deprived of her nails, the bears obtain their freedom; amputation of the first joint liberates the netsiq (*Pagomys*); while that of the second loosens the ugjuq (*Phoca*). Should the knuckles be detached whole herds of walrus rise to the surface; and should the adventurous angakoq succeed in cutting through the lower part of the metacarpal bones, the monstrous whales are disenthralled and delightedly join the other creatures of the deep. * * * Her house is exceedingly fine, and very like a Kabluna (European) looking-glass (?) ; and, what is still more attractive to an Eskimo, it contains plenty of food. Immediately within the door of the dwelling, which has a long passage of entrance, is stationed a very large and fierce dog, which has no tail, and whose hinder quarters are black. * * * Aiviliajoq is described as being equally wonderful in her personal appearance as in her actions. She is very tall and has but one eye, which is the left, the place of the other being covered by a profusion of black hair. She has one pigtail only, contrary to the established fashion in the upper Eskimo world, which is to wear one on each side of the face, and this is of such immense magnitude, that a man can scarcely grasp it with both hands. Its length is exactly twice that of her arm, and it descends to her knee. The hood of her jacket is always worn up. * * *

Her father has but one arm, the hand of which is covered by a very large mitten of bearskin. * * * He is not larger than a boy of ten years of age. He bears the character of a good, quiet sort of person and is master of a very nice house, which, however, is not approachable, on account of the vast herds of walrus lying round it, which, with numerous bears, make a terrific howling. * * * He has nothing to eat, and does not even require it; in which particular he differs widely from his daughter, who has a most voracious appetite. I know not if he is the father of all terrestrial animals, but he is certainly their patron, and withholds them at times from the Eskimo.

The name of the father, Anautalik (An-now-ta-lig), i. e., the man with something to cut (with a knife), is very remarkable. Besides, it is interesting that the angakoq who visits the dwelling of Nuliajoq has to cut off her hand in order to liberate the sea animals. In the tradition related in the foregoing, Sedna has another name, to wit, Uinigumisuitung, i. e., she who would not have a husband; her father, Savirqong, i. e., the man with the knife. Often he is only called Anguta, her father.

It is evident that Nuliajoq is identical with Sedna, though some peculiarities exist in the tradition as related by Lyon which it is rather difficult to reconcile with the myth as it is related among the Oqomiut. It seems to me that this difficulty arises from the mixing up of the angakoq's visit to Sedna with the tradition itself. Indeed Lyon only refers to the angakoq's visit to Nuliajoq, whom he considers a genius of a great angakoq, though he remarks in another place (p. 363) that she "has a boundless command over the lives and destinies of mankind."

The tale of the angakoq's visit makes the tradition very similar to the Greenland myth of Arnaquagsaq, i. e., the old woman. According to Cranz (p. 264) and to Rink (p. 40) this spirit has her abode in the depth of the ocean. She represents the source of nourishment, supplying the physical wants of mankind. She sits in her dwelling in front of a lamp, beneath which is placed a vessel which receives the oil that keeps flowing down from the lamp. From this vessel, as well as from the dark interior of her hut, she sends out all the animals which serve for food, but in certain cases withholds the supply, thus causing want and famine. The reason for thus withholding the supply was that certain filthy and noxious parasites fastened themselves upon her head, of which she could only be relieved by an angakoq. Then she could be induced again to send out the animals for the benefit of man. In going to her he (the angakoq) had first to pass the Arsissut and then to cross an abyss, in which, according to the earliest authors, a wheel as slippery as ice was constantly turning around; then, having safely passed a boiling kettle with seals in it, he arrived at the house, in front of which watch was kept by terrible animals, sometimes described as seals, sometimes as dogs; and, lastly, within the house passage itself, he had to cross an abyss by means of a bridge as narrow as a knife edge.

About the same tale is found among the Baffin Land tribes; according to Captain Spicer, of Groton, Conn., she is called Nanoquag͘saq by the Akuliarmiut. She is visited by the angakut, who liberate the sea animals by subduing her or rather by depriving her of a charm by which she restrains the animals.

I am inclined to think that the form in which Lyon gives this tradition is not quite correct, but is a mixture of the Sedna myth and that of the angakoq's visit to Arnaquagsaq. This seems the more probable from a Greenland tale which Dr. Rink kindly communicated to me, in which it is related that the grandfather of Arnaquagsaq cut off her fingers, which were changed into sea animals.

For this reason it is most probable that Arnaquagsaq, Sedna, and Nuliajoq proceed from the same myth, though the traditions differ from one another as they are related by the travelers. In the mythology of the central tribes this character has a much more decided influence upon their religious belief than the Arnaquagsaq of the Greenlanders seems to have had.

The myth of Sedna is confused with another which treats of the origin of the Europeans and of the Adlet (see p. 229). The legends are in part almost identical. Sedna orders her dog to gnaw off her father's feet; Uinigumisuitung's children maim their grandfather in the same way; and, besides, Sedna's second name is also Uinigumisuitung. In both tales the father is called Savirqong. In Lyon's Private Journal (p. 363) an important statement is found to the effect that the dog which protects Nuliajoq's dwelling is by some natives called her husband, by others merely her dog, but that he is generally considered the father of Erqigdlit (identical with Adlet, p. 637) and Qadlunait (Europeans).

Finally, I must record the legend of the origin of the walrus and the reindeer, which is closely related to the Sedna tradition. I could never learn any other reason why the use of sea animals and reindeer at the same period should be forbidden, except the fear of offending Sedna. She is represented as disliking the deer, which accordingly are not found in her house. Any reason for this dislike is not given. The Akuliarmiut, however, have a tradition that a woman, most probably Sedna herself, created the walrus and the reindeer during a famine. She opened her belly and took out a small piece of fat which she carried up the hills where it was transformed by a magic spell into a reindeer. As soon as she saw the animal she became frightened and ordered it to run away, but the deer turned upon her and would not go; then she became angry and knocked out its teeth.

It turned round at once, but before it could leave she gave it a kick which lopped off its tail. Thus it happened that the deer is deficient as to certain teeth and has scarcely any tail. The woman, however, continued to hate the deer. Afterward she descended to the beach and threw another piece of fat into the water. It was transformed into a walrus, which swam away at once. (According to a communication of Captain Spicer.)

The form of this tradition as related by the Akudnirmiut is somewhat different. During a famine a woman (I could not learn whether she was identical with Sedna or not) carried her boots to the hills and transformed them by magic into deer, which spread all over the country. Then she carried her breeches to the sea, where they were changed into walrus. The first deer, however, had large tusks and no horns, while the walrus had horns and no tusks. The Eskimo soon found that this was very dangerous for the hunter, as the deer killed pursuers with their tusks, while the walrus upset the boats. Therefore an old man transferred the horns to the deer and the tusks to the walrus.

It is very probable that this woman was Sedna, as the Eskimo affirm that the observances referring to walrus and deer are commanded by Sedna and as the first tradition accounts for her dislike of the deer.

I could not find any trace of the tradition reported by Lyon, that Anautalik, Nuliajoq's father, is the protector of land animals, nor of that of a being to whom he refers by the name of Pukimna (derived from pukiq, the white parts of a deerskin), who lives in a fine country far to the west and who is the immediate protectress of deer, which animals roam in immense herds around her dwelling.

Sedna is the mistress of one of the countries to which the souls go after death. It has been related in the foregoing tradition of Sedna and the fulmar that she descended to Adlivun; since that time she has been the mistress of the country, and when invoked as such has the name of Idliragijenget. She has a large house, in which no deerskins are found. There she lives with her father, each occupying one side of it. The father, who is unable to move, lies on the ledge and is covered with old skins. In the entrance across the threshold lies Sedna's dog watching her house. Like her, the father has only one eye, and he never moves from his place while in the house.

The dead, who are seized by Sedna's father, Anguta, are carried to this dwelling. The dog moves aside only a little, just enough to allow the souls to pass. They have to stay in this dismal abode during a whole year, lying by the side of Anguta, who pinches them.

The happy land is heaven and is called Qudlivun (the uppermost ones). It abounds with deer, which are easily caught, and no ice or snow ever visits it.

The Oqomiut and the Akudnirmiut make a distinction between Adlivun and Adliparmiut. Adlivun means "those who live beneath us;" Adliparmiut, "the inhabitants of the country farthest below us;" and the same difference exists between Qudlivun and Qudliparmiut. Though these names intimate the probability that the Eskimo believe in a series of places, located in a descending scale, each below the other, I could not find any more detailed description of the conception.

Hall's observations agree fairly with my own. He says (I, p. 524):

Qudliparmiut (heaven) is upward. Everybody happy ther . All the time light; no snow, no ice, no storms; always pleasant; no trouble; never tired; sing and play all the time—all this to continue without end.

Adliparmiut (hell) is downward. Always dark there. No sun ; trouble there continually ; snow flying all the time, terrible storms; cold, very cold; and a great deal of ice there. All who go there must always remain.

All Inuit who have been good go to Qudliparmiut; that is, who have been kind to the poor and hungry, all who have been happy while living on this earth. Any one who has been killed by accident, or who has committed suicide, certainly goes to the happy place.

All Inuit who have been bad—that is, unkind one to another—all who have been unhappy while on this earth, will go to Adliparmiut. If an Inung kills another because he is mad at him, he will certainly go to Adliparmiut.

Kumlien's remarks on this subject, as well as on other ethnographic subjects, are not trustworthy. He has transferred Greenland tales to Cumberland Sound, though the traditions of these tribes differ materially one from the other. I tried hard to corroborate his statements concerning the amaroq and the tornarsuq, concerning certain customs, &c., and am convinced that they are totally unknown to all the natives of Baffin Land from Nugumiut to Tununirn.

Kumlien states that the better land is below the surface of the earth and that those who are killed by violence descend after death. According to Hall and to replies to my own inquiries, it is quite the reverse. Lyon's report is extremely interesting, particularly his description of the stages of the nether world, of which I could only find a scanty hint in the names. He says (p. 372):

There are two places appointed to receive the souls of the good: one of these is in the center of the earth, the other in qilaq, or heaven. To the latter place, such as are drowned at sea, starved to death, murdered, or killed by walruses or bears, are instantly wafted, and dwell in a charming country, which, however, has never been seen by any angakoq.   *   *   *

The place of souls in the world below is called Adli generally; but there are, properly, four distinct states of blessedness, and each rank has a world to itself, the lowest land being the last and best, which all hope to reach. The day on which a good person dies and is buried, the soul goes to a land immediately under the visible world; and, still descending, it arrives the second day at one yet lower; the third day it goes farther yet; and on the fourth it finds, "below the lowest deep, a deeper still." This is the "good land," and the soul which reaches it is for ever happy. The three first stages are bad uncomfortable places for in each the sky is so close to the earth, that a man cannot walk erect : yet these regions are inhabited; and the good soul, in passing through them, sees multitudes of the dead, who, having lost their way, or, not being entitled to the "good land," are always wandering about and in great distress. Whether these unhappy souls are in purgatory or not, I was unable to learn; but they suffer no other pain than what we would call the "fidgets." In the lowest Adli a perpetual and delightful summer prevails.

The belief of these tribes undoubtedly is that all who die by accident or by violence and women who die in childbirth are taken to the upper world. I never heard a different opinion expressed by any native. I do not know whether they believe in a series of upper worlds similar to the nether worlds of the Iglulirmiut, but it is probable, from the names Qudlivun and Qudliparmiut. In the Greenland tradition the upper world is represented as a country with hills and valleys, over which the solid blue sky is expanded. Sedna of the Oqomiut lives in Adlivun, and here the souls must stay one year after death. Everybody who dies from disease or who has offended Sedna by infringing her orders is taken to her. The Eskimo are in great fear of the terrors of her abode. Murderers and offenders against human laws, after they have entered Sedna's house, will never leave it: the other souls, however, are taken to the Adliparmiut, where they live comparatively at their ease, although they are not nearly so blessed as the Qudliparmiut. They hunt whales and walrus and are almost always troubled by ice and snow.

The older authors on Greenland mythology state that the conceptions of the natives do not coincide (Cranz). According to one tradition the good land is below, and tornarsuq, the supreme tornaq, is master of it. Here continuous summer prevails and there is plenty of fresh water, with a profusion of game. Only those people are allowed to come here who have been good hunters and workers, who have accomplished great exploits, caught many seals, who have suffered much, or have died by violence or in childbirth. The souls of the deceased must slide for five days, or even longer, down a steep rock, which has become quite slippery from the blood which has been sprinkled over it. Those who have been lazy and unfit for working go to the upper world, where they suffer from scarcity of food. Particularly the bad and witches are taken to this country, where they are tormented by ravens.

Another tradition places the good land in heaven. The souls travel on the rainbow to the moon, near which they find a large lake abounding with fowls and fish. Rink gives the following statement on this subject (p. 37):

After death, human souls either go to the upper or to the under world. The latter is decidedly to be preferred, as being warm and rich in food. There are the dwellings of the happy dead called arsissut,—viz, those who live in abundance. On the contrary, those who go to the upper world will suffer from cold and famine; and these are called the arssartut, or ball players, on account of their playing at ball with a walrus head, which gives rise to the aurora borealis.

While the Iglulirmiut believe that the soul leaves the body immediately after death and descends to Adli, the tribes of Davis Strait suppose that it lingers three days around the body, unable to leave it. Then it descends to Sedna's house. During its stay in Adlivun the soul is called tupilaq, which is represented by the figure of a man with wide, loose, shabby clothing. It is looked upon as a malevolent spirit, frequently roaming around the villages. The tupilaq is not allowed to enter the houses, and if the angakoq perceives and announces his presence no one would dare to leave the houses. His touch kills men at once, the sight of him causes sickness and mischief. As soon as the soul has become an adliparmio, it is at rest and ceases to be feared as a tupilaq.

It is worth remarking that the Greenlanders designate with the name of tupilaq a supernatural being made by men for the purpose of destroying their enemies (Rink, p. 53). It is composed of various parts of different animals and is enabled to act in the shape of any of them at will. I have not found any trace of this idea among the Central Eskimo.

THE TORNAIT AND THE ANGAKUT.

A consideration of the religious ideas of the Eskimo shows that the tornait, the invisible rulers of every object, are the most remarkable beings next to Sedna. Everything has its inua (owner), which may become the genius of man who thus obtains the qualities of angakunirn. I am not quite sure that every inua can become the tornaq of a man, though with the Greenlanders this was possible. I learned of three kinds of spirits only, who are protectors of angakut: those in the shape of men, of stones, and of bears. These spirits enable the angakut to have intercourse with the others who are considered malevolent to mankind, and though those three species are kind to their angakut they would hurt strangers who might happen to see them. The bear seems to be the most powerful among these spirits. The tornait of the stones live in the large bowlders scattered over the country. The Eskimo believe that these rocks are hollow and form a nice house, the entrance of which is only visible to the angakoq whose genius lives in the stone. The tornaq is a woman with only one eye, in the middle of the brow. Another kind of tornaq lives in the stones that roll down the hills in spring when the snow begins to melt. If a native happens to meet such a stone, which is about to become his tornaq, the latter addresses him: " I jumped down in long leaps from my place on the cliff. As the snow melts, as water is formed on the hills, I jump down." Then it asks the native whether he is willing to have it for his tornaq, and if he answers in the affirmative it accompanies him, wabbling along, as it has no legs.

The bear tornaq is represented as a huge animal without any hair except on the points of the ears and of the tail and at the mouth. If a man wishes to obtain a bear for his tornaq he must travel all alone to the edge of the land floe and summon the bears. Then a large herd will approach and frighten him almost to death. He falls down at once. Should he fall backward he would die at once. If he falls upon his face, however, one bear out of the herd steps forward and asks him if he wishes him to become his tornaq. He then recovers and takes the bear for his spirit and is accompanied by him on the return journey. On the way home, they pass a seal hole and the bear captures the animal for his master. The Eskimo is now a great angakoq, and whenever he wants help he is sure to get it from his bear.

The Eskimo do not make images of the tornait or other supernatural beings in whom they believe, but use to a great extent amulets (armgoaq), some of which are given by the tornait, while others are inherited. The most common varieties of amulets are the feather of an owl, a bear's tooth, and the like, which are always worn on the middle of the back of the inner jacket. Rare minerals (e. g., iron) sewed up in a piece of skin are sometimes used for the same purpose. A small part of the first gown worn by a child is considered a powerful amulet and is preserved for this reason. It is worn at the point of the hood at a great feast celebrated every fall (see pp. 197, 203) and is called koukparmiutang.

Lyon (p. 367) gives the following account of the use of amulets in Iglulik:

Bones and teeth of animals, hanging as solitary pendants, or strung in great numbers, have peculiar virtues, and the bones of the feet of the kabliaqdjuq, which I imagine to be the wolverine, are the most in request. The front teeth of musk oxen are considered as jewels, while the grinders, one or two together, are much esteemed as tassels for the strings used to tie up the breeches of the women. Eye teeth of foxes are sometimes seen to the number of hundreds, neatly perforated and arranged as a kind of fringe round caps or dresses, and even the bones and teeth of fish have their value.

Leather cases of the size of a quill, and containing small pieces of deer's or other flesh, are frequently attached to the caps or hoods of children, but whether to render them expert hunters, or to preserve their health, I could not discover. I was assured that broken spear heads, and other equally cumbrous pendants, worn round the necks of young girls, were spells for the preservation of their chastity, while the same ornaments caused the women to be prolific.

The principal office of the angakut is to find out the reason of sickness and death or of any other misfortune visiting the natives.

The Eskimo believes that he is obliged to answer the angakoq's questions truthfully. The lamps being lowered, the angakoq strips off his outer jacket, pulls the hood over his head, and sits down in the back part of the hut facing the wall. He claps his hands, which are covered with mittens, and, shaking his whole body, utters sounds which one would hardly recognize as human.

Thus he invokes his tornaq, singing and shouting alternately, the listeners, who sit on the edge of the bed, joining the chorus and answering his questions. Then he asks the sick person: "Did you work when it was forbidden?" "Did you eat when you were not allowed to eat?" And if the poor fellow happens to remember any transgression of such laws, he cries: "Yes, I have worked." "Yes, I have eaten." And the angakoq rejoins "I thought so" and issues his commands as to the manner of atonement.

These are manifold. Exchange of wives between two men or adoption of a sick child by another family in order to save its life are frequently demanded. The inhabitants of a village are forbidden to wash themselves for a number of days, to scrape the ice from the windows, and to clean their urine pots before sunrise. Sometimes the angakoq commands that the clothing be thrown away or gives regulations for diet, particularly forbidding the eating of venison, working on deerskins, filing iron, &c.

Disorders of women are considered as a punishment for the neglect to observe the regulations referring to their behavior at certain periods, which regulations were established by Sedna. The same is stated by Lyon (p. 363).

A method of finding out the reason of a disease is by "head lifting." A thong is tied round the head of the sick person or of a relative, who must lie down on the bed, the angakoq holding the thong. Then he asks his tornaq the reason of the sickness and the remedy. If the tornaq answers a question of the angakoq in the affirmative the head is easily lifted. In the other case it feels so heavy that he is unable to move it. Another method is by lifting a boot or a stone, which has been placed under the pillow of the patient. The angakut believe that the boot or stone becomes heavy and cannot be lifted when the tornaq answers their incantations.

At the beginning of some of their performances I have observed the angakoq crawling about in the passage of the hut, howling and shouting, while those inside kept on singing. Then he entered the hut and continued the incantations on the back part of the bed.

Sometimes their cure for sickness is laying a piece of burning wick upon the diseased part of the body and blowing it up into the air or merely blowing upon it.

Storm and bad weather, when lasting a long time and causing want of food, are conjured by making a large whip of seaweed, stepping to the beach, and striking out in the direction whence the wind blows, at the same time crying Taba (It is enough).

A great number of the performances of the angakut require much skill and expertness. Thus in invoking a tornaq or flying to a distant place they can imitate a distant voice by a sort of ventriloquism. In these performances they always have the lamps extinguished and hide themselves behind a screen hung up in the back part of the hut. The tornaq, being invoked, is heard approaching and shaking the hut. The angakoq believes that it is unroofed and flies with his spirit to their place of destination, to propitiate the wrath of a hostile tornaq, to visit the moon or Sedna's dismal abode.

Part of their performances might almost be called juggling. Hall (II, p. 101) describes one of these performances:

The angakoq (Ar-too-a) now made use of three walrus spears. One of these he thrust into the wall of the snow house, and * * * ran with it outside of the igdlu [house] where his ejaculations were responded to by the party inside with the cries of " Atte ! Atte !" [Go on ! Go on !]. Returning with his spear to the door, he had a severe wrestling match with four of the men, who overcame him. But coming again into the central igdlu, and having the lights which had been at the first patted down, relit, he showed the points of two spears apparently covered with fresh blood, which he held up in the presence of all.

The performance of the angakut in the Sedna feast, which will be described hereafter (p. 196) is quite astonishing. Some pierce their bodies with harpoons, evidently having bladders filled with blood fastened under their jackets beforehand, and bleed profusely as they enter the hut. (See Appendix, Note 5.)

A memorable ceremony has been described by Hall (I, p. 469):

I heard a loud shout just outside [the hut]. As quick as thought, the Eskimo sprang for the long knives lying around, and hid them wherever they could find places. * * * Immediately there came crawling into the low entrance to the hut a man with long hair completely covering his face and eyes. He remained on his knees on the floor of the hut, feeling round like a blind man at each side of the entrance, back of the firelight, the place where meat is usually kept, and where knives may generally be found. Not finding any, the angakoq slowly withdrew. * * * If he had found a knife he would have stabbed himself in the breast.

It is one of their favorite tricks to have their hands tied up and a thong fastened around their knees and neck. Then they begin invoking their tornaq, and all of a sudden the body lies motionless while the soul flies to any place which they wish to visit. After returning, the thongs are found untied, though they had been fastened by firm knots. The resemblance of this performance to the experiments of modern spiritualists is striking.

The angakut use a sacred language in their songs and incantations. A great number of words have a symbolic meaning, but others are old roots, which have been lost from common use in the lapse of time. These archaic words are very interesting from a linguistic point of view. Indeed, some are found which are still in use in Greenland, though lost in the other dialects, and others which are only used in Alaska.

I ought to add here that most of the angakut themselves believe in their performances, as by continued shouting and invoking they fall into an ecstasy and really imagine they accomplish the flights and see the spirits.

The angakoq, who must be paid at once for curing a sick person, receives pretty large fees for services of this kind.

Although witchcraft occupied a prominent place in the belief of the Greenlanders I could only find very faint traces of it in Baffin Land, to wit, the opinion that a man has the power of injuring a distant enemy by some means the details of which I did not learn.

I shall add here the numerous regulations referring to eating and working, many of which are connected with the Sedna tradition, and the observance of which is watched by the angakut. As all sea animals have originated from her fingers the Eskimo must make an atonement for every animal he kills. When a seal is brought into the hut the women must stop working until it is cut up. After the capture of a ground seal, walrus, or whale they must rest for three days. Not all kinds of work, however, are forbidden, for they are allowed to mend articles made of sealskin, but they must not make anything new. For instance, an old tent cover may be enlarged in order to build a larger hut, but it is not permitted to make a new one. Working on new deerskins is strictly forbidden. No skins of this kind obtained in summer may be prepared before the ice has formed and the first seal is caught with the harpoon. Later, as soon as the first walrus is caught, the work must stop again until the next fall. For this reason all families are eager to finish the work on deerskins as quickly as possible, as the walrusing season is not commenced until that is done.

The laws prohibiting contact with deer and sea animals at the same time are very strict. According to the Eskimo themselves Sedna dislikes the deer (probably for some reason connected with the tradition of its origin,) and therefore they are not allowed to bring it in contact with her favorites. The meat of the whale, seal, or walrus must not be eaten on the same day with venison. It is not permitted that both sorts of meat lie on the floor of the hut or behind the lamps at the same time. If a man who has eaten venison in the morning happens to enter a hut in which seal meat is being cooked he is allowed to eat venison on the bed, but it must be wrapped up before being carried into the hut and he must take care to keep clear of the floor. Before changing from one food to the other the Eskimo must wash themselves. For the same reason walrus hide must not be carried to Lake Nettilling, which is considered the domain of deer.

A similar custom requires that the Ukusiksalirmiut carry salmon into a hut by a separate entrance, for it must not pass through the same one as seal oil. Besides, the fish must only be cooked at the distance of a day's journey from the place where they have been caught. If eaten on the spot they must be eaten raw (Klutschak, p. 158).

Their customs referring to hunting are manifold. When skinning a deer they must not break a single bone ; then they cut off bits of different parts of the animal and bury them in the ground or under stones (Hall I, p. 386). I have never noticed this custom myself.

On the west shore of Hudson Bay dogs are not allowed to gnaw deer bones during the deer hunting season or seal bones during the sealing season (Klutschak, p. 123). Deer bones must not be broken while walrus are hunted (Hall II, p. 155).

When the men go out hunting in their kayaks the women of the Aivillirmiut take a cup down to the shore and leave it there, believing that it will bring luck (Hall II, p. 103). On Davis Strait they throw a piece of seal's blubber on their husband's kayak when he is about to go hunting (Kumlien, p. 45). After the capture of a whale the Aivillirmiut are not allowed to burn shrubs, but use bones of the whale instead, which are mixed with blubber (Hall II, p. 364). If an animal that is with young is killed the fetus must not be taken and used for food (Hall II, p. 253). When a bear is caught the Nugumiut and the Oqomiut are accustomed to fasten its bladder to a stick which is placed upright near the hut or encampment for three days.

When a house is deserted the Aivillirmiut are in the habit of carrying all the bones lying inside to some distance and putting them upon the ice (Hall II, p. 175). If they intend to move to a place some distance away they are in the habit of burying some of their clothing. Klutschak observed this custom among the Netchillirmiut ; I myself, among the Akudnirmiut. If a great number of families leave a village those who remain build new houses, as they believe that they would otherwise have bad luck in hunting.

A great number of regulations refer to the behavior of women during menstruation. They are not allowed to eat raw meat, they must cook in separate pots, and are not permitted to join in festivals, being looked upon as unclean during this period. Customs referring to childbirth and sickness will be found further on (see p. 201).

When a traveling party visits a neighboring tribe it is obliged to adopt the customs and regulations of the latter.

This account does not by any means include all the peculiar customs of these people, for they are so numerous and the difficulty of finding out anything pertaining to this subject is so great that it is probable that the greater part of them have escaped notice.

I shall also mention a few customs that are peculiar to certain places. At Qeqertelung, east of Naujateling, in Cumberland Sound, the Eskimo dig potstone, but must buy it from the rock: that is, having dug out a piece, they must give the rock something in exchange; for example, ivory carvings, beads, food, or the like.

At Arligaulik, near Wager River, the Eskimo address a large rock and bid it farewell when passing (Hall II, p. 174).

In Cumberland Sound there is a cape called Iliqimisarbing, i. e., the place of headshaking. The place is very dangerous, as heavy squalls sweep down the steep rocks and slides frequently occur. Therefore the natives never pass it without shaking their heads, at the same time uttering a deep murmur.

Besides the tornait already mentioned, a number of others are known which cannot become genii of men. A spirit of the sea, Kalopaling or Mitiling, is described in a tradition (see p. 212). In Erdmann's Wörterbuch des Labradordialectes "Mitiling" is translated Gespenst, i. e., ghost. No doubt it is the name of the same spirit or at least of a similar one which is recognized among the northern tribes, the literal translation being "with eider ducks." Another spirit of which the natives are in great fear is Qiqirn, a phantom in the shape of a huge dog almost without hair. Like the bear which has been alluded to, it has hair only at the mouth, the feet, and the points of the ears and the tail. If it comes near dogs or men they fall into fits and only recover when Qiqirn has left. It is exceedingly afraid of men and runs away as soon as an angakoq descries it.

A very remarkable tornaq is the qaggim inua, i. e., master of the dancing house. The natives build large houses for feasting, singing, and dancing, which are devoted to spirits. This tornaq has the shape of a bandy legged man, his knees being bent outward and forward. He has not a single hair upon his entire body and no bones at the back of his head. To touch him would result in immediate death (see p. 228).

Besides these tornait, more powerful supernatural beings are known, who are "owners" (inua) of the stars and constellations and of meteorologic processes. Moon and sun are considered brother and sister, and in this the tradition of the Central Eskimo exactly corresponds with that of the Greenlanders. It is even known among the Eskimo of Point Barrow (Simpson, p. 940). From Repulse Bay (Aivillirmiut) a few scanty traces of this tradition are recorded by Rae (I, p. 79). He relates as follows:

It is said that many years ago, not long after the creation of the world, there was a mighty conjurer, who gained so much power that at last he raised himself up into the heavens, taking with him his sister (a beautiful girl) and a fire. To the latter he added great quantities of fuel, which thus formed the sun. For some time he and his sister lived in great harmony, but at last they disagreed, and he, in addition to maltreating the lady in many ways, at last scorched the side of her face. She had suffered patiently all sorts of indignities, but the spoiling of her beauty was not to be borne; she therefore ran away from him and formed the moon, and continues so until this day. Her brother is still in chase of her, but although he gets near, he will never overtake her. When it is new moon, the burnt side of the face is towards us; when full moon, the reverse is the case.

The following form of the legend, which I received from some Akudnirmiut and Oqomiut, is almost identical with the Greenland one:

In olden times a brother and his sister lived in a large village in which there was a singing house, and every night the sister with her playfellows enjoyed themselves in this house. Once upon a time, when all the lamps in the singing house were extinguished, somebody came in and outraged her. She was unable to recognize him; but she blackened her hands with soot and when the same again happened besmeared the man's back with it. When the lamps were relighted she saw that the violator was her brother. In great anger she sharpened a knife and cut off her breasts, which she offered to him, saying: "Since you seem to relish me, eat this." Her brother fell into a passion and she fled from him, running about the room. She seized a piece of wood (with which the lamps are kept in order) which was burning brightly and rushed out of the house. The brother took another one, but in his pursuit he fell down and extinguished his light, which continued to glow only faintly. Gradually both were lifted up and continued their course in the sky, the sister being transformed into the sun, the brother into the moon. Whenever the new moon first appears she sings:

Aningaga tapika, takirn tapika qaumidjatedlirpoq; qaumatitaudle.
Aningaga tapika, tikipoq tapika.
(My brother up there, the moon up there begins to shine; he will be bright.
My brother up there, he is coming up there.)

THE FLIGHT TO THE MOON.

There exists another tradition in regard to the spirit of the moon, which is also known to the Greenlanders. While in the first tradition the moon is a man carrying a glowing light, in the other she is the moon man's house (Rink, p. 440). The legend, as told by the Oqomiut and Akudnirmiut, is the narrative of the flight of an angakoq to the moon and is as follows:

A mighty angakoq, who had a bear for his tornaq, resolved to pay a visit to the moon. He sat down in the rear of his hut, turning his back toward the lamps, which had been extinguished. He had his hands tied up and a thong fastened around his knees and neck. Then he summoned his tornaq, which carried him rapidly through the air and brought him to the moon. He observed that the moon was a house, nicely covered with white deerskins, which the man in the moon used to dry near it. On each side of the entrance was the upper portion of the body of an enormous walrus, which threatened to tear in pieces the bold intruder. Though it was dangerous to pass by the fierce animals, the angakoq, by help of his tornaq, succeeded in entering the house.

In the passage he saw the only dog of the man of the moon, which is called Tirie'tiang and is dappled white and red. On entering the main room he perceived, to the left, a small additional building, in which a beautiful woman, the sun, sat before her lamp. As soon as she saw the angakoq entering she blew her fire, behind the blaze of which she hid herself. The man in the moon came to meet him kindly, stepping from the seat on the ledge and bidding the stranger welcome. Behind the lamps great heaps of venison and seal meat were piled up, but the man of the moon did not yet offer him anything. He said: "My wife, Ululiernang, will soon enter and we will perform a dance. Mind that you do not laugh, else she will slit open your belly with her knife, take out your intestines, and give them to my ermine which lives in yon little house outside."

Before long a woman entered carrying an oblong vessel in which her ulo (see p. 110) lay. She put it on the floor and stooped forward, turning the vessel like a whirligig. Then she commenced dancing, and when she turned her back toward the angakoq it was made manifest that she was hollow. She had no back, backbone, or entrails, but only lungs and heart.

The man joined her dance and their attitudes and grimaces looked so funny that the angakoq could scarcely keep from laughing. But just at the right moment he called to mind the warnings of the man in the moon and rushed out of the house. The man cried after him, "Uqsureliktaleqdjuin" ("Provide yourself with your large white bear tornaq").[1] Thus he escaped unhurt.

Upon another visit he succeeded in mastering his inclination to laugh and was hospitably received by the man after the performance was finished. He showed him all around the house and let him look into a small additional building near the entrance. There he saw large herds of deer apparently roaming over vast plains, and the man of the moon allowed him to choose one animal, which fell immediately through a hole upon the earth. In another building he saw a profusion of seals swimming in an ocean and was allowed to pick out one of these also. At last the man in the moon sent him away, when his tornaq carried him back to his hut as quickly as he had left it.

During his visit to the moon his body had lain motionless and soulless, but now it revived. The thongs with which his hands had been fastened had fallen down, though they had been tied in firm knots. The angakoq felt almost exhausted, and when the lamps were relighted he related to the eagerly listening men his adventures during his flight to the moon.

It is related in the course of this tradition that the man in the moon has a qaumat, some kind of light or fire, but I could not reach a satisfactory understanding of the meaning of this word. It is derived from qauq (daylight) and is used in Greenland for the moon herself. Among the Eskimo of Baffin Land it is only employed in the angakoq language, in which the moon is called qaumavun, the sun qaumativun. Another name of the moon is aninga (her brother), in reference to the first legend. The natives also believe that the man in the moon makes the snow. He is generally considered a protector of orphans and of the poor, and sometimes descends from his house on a sledge drawn by his dog, Tirie'tiang, in order to help them (see the tradition of Qaudjaqdjuq, p. 222).

---

[1] Uqsurelik, with blubber, signifies in the language of the angakut the white bear; lauk, large; -leqdjorpoq, he provides himself with.

KADLU THE THUNDERER.

It is said that three sisters make the lightning, the thunder, and the rain. The names of two of them are Ingnirtung (the one who strikes the fire) and Udluqtung (the one who rubs the skins), whose second name is Kadlu (thunder), while that of the third I could not ascertain. They live in a large house the walls of which are supported by whale ribs. It stands in the far west, at a great distance from the sea, as Kadlu and her sisters do not like to go near it. If an Eskimo should happen to enter the house he must hasten away or Ingnirtung will immediately kill him with her lightning. Even the stones are afraid of her and jump down the hills whenever they see the lightning and hear the thunder. The faces of the sisters are entirely black and they wear no clothes at all. (?) Ingnirtung makes the lightning by striking two red stones together (flint). Kadlu makes the thunder by rubbing sealskins and singing. The third sister makes the rain by urinating. They procure food by striking reindeer with the lightning, which singes their skins and roasts their flesh. The Akudnirmiut say that beyond Iglulik, on the continent of America, a large tribe of Eskimo live whom they call Kakī'joq. The women of the tribe are said to have rings tattooed round their eyes. These natives offer the dried skins of a species of small seals to Kadlu, who uses them for making the thunder.

FEASTS, RELIGIOUS AND SECULAR.

The Eskimo have some very interesting feasts, most of which are closely connected with their religious notions. In summer feasts are celebrated in the open air, but in winter a house, called qaggi, or, as we may call it, singing house, is built for that purpose.

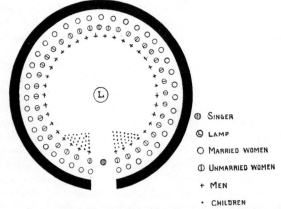

SINGER
LAMP
MARRIED WOMEN
UNMARRIED WOMEN
MEN
CHILDREN

Fig. 142. Diagram showing interior of qaggi or singing house among eastern tribes.

The plan of the house which is used by the eastern tribes is represented in Fig. 142. It is a large snow dome about fifteen feet in

eight and twenty feet in diameter, without any lining.   In the
center there is a snow pillar five feet high, on which the lamps
stand.   When the inhabitants of a village assemble in this building for singing and dancing the married women stand in a row next
the wall.   The unmarried women form a circle inside the former,
while the men sit in the innermost row.   The children stand in two
groups, one at each side of the door.   When the feast begins, a man
takes up the drum (kilaut), which will be described presently, steps
into the open space next the door, and begins singing and dancing.
Among the stone foundations of Niutang, in Kingnait (Cumberland
Sound), there is a qaggi built on the same plan as the snow structure.
Probably it was covered with a snow roof when in use.

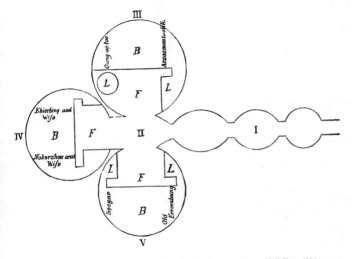

Fig. 143 Plan of Hudson Bay qaggi or singing house.   (From Hall II, p. 220.)

Hall gives the plan of the Hudson Bay qaggi (Fig. 143), a copy of
which is here introduced, as well as his description of the drum (Fig.
144), which I have never seen made (Hall II, p. 96):

The drum is made from the skin of the deer [or seal], which is stretched over a
hoop made of wood, or of bone from the fin of a whale, by the use of a strong,
braided cord of sinew passed around a groove on the outside.   The hoop is about 2½
inches wide, 1½ inches thick, and 3 feet in diameter, the whole instrument weighing
about 4 pounds.   The wooden drumstick, 10 inches in length and 3 inches in diameter, is called a kentun.   * * *

The deerskin which is to be the head of the instrument is kept frozen when not
in use.   It is then thoroughly saturated with water, drawn over the hoop, and temporarily fastened in its place by a piece of sinew.   A line of heavy, twisted sinew,
about 50 feet long, is now wound tightly on the groove on the outside of the
hoop, binding down the skin.   This cord is fastened to the handle of the kilaut
[drum], which is made to turn by the force of several men (while its other end is

held firmly), and the line eased out as required.   To do this a man sits on the bed
plat orm, "having one or two turns of the line about his body, which is encased i
furred deerskins, and empaled by four upright pieces of wood."   Tension is secure
by using a round stick of wood as a lever on the edge of the skin, drawing it from
beneath the cord.   When any whirring sound is heard, little whisps of reindeer hai
are tucked in between the skin and the hoop, until the head is as tight as a drum

Fig. 144. Kilaut or drum.

When the drum is played, the drum handle is held in the left hand of the per
former, who strikes the edge of the rim opposite that over which the skin is stretched
He holds the drum in different positions, but keeps it in a constant fan-like motion
by his hand and by the blows of the kentun struck alternately on the opposite side
of the edge.   Skillfully keeping the drum vibrating on the handle, he accompanie
this with grotesque motions of the body, and at intervals with a song, while th
women keep up their own Inuit songs, one after another, through the whole per
formance.

The feast is described as follows:

As usual the women sat on the platform Turk fashion; the men, behind them with
extended legs.   The women were gayly dressed.   They wore on each side of th
face an enormous pigtail, made by wrapping their hair on a small wooden roller a
foot in length; strips of reindeer-fur being wrapped with the hair [see p. 151].   These
were black and white for those who had sons and black only for those who had
none.   Shining ornaments were worn on the head and on the breast they had
masonic-like aprons, the groundwork of which was of a flaming red color, orna
mented with glass beads of many colors.

In Cumberland Sound the women also wear pigtails at the celebra
tion of these feasts.   The drum is sometimes played with the wrist
of the right hand instead of the beater.

Every singing house is dedicated to a tornaq, the qaggim inua
as mentioned above.   For this reason all these performances may be
considered religious feasts.

The songs are always composed by the singer himself.   Satiric
songs are great favorites on these occasions.   While the men listen
in silence the women join in the chorus, amna aya, the never failing

nd of each verse.   The dancer remains on one spot only, stamping
rythmically with the feet, swinging the upper part of his body, and
t the same time playing the kilaut.   While dancing he always strips
he upper part of the body, keeping on only trousers and boots.   Sing-
ng and dancing are alternated with wrestling matches and playing
t hook and crook.   Almost every great success in hunting is cele-
rated in the qaggi, and especially the capture of a whale.   Such
 feast has been described by Parry.

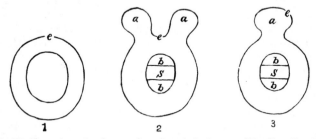

FIG. 145. Plans of remains of supposed qaggin or singing houses.   (From Parry II, p. 362.)

The stone foundations observed by Parry and copied here (Fig. 145)
re probably the remains of singing houses.   Parry's description is
s follows (II, p. 362):

It appears that the whole whale or a principal part of it is dragged into the en-
losure, where some of the men are employed in cutting it up and throwing the
ieces over the wall to the rest, who stand ready to receive them outside; while within
he women range themselves in a circle around the whale and continue singing
uring the operation.   * * *   Each of these structures * * *   was the distinct
roperty of a particular individual ; and had probably, in its turn, been the seat of
easting and merriment either to the present owner, or those from whom he had in-
erited it.

Great feasts closely connected with the Sedna tradition are cele-
rated every fall.

When late in the fall storms rage over the land and release the sea
rom the icy fetters by which it is as yet but slightly bound, when the
oosened floes are driven one against the other and break up with
ud crashes, when the cakes of ice are piled in wild disorder one
pon another, the Eskimo believes he hears the voices of spirits which
hhabit the mischief laden air.

The spirits of the dead, the tupilaq, knock wildly at the huts, which
hey cannot enter, and woe to the unhappy person whom they can
y hold of.   He immediately sickens and a speedy death is regarded
s sure to come.   The wicked qiqirn pursues the dogs, which die with
onvulsions and cramps as soon as they see him.   All the countless
pirits of evil are aroused, striving to bring sickness and death, bad
reather, and failure in hunting.   The worst visitors are Sedna, mis-
ess of the under world, and her father, to whose share the dead

Inuit fall. While the other spirits fill the air and the water, she rises from under the ground.

It is then a busy season for the wizards. In every hut we may hear them singing and praying; conjuring of the spirits is going on in every house. The lamps burn low. The wizard sits in a mystic gloom in the rear of the hut. He has thrown off his outer coat and drawn the hood of his inner garment over his head, while he mutters indescribable sounds, unnatural to a human voice. At last the guardian spirit responds to the invocation. The angakoq lies in a trance and when he comes to himself he promises in incoherent phrases the help of the good spirit against the tupilaq and informs the credulous, affrighted Inuit how they can escape from the dreaded ghosts.

The hardest task, that of driving away Sedna, is reserved for the most powerful angakoq. A rope is coiled on the floor of a large hut in such a manner as to leave a small opening at the top, which represents the breathing hole of a seal. Two angakut stand by the side of it, one of them holding the seal spear in his left hand, as if he were watching at the seal hole in the winter, the other holding the harpoon line. Another angakoq, whose office it is to lure Sedna up with a magic song, sits at the back of the hut. At last she comes up through the hard rocks and the wizard hears her heavy breathing; now she emerges from the ground and meets the angakoq waiting at the hole. She is harpooned and sinks away in angry haste, drawing after her the harpoon, to which the two men hold with all their strength. Only by a desperate effort does she tear herself away from it and return to her dwelling in Adlivun. Nothing is left with the two men but the blood sprinkled harpoon, which they proudly show to the Inuit.

Sedna and the other evil spirits are at last driven away, and on the following day a great festival for young and old is celebrated in honor of the event. But they must still be careful, for the wounded Sedna is greatly enraged and will seize any one whom she can find out of his hut; so on this day they all wear protecting amulets (koukparmiutang) on the tops of their hoods. Parts of the first garment which they wore after birth are used for this purpose.

The men assemble early in the morning in the middle of the settlement. As soon as they have all got together they run screaming and jumping around the houses, following the course of the sun (nunajisartung or kaivitijung). A few, dressed in women's jackets run in the opposite direction. These are those who were born in abnormal presentations. The circuit made, they visit every hut and the woman of the house must always be in waiting for them. When she hears the noise of the band she comes out and throws a dish containing little gifts of meat, ivory trinkets, and articles of sealskin into the yelling crowd, of which each one helps himself to what he can get. No hut is omitted in this round (irqatatung).

The crowd next divides itself into two parties, the ptarmigans (aχigirn), those who were born in the winter, and the ducks (aggirn), or the children of summer. A large rope of sealskin is stretched out. One party takes one end of it and tries with all its might to drag the opposite party over to its side. The others hold fast to the rope and try as hard to make ground for themselves. If the ptarmigans give way the summer has won the game and fine weather may be expected to prevail through the winter (nussueraqtung).

The contest of the seasons having been decided, the women bring out of a hut a large kettle of water and each person takes his drinking cup. They all stand as near the kettle as possible, while the oldest man among them steps out first. He dips a cup of water from the vessel, sprinkles a few drops on the ground, turns his face toward the home of his youth, and tells his name and the place of his birth (oχsoaχsavepunga——me, I was born in——). He is followed by an aged woman, who announces her name and home, and then all the others do the same, down to the young children, who are represented by their mothers. Only the parents of children born during the last year are forbidden to partake in this ceremony. As the words of the old are listened to respectfully, so those of the distinguished hunters are received with demonstrative applause and those of the others with varying degrees of attention, in some cases even with joking and raillery (imitijung).

Now arises a cry of surprise and all eyes are turned toward a hut out of which stalk two gigantic figures. They wear heavy boots; their legs are swelled out to a wonderful thickness with several pairs of breeches; the shoulders of each are covered by a woman's over-jacket and the faces by tattooed masks of sealskins. In the right hand each carries the seal spear, on the back of each is an inflated buoy of sealskin, and in the left hand the scraper. Silently, with long strides, the qailertetang (Fig. 146) approach the assembly, who, screaming, press back from them. The pair solemnly lead the men to a suitable spot and set them in a row, and the women in another opposite them. They match the men and women in pairs and these pairs run, pursued by the qailertetang, to the hut of the woman, where they are for the following day and night man and wife (nuli-anititijung). Having performed this duty, the qailertetang stride down to the shore and invoke the good north wind, which brings fair weather, while they warn off the unfavorable south wind.

As soon as the incantation is over, all the men attack the qailertetang with great noise. They act as if they had weapons in their hands and would kill both spirits. One pretends to probe them with a spear, another to stab them with a knife, one to cut off their arms and legs, another to beat them unmercifully on the head. The buoys which they carry on their backs are ripped open and collapse and soon they both lie as if dead beside their broken weapons (pilektung).

The Eskimo leave them to get their drinking cups and the qailertetang awake to new life. Each man fills his sealskin with water,
passes a cup to them, and inquires about the future, about the
fortunes of the hunt and the events of life. The qailertetang answer
in murmurs which the questioner must interpret for himself.

FIG. 146. Qailertetang, a masked figure. (From a sketch by the author.)

The evening is spent in playing ball, which is whipped all around
the settlement (ajuktaqtung). (See Appendix, Note 6.)

This feast is celebrated as here described in Cumberland Sound and
Nugumiut. Hall and Kumlien make a few observations in regard
to it, but the latter has evidently misunderstood its meaning. His
description is as follows (p. 43):

An angakoq dresses himself up in the most hideous manner, having several pairs
of pants on among the rest, and a horrid looking mask of skins. The men and
women now range themselves in separate and opposite ranks, and the angakoq takes

is place between them. He then picks out a man and conducts him to a woman in he opposite ranks. This couple then go to the woman's hut and have a grand spree or a day or two. This manner of proceeding is kept up till all the women but one re disposed of. This one is always the angakoq's choice, and her he reserves for imself.

Another description by Kumlien (p. 19) evidently refers to the ame feast:

They have an interesting custom or superstition, namely, the killing of the evil pirit of the deer; sometime during the winter or early in spring, at any rate be-ore they can go deer hunting, they congregate together and dispose of this imag-nary evil. The chief ancut [angakoq], or medicine man, is the main performer. le goes through a number of gyrations and contortions, constantly hallooing and alling, till suddenly the imaginary deer is among them. Now begins a lively time. Every one is screaming, runn ng, jumping, spearing, and stabbing at the imagi-ary deer. till one would think a whole madhouse was let loose. Often this deer roves very agile, and must be hard to kill, for I have known them to keep this erformance up for days ; in fact, till they were completely exhausted.

During one of these performances an old man speared the deer, another knocked ut an eye, a third stabbed him, and so on till he was dead. Those who are able or ortunate enough to inflict some injury on this bad deer, especially he who inflicts he death blow, is considered extremely lucky, as he will have no difficulty in rocuring as many deer as he wants, for there is no longer an evil spirit to turn is bullets or arrows from their course.

I could not learn anything about this ceremony, though I asked all he persons with whom Kumlien had had intercourse. Probably here was some misunderstanding as to the meaning of their feast luring the autumn which induced him to give this report.

Hall describes the feast as celebrated by the Nugumiut (I, p. 528), s follows:

At a time of the year apparently answering to our Christmas, they have a general meeting in a large igdlu [snow house] on a certain evening. There the angakoq rays on behalf of the people for the public prosperity through the subsequent year. hen follows something like a feast. The next day all go out into the open air and orm in a circle; in the centre is placed a vessel of water, and each member of the ompany brings a piece of meat, the kind being immaterial. The circle being formed, ach person eats his or her meat in silence, thinking of Sedna. and wishing for good hings. Then one in the circle takes a cup, dips up some of the water, all the time hinking of Sedna, and drinks it ; and then, before passing the cup to another, tates audibly the time and the place of his or her birth. This ceremony is per-ormed by all in succession. Finally, presents of various articles are thrown from ne to another, with the idea that each will receive of Sedna good things in propor-ion to the liberality here shown.

Soon after this occasion. at a time which answers to our New Year's day, two nen start out, one of them being dressed to represent a woman. and go to every ouse in the village, blowing out the light in each. The lights are afterwards ekindled from a fresh fire. When Taqulitu [Hall's well known companion in is journeys] was asked the meaning of this, she replied. " New sun — new light," mplying a belief that the sun was at that time renewed for the year.

Inasmuch as Hall did not see the feast himself. but had only a lescription by an Eskimo. into which he introduced points of simi-arity with Christian feasts. it may be looked upon as fairly agreeing with the feast of the Oqomiut. The latter part corresponds to the celebration of the feast as it is celebrated in Akudnirn.[1]

According to a statement in the journal of Hall's second expedition (II, p. 219) masks are also used on the western shore of Hudson Bay, where it seems that all the natives disguise themselves on this occasion.

The Akudnirmiut celebrate the feast in the following way: The qailertetang do not act a part there, but other masks take their place. They are called mirqussang and represent a man and his wife. They wear masks of the skin of the ground seal, only that of the woman being tattooed. The hair of the man is arranged in a bunch protruding from the forehead (sulubaut), that of the woman in a pigtail on each side and a large knot at the back of the head. Their left legs are tied up by a thong running around the neck and the knee, compelling them to hobble. They have neither seal float and spear nor inflated legs, but carry the skin scraper. They must try to enter the huts while the Inuit hold a long sealskin thong before them to keep them off. If they fall down in the attempt to cross it they are thoroughly beaten with a short whip or with sticks. After having succeeded in entering the huts they blow out all the fires.

The parts of the feast already described as celebrated in Cumberland Sound seem not to be customary in Akudnirn, the conjuration of Sedna and the exchanges of wives excepted, which are also practiced here. Sometimes the latter ceremony takes place the night before the feast. It is called suluiting or quvietung.

When it is quite dark a number of Inuit come out of their huts and run crying all round their settlements. Wherever anybody is asleep they climb upon the roof of his hut and rouse him by screaming and shouting until all have assembled outside. Then a woman and a man (the mirqussang) sit down in the snow. The man holds a knife (sulung) in his hand, from which the feast takes its name, and sings:

> Oangaja jaja jajaja aja.
> Pissiungmipadlo panginejernago
> Qodlungutaokpan panginejerlugping
> Pissiungmipadlo panginejernago.

To this song the woman keeps time by moving her body and her arms, at the same time flinging snow on the bystanders. Then the whole company goes into the singing house and joins in dancing and singing. This done, the men must leave the house and stand outside while the mirqussang watch the entrance. The women continue singing and leave the house one by one. They are awaited by the mirqussang, who lead every one to one of the men standing about. The pair must re-enter the singing house and walk around the lamp

[1] Since the above was written I learn from a paper by Mr. Lucien M. Turner that a similar feast is celebrated in Ungava Bay. (American Naturalist, August, 1887

all the men and women crying, " Hrr! hrr!" from both corners of the mouth. Then they go to the woman's hut, where they stay during the ensuing night. The feast is frequently celebrated by all the tribes of Davis and Hudson Strait, and even independently of the great feast described above.

The day after, the men frequently join in a shooting match. A target is set up, at which they shoot their arrows. As soon as a man hits, the women, who stand looking on, rush forward and rub noses with him.

If a stranger unknown to the inhabitants of a settlement arrives on a visit he is welcomed by the celebration of a great feast. Among the southeastern tribes the natives arrange themselves in a row, one man standing in front of it. The stranger approaches slowly, his arms folded and his head inclined toward the right side. Then the native strikes him with all his strength on the right cheek and in his turn inclines his head awaiting the stranger's blow (tigluiqdjung). While this is going on the other men are playing at ball and singing (igdlukitaqtung). Thus they continue until one of the combatants is vanquished.

The ceremonies of greeting among the western tribes are similar to those of the eastern, but in addition "boxing, wrestling, and knife testing" are mentioned by travelers who have visited them. In Davis Strait and probably in all the other countries the game of "hook and crook" is always played on the arrival of a stranger (pakijumijartung). Two men sit down on a large skin, after having stripped the upper part of their bodies, and each tries to stretch out the bent arm of the other. These games are sometimes dangerous, as the victor has the right to kill his adversary; but generally the feast ends peaceably. The ceremonies of the western tribes in greeting a stranger are much feared by their eastern neighbors and therefore intercourse is somewhat restricted. The meaning of the duel, according to the natives themselves, is "that the two men in meeting wish to know which of them is the better man." The similarity of these ceremonies with those of Greenland, where the game of hook and crook and wrestling matches have been customary, is quite striking, as is that of the explanation of these ceremonies.

The word for greeting on Davis Strait and Hudson Strait, is Assojutidlin? (Are you quite well?) and the answer, Tabaujuradlu (Very well). The word Taima! which is used in Hudson Strait, and Mane taima! of the Netchillirmiut seem to be similar to our Halloo! The Ukusiksalirmiut say Ilaga! (My friend!)

CUSTOMS AND REGULATIONS CONCERNING BIRTH, SICKNESS, AND DEATH.

I have mentioned that it is extremely difficult to find out the innumerable regulations connected with the religious ideas and customs of the Eskimo. The difficulty is even greater in regard to the customs which refer to birth, sickness, and death, and it is no wonder that, while some of the accounts of different writers coincide tolerably well, there are great discrepancies in others, particularly as the customs vary to a great extent among the different tribes.

Before the child is born a small hut or snow house is built for the mother, in which she awaits her delivery. Sick persons are isolated in the same way, the reason being that in case of death everything that had been in contact with the deceased must be destroyed. According to Kumlien (p. 28) the woman is left with only one attendant, a young girl appointed by the head ancut (angakoq) of the encampment; but this, no doubt, is an error. She may be visited by her friends, who, however, must leave her when parturition takes place. She must cut the navel string herself, and in Davis Strait this is done by tying it through with deer sinews; in Iglulik (Lyon, p. 370), by cutting it with a stone spear head. The child is cleaned with a birdskin and clothed in a small gown of the same material. According to Lyon the Iglulirmiut swathe it with the dried intestines of some animal.

Kumlien describes a remarkable custom of which I could find no trace, not even upon direct inquiry (p. 281) :

As soon as the mother with her new born babe is able to get up and go out, usually but a few hours, they are taken in charge by an aged female angakoq, who seems to have some particular mission to perform in such cases. She conducts them to some level spot on the ice, if near the sea, and begins a sort of march in circles on the ice, the mother following with the child on her back; this manœuvre is kept up for some time, the old woman going through a number of performances the nature of which we could not learn and continually muttering something equally unintelligible to us. The next act is to wade through snowdrifts, the aged angakoq leading the way. We have been informed that it is customary for the mother to wade thus bare-legged.

Lyon says (p. 370) :

After a few days, or according to the fancy of the parents, an angakoq, who by relationship or long acquaintance is a friend of the family, makes use of some vessel, and with the urine the mother washes the infant, while all the gossips around pour forth their good wishes for the little one to prove an active man, if a boy, or, if a girl, the mother of plenty of children. This ceremony, I believe, is never omitted, and is called qoqsiuariva.

Though I heard about the washing with urine, I did not learn anything about the rest of the ceremony in Cumberland Sound and Davis Strait.

A few days after birth the first dress of the child is exchanged for another. A small hood made from the skin of a hare's head is fitted snugly upon the head, a jacket for the upper part of the body is made of the skin of a fawn, and two small boots, made of the same kind of a skin, the left one being wreathed with seaweed (*Fucus*), cover the legs. While the child wears this clothing that which was first worn is fastened to a pole which is secured to the roof of the hut. In two months the child gets a third suit of clothes the same as formerly described (p. 149). Then the second gown is exposed for some time on the top of the hut, the first one being taken down, and both are carefully preserved for a year. After this time has expired both are once more exposed on the top of a pole and then sunk into the sea, a portion of the birdskin dress alone being kept, for this is considered a powerful amulet and is held in high esteem and worn every fall at the Sedna feast on the point of the hood (see p. 196). I have stated that those who were born in abnormal presentations wear women's dresses at this feast and must make their round in a direction opposite to the movement of the sun. Captain Spicer, of Groton, Conn., affirms that the bird used for the first clothing is chosen according to a strict law, every month having its own bird. So far as I know, waterfowl are used in summer and the ptarmigan in winter, and accordingly the men are called at the great autumn feast the ducks and ptarmigans, the former including those who were born in summer, the latter those born in winter.

As long as any portion of the navel string remains a strip of sealskin is worn around the belly.

After the birth of her child the mother must observe a great number of regulations, referring particularly to food and work. She is not allowed for a whole year to eat raw meat or a part of any animal killed by being shot through the heart. In Cumberland Sound she must not eat for five days anything except meat of an animal killed by her husband or by a boy on his first hunting expedition. This custom seems to be observed more strictly, however, and for a longer period if the new born child dies. Two months after delivery she must make a call at every hut, while before that time she is not allowed to enter any but her own. At the end of this period she must also throw away her old clothing. The same custom was observed by Hall among the Nugumiut (I, p. 426). On the western shore of Hudson Bay she is permitted to re-enter the hut a few days after delivery, but must pass in by a separate entrance. An opening is cut for the purpose through the snow wall. She must keep a little skin bag hung up near her, into which she must put a little of her food after each meal, having first put it up to her mouth. This is called laying up food for the infant, although none is given to it (Hall II, p. 173). I have already mentioned that the parents are not allowed in the first year after the birth of a child to take part in the Sedna feast.

The customs which are associated with the death of an infant are very complicated. For a whole year, when outside the hut, the mother must have her head covered with a cap, or at least with a piece of skin. If a ground seal is caught she must throw away the old cap and have a new one made. The boots of the deceased are always carried about by the parents when traveling, and whenever they stop these are buried in the snow or under stones. Neither parent is allowed to eat raw flesh during the following year. The woman must cook her food in a small pot which is exclusively used by her. If she is about to enter a hut the men who may be sitting inside must come out first, and not until they have come out is she allowed to enter. If she wants to go out of the hut she must walk around all the men who may happen to be there.

The child is sometimes named before it is born. Lyon says upon this subject (p. 369):

Some relative or friend lays her hand on the mother's stomach, and decides what the infant is to be called, and, as the names serve for either sex, it is of no consequence whether it proves a girl or a boy.

On Davis Strait it is always named after the persons who have died since the last birth took place, and therefore the number of names of an Eskimo is sometimes rather large. If a relative dies while the child is younger than four years or so, his name is added to the old ones and becomes the proper name by which it is called. It is possible that children receive the names of all the persons in the settlement who die while the children are quite young, but of this I am not absolutely certain. When a person falls sick the angakut change his name in order to ward off the disease or they consecrate him as a dog to Sedna. In the latter event he gets a dog's name and must wear throughout life a harness over the inner jacket. Thus it may happen that Eskimo are known in different tribes by different names. It may also be mentioned here that friends sometimes exchange names and dogs are called by the name of a friend as a token of regard.

The treatment of the sick is the task of the angakoq, whose manipulations have been described.

If it is feared that a disease will prove fatal, a small snow house or a hut is built, according to the season, into which the patient is carried through an opening at the back. This opening is then closed, and subsequently a door is cut out. A small quantity of food is placed in the hut, but the patient is left without attendants. As long as there is no fear of sudden death the relatives and friends may come to visit him, but when death is impending the house is shut up and he is left alone to die. If it should happen that a person dies in a hut among its inmates, everything belonging to the hut must be destroyed or thrown away, even the tools &c. lying inside becoming useless to the survivors, but the tent poles may be used again after a year has elapsed. No doubt this custom explains the isolation of the sick. If a child dies in a hut and the mother immediately rushes out with it, the contents of the hut may be saved.

Though the Eskimo feel the greatest awe in touching a dead body, the sick await their death with admirable coolness and without the east sign of fear or unwillingness to die. I remember a young girl who sent for me a few hours before her death and asked me to give her some tobacco and bread, which she wanted to take to her mother, who had died a few weeks before.

Only the relatives are allowed to touch the body of the deceased. They clothe it or wrap it in deerskins and bury it at once. In former times they always built a tomb, at least when death occurred in the summer. From its usual dimensions one would suppose that the body was buried with the legs doubled up, for all of them are too short for grown persons. If the person to be buried is young, his feet are placed in the direction of the rising sun, those of the aged in the opposite direction. According to Lyon the Iglulirmiut bury half grown children with the feet towards the southeast, young men and women with the feet towards the south, and middle aged persons with the feet towards the southwest. This agrees with the fact that the graves in Cumberland Sound do not all lie east and west. The tomb is always vaulted, as any stone or piece of snow resting upon the body is believed to be a burden to the soul of the deceased. The man's hunting implements and other utensils are placed by the side of his grave; the pots, the lamps, knives, &c., by the side of that of the woman; toys, by that of a child. Hall (I, p. 103) observed in a grave a small kettle hung up over a lamp. These objects are held in great respect and are never removed, at least as long as it is known to whose grave they belong. Sometimes models of implements are used for this purpose instead of the objects themselves. Figure 147 represents a model of a lamp found in a grave of Cumberland Sound. Nowadays the Eskimo place the body in a box, if they can procure one, or cover it very slightly with stones or snow. It is strange that, though the ceremonies of burying are very strictly attended to and though they take care to give the dead their belongings, they do not heed the opening of the graves by dogs or wolves and the devouring of the bodies and do not attempt to recover them when the graves are invaded by animals.

Fig. 147. Model of lamp from a grave in Cumberland Sound. (Museum für Völkerkunde, Berlin.)

The body must be carried to the place of burial by the nearest relatives, a few others only accompanying it. For this purpose they rarely avail themselves of a sledge, as it cannot be used afterward, but must be left with the deceased. Dogs are never allowed to drag the sledge on such an occasion. After returning from the burial the relatives must lock themselves up in the old hut for three days, during which they mourn the loss of the deceased. During this time they do not dress their hair and they have their nostrils closed with a piece of deerskin. After this they leave the hut forever. The dog are thrown into it through the window and allowed to devour what ever they can get at. For some time afterward the mourners mus cook their meals in a separate pot. A strange custom was observe by Hall in Hudson Bay (II, p. 186). The mourners did not smoke They kept their hoods on from morning till night. To the hood the skin and feathers of the head of *Uria grylle* were fastened and a feather of the same waterfowl to each arm just above the elbow All male relatives of the deceased wore a belt around the waist besides which they constantly wore mittens. It is probable that at the present time all Eskimo when in mourning avoid using imple ments of European manufacture and suspend the use of tobacco It has already been stated that women who have lost a child mus keep their heads covered.

Parry, Lyon (p. 369), and Klutschak (p. 201) state that when th Eskimo first hear of the death of a relative they throw themselve upon the ground and cry, not for grief, but as a mourning cere mony.

For three or sometimes even four days after a death the inhabitant of a village must not use their dogs, but must walk to the huntin ground, and for one day at least they are not allowed to go huntin at all. The women must stop all kinds of work.

On the third day after death the relatives visit the tomb and trave around it three times in the same direction as the sun is moving, a the same time talking to the deceased and promising that the will bring him something to eat. According to Lyon the Igluli miut chant forth inquiries as to the welfare of the departed sou whether it has reached the land Adli, if it has plenty of food, &c at each question stopping at the head of the grave and repeatin some ceremonial words (p. 371).

These visits to the grave are repeated a year after death and when ever they pass it in traveling. Sometimes they carry food to th deceased, which he is expected to return greatly increased. Ha describes this custom as practiced by the Nugumiut (I, p. 426). H says:

They took down small pieces of [deer] skin with the fur on, and of [fat]. Whe there they stood around [the] grave [of the woman] upon which they placed th articles they had brought. Then one of them stepped up, took a piece of the [dee meat], cut a slice and ate it, at the same time cutting off another slice and placin it under a stone by the grave. Then the knife was passed from one hand to th other, both hands being thrown behind the person. This form of shifting the im plement was continued for perhaps a minute, the motions being accompanied b constant talk with the dead. Then a piece of [deer] fur and some [fat] were place under the stone with an exclamation signifying, "Here is something to eat ar something to keep you warm." Each of the [natives] also went through the sam forms. They never visit the grave of a departed friend until some months aft death, and even then only when all the surviving members of the family have removed to another place. Whenever they return to the vicinity of their kindred's grave, a visit is made to it with the best of food as a present for the departed one. Neither seal, polar bear, nor walrus, however, is taken.

According to Klutschak (p. 154), the natives of Hudson Bay avoid staying a long time on the salt water ice near the grave of a relative. On the fourth day after death the relatives may go for the first time upon the ice, but the men are not allowed to hunt; on the next day they must go sealing, but without dogs and sledge, walking to the hunting ground and dragging the seal home. On the sixth day they are at liberty to use their dogs again. For a whole year they must not join in any festival and are not allowed to sing certain songs.

If a married woman dies the widower is not permitted to keep any part of the first seal he catches after her death except the flesh. Skin, blubber, bones, and entrails must be sunk in the sea.

All the relatives must have new suits of clothes made and before the others are cast away they are not allowed to enter a hut without having asked and obtained permission. (See Appendix, Note 7.)

Lyon (p. 368) makes the following statement on the mourning ceremonies in Iglulik:

Widows are forbidden for six months to taste of unboiled flesh; they wear no * * * pigtails, and cut off a portion of their long hair in token of grief, while the remaining locks hang in loose disorder about their shoulders. * * * After six months, the disconsolate ladies are at liberty to eat raw meat, to dress their pigtails and to marry as fast as they please; while in the meantime they either cohabit with their future husbands, if they have one, or distribute their favors more generally. A widower and his children remain during three days within the hut where his wife died, after which it is customary to remove to another. He is not allowed to fish or hunt for a whole season, or in that period to marry again. During the three days of lamentation all the relatives of the deceased are quite careless of their dress; their hair hangs wildly about, and, if possible, they are more than usually dirty in their persons. All visitors to a mourning family consider it as indispensably necessary to howl at their first entry.

I may add here that suicide is not of rare occurrence, as according to the religious ideas of the Eskimo the souls of those who die by violence go to Qudlivun, the happy land. For the same reason it is considered lawful for a man to kill his aged parents. In suicide death is generally brought about by hanging.

TALES AND TRADITIONS.

ITITAUJANG.

A long, long time ago, a young man, whose name was Ititaujang, lived in a village with many of his friends. When he became grown he wished to take a wife and went to a hut in which he knew an orphan girl was living. However, as he was bashful and was afraid to speak to the young girl himself, he called her little brother, who was playing before the hut, and said, "Go to your sister and ask her if she will marry me." The boy ran to his sister and delivered the message. The young girl sent him back and bade him ask the name of her suitor. When she heard that his name was Ititaujang she told him to go away and look for another wife, as she was not willing to marry a man with such an ugly name.[1] But Ititaujang did not submit and sent the boy once more to his sister. "Tell her that Nettirsuaqdjung is my other name," said he. The boy, however, said upon entering, "Ititaujang is standing before the doorway and wants to marry you." Again the sister said "I will not have a man with that ugly name." When the boy returned to Ititaujang and repeated his sister's speech, he sent him back once more and said, "Tell her that Nettirsuaqdjung is my other name." Again the boy entered and said, "Ititaujang is standing before the doorway and wants to marry you." The sister answered, "I will not have a man with that ugly name." When the boy returned to Ititaujang and told him to go away, he was sent in the third time on the same commission, but to no better effect. Again the young girl declined his offer, and upon that Ititaujang went away in great anger. He did not care for any other girl of his tribe, but left the country altogether and wandered over hills and through valleys up the country many days and many nights.

At last he arrived in the land of the birds and saw a lakelet in which many geese were swimming. On the shore he saw a great number of boots; cautiously he crept nearer and stole as many as he could get hold of. A short time after the birds left the water and finding the boots gone became greatly alarmed and flew away. Only one of the flock remained behind, crying, "I want to have my boots; I want to have my boots." Ititaujang came forth now and answered, "I will give you your boots if you will become my wife." She objected, but when Ititaujang turned round to go away with the boots she agreed, though rather reluctantly.

Having put on the boots she was transformed into a woman and they wandered down to the seaside, where they settled in a large village. Here they lived together for some years and had a son. In time Ititaujang became a highly respected man, as he was by far the best whaler among the Inuit.

Once upon a time the Inuit had killed a whale and were busy cutting it up and carrying the meat and the blubber to their huts. Though Ititaujang was hard at work his wife stood lazily by. When he called her and asked her to help as the other women did she objected, crying, "My food is not from the sea; my food is from the land; I will not eat the meat of a whale; I will not help."

---

[1] Ititaujang means "similar to the anus." This tradition is curtailed, as some parts were considered inappropriate for this publication. The full text will be found in the Verhandlungen der Berliner Gesellschaft für Anthropologie, Ethnologie und Urgeschichte, Berlin, 1888.

Ititaujang answered, "You must eat of the whale; that will fill your stomach." Then she began crying and exclaimed, "I will not eat it; I will not soil my nice white clothing."

She descended to the beach, eagerly looking for birds' feathers. Having found a few she put them between her fingers and between those of her child; both were transformed into geese and flew away.

When the Inuit saw this they called out, "Ititaujang, your wife is flying away." Ititaujang became very sad ; he cried for his wife and did not care for the abundance of meat and blubber, nor for the whales spouting near the shore. He followed his wife and ascended the land in search of her.

After having traveled for many weary months he came to a river. There he saw a man who was busy chopping chips from a piece of wood with a large hatchet. As soon as the chips fell off he polished them neatly and they were transformed into salmon, becoming so slippery that they glided from his hands and fell into the river, which they descended to a large lake near by. The name of the man was Eχaluqdjung (the little salmon).

On approaching, Ititaujang was frightened almost to death, for he saw that the back of this man was altogether hollow and that he could look from behind right through his mouth. Cautiously he crept back and by a circuitous way approached him from the opposite direction.

When Eχaluqdjung saw him coming he stopped chopping and asked, "Which way did you approach me?" Ititaujang, pointing in the direction he had come last and from which he could not see the hollow back of Eχaluqdjung, answered, "It is there I have come from." Eχaluqdjung, on hearing this, said, "That is lucky for you. If you had come from the other side and had seen my back I should have immediately killed you with my hatchet." Ititaujang was very glad that he had turned back and thus deceived the salmon maker. He asked him, "Have you not seen my wife, who has left me, coming this way?" Eχaluqdjung had seen her and said, "Do you see yon little island in the large lake? There she lives now and has taken another husband."

When Ititaujang heard this report he almost despaired, as he did not know how to reach the island; but Eχaluqdjung kindly promised to help him. They descended to the beach; Eχaluqdjung gave him the backbone of a salmon and said, "Now shut your eyes. The backbone will turn into a kayak and carry you safely to the island. But mind you do not open your eyes, else the boat will upset."

Ititaujang promised to obey. He shut his eyes, the backbone became a kayak, and away he went over the lake. As he did not hear any splashing of water, he was anxious to see whether the boat moved on, and opened his eyes just a little. But he had scarcely taken a short glimpse when the kayak began to swing violently and he felt that it became a backbone again. He quickly shut his eyes, the boat went steadily on, and a short time after he was landed on the island.

There he saw the hut and his son playing on the beach near it. The boy on looking up saw Ititaujang and ran to his mother crying, "Mother, father is here and is coming to our hut." The mother answered, "Go, play on; your father is far away and cannot find us." The child obeyed; but as he saw Ititaujang approaching he re-entered the hut and said, "Mother, father is here and is coming to our hut." Again the mother sent him away, but he returned very soon, saying that Ititaujang was quite near.

Scarcely had the boy said so when Ititaujang opened the door. When the new husband saw him he told his wife to open a box which was in a corner of the hut. She did so, and many feathers flew out of it and stuck to them. The woman, her new husband, and the child were thus again transformed into geese. The hut disappeared; but when Ititaujang saw them about to fly away he got furious and cut open the belly of his wife before she could escape. Then many eggs fell down.

THE EMIGRATION OF THE SAGDLIRMIUT.

In the beginning all the Inuit lived near Ussualung, in Tiniqdjuarbing (Cumberland Sound). The Igdlumiut, the Nugumiut, and the Talirpingmiut in the south, the Aggomiut in the far north, and the Inuit, who tattoo rings round their eyes, in the far west, all once lived together. There is a tradition concerning the emigration of the Sagdlirmiut (see p. 43) who live east of Iglulik. The Akudnirmiut say that the following events did not happen in Tiniqdjuarbing, but in Aggo, a country where nobody lives nowadays. Ikeraping, an Akudnirmio, heard the story related by a Tununirmio, who had seen the place himself, but all the Oqomiut assert that Ussualung is the place where the events in the story happened.

An old woman, the sister of Mitiq, the angakoq, told the story as follows:

Near Ussualung there are two places, Qerniqdjuaq and Eχaluqdjuaq. In each of these was a large house, in which many families lived together. They used to keep company during the summer when they went deer hunting, but returned to their separate houses in the fall.

Once upon a time it happened that the men of Qerniqdjuaq had been very successful, while those of Eχaluqdjuaq had caught scarcely any deer. Therefore the latter got very angry and resolved to kill the other party, but they preferred to wait until the winter. Later in the season many deer were caught and put up in depots. They were to be carried down to the winter settlements by means of sledges.

One day both parties agreed upon a journey to these depots and the men of Eχaluqdjuaq resolved to kill their enemies on this occa-

sion. They set out with their dogs and sledges, and when they were
fairly inland they suddenly attacked their unsuspecting companions
and killed them. For fear that the wives and children of the murdered men might be suspicious if the dogs returned without their
masters, they killed them too. After a short time they returned and
said they had lost the other party and did not know what had happened to them.

A young man of Eɤaluqdjuaq was the suitor of a girl of Qerniqdjuaq and used to visit her every night. He did not stop his visits
now. He was kindly received by the woman and lay down to sleep
with his young wife.

Under the snow bench there was a little boy who had seen the young
man of Eɤaluqdjuaq coming. When everybody was sleeping he heard
somebody calling and soon recognized the spirits of the murdered men,
who told him what had happened and asked him to kill the young
man in revenge. The boy crept from his place under the bed, took a
knife, and put it into the young man's breast. As he was a small boy
and very weak, the knife glided from the ribs and entered deep into
the heart, thus killing the young man.

Then he roused the other inhabitants of the hut and told them that
the spirits of the dead men had come to him, that they had told him
of their murder, and had ordered him to kill the young man. The
women and children got very much frightened and did not know
what to do. At last they resolved to follow the advice of an old
woman and to flee from their cruel neighbors. As their dogs were
killed, the sledges were of no use, but by chance a bitch with pups
was in the hut and the old woman, who was a great angakoq, ordered
them to go and whip the young dogs, which would thus grow up
quickly. They did so and in a short time the pups were large and
strong. They harnessed them and set off as quickly as possible. In
order to deceive their neighbors they left everything behind and did
not even extinguish their lamps, that they might not excite suspicion.

The next morning the men of Eɤaluqdjuaq wondered why their
companion had not returned and went to the hut in Qernirtung.
They peeped through the spy hole in the window and saw the lamps
burning, but nobody inside. At last they discovered the body of the
young man, and, finding the tracks of the sledges, they hurriedly put
their sledges in order and pursued the fugitives.

Though the latter had journeyed rapidly their pursuers followed
still more rapidly and seemed likely to overtake them in a short time.
They therefore became very much frightened, fearing the revenge of
their pursuers.

When the sledge of the men drew near and the women saw that
they were unable to escape, a young woman asked the old angakoq:
"Don't you know how to cut the ice?" The matron answered in the
affirmative and slowly drew a line over the ice with her first finger

across the path of their pursuers. The ice gave a loud crack. Once more she drew the line, when a crack opened and quickly widened as she passed on. The floe began moving and when the men arrived they could not cross over the wide space of water. Thus the party were saved by the art of their angakoq.

For many days they drifted to and fro, but finally they landed on the island of Sagdlirn, where they took up their abode and became the mothers of the Sagdlirmiut.

KALOPALING.

Kalopaling is a fabulous being that lives in the sea. His body is like that of a human being and he wears clothing made of eider ducks' skins. Therefore he is sometimes called Mitiling (with eider ducks). As these birds have a black back and a white belly, his gown looked speckled all over. His jacket has an enormous hood, which is an object of fear to the Inuit. If a kayak capsizes and the boatman is drowned Kalopaling puts him into this hood. He cannot speak, but can only cry, "Be, be! Be, be!" His feet are very large and look like inflated sealskin floats.

The Inuit believe that in olden times there were a great number of Kalopalit, but gradually their number diminished and there are now very few left. They may be seen from the land swimming very rapidly under the water and sometimes rising to the surface. While swimming they make a great noise by splashing with arms and legs. In summer they like to bask on rocks and in winter they sometimes sit on the ice near cracks or at the edge of drifting floes. As they pursue the hunters the most daring men try to kill them whenever they can get near them. Cautiously they approach the sleeping Kalopaling, and as soon as they come near enough they throw the walrus harpoon at him. They must shut their eyes immediately until the Kalopaling is dead, else he will capsize the boat and kill the hunters. The flesh of the Kalopaling is said to be poisonous, but good enough for dog's food.

An old tradition is handed down which refers to a Kalopaling:

An old woman lived with her grandson in a small hut. As they had no kinsmen they were very poor. A few Inuit only took pity on them and brought them seal's meat and blubber for their lamps. Once upon a time they were very hungry and the boy cried. The grandmother told him to be quiet, but as he did not obey she became angry and called Kalopaling to come and take him away. He entered at once and the woman put the boy into the large hood, in which he disappeared almost immediately.

Later on the Inuit were more successful in sealing and they had an abundance of meat. Then the grandmother was sorry that she had so rashly given the boy to Kalopaling and wished to see him back again. She lamented about it to the Inuit, and at length a man and his wife promised to help her.

When the ice had consolidated and deep cracks were formed near the shore by the rise and fall of the tide, the boy used to rise and sit alongside the cracks, playing with a whip of seaweed. Kalopaling, however, was afraid that somebody might carry the boy away and had fastened him to a string of seaweed, which he held in his hands. The Inuit who had seen the boy went toward him, but as soon as he saw them coming he sang, " Two men are coming, one with a double jacket, the other with a foxskin jacket" (Inung maqong tikitong, aipa mirqosailing, aipa kapiteling). Then Kalopaling pulled on the rope and the boy disappeared. He did not want to return to his grandmother, who had abused him.

Some time afterward the Inuit saw him again sitting near a crack. They took the utmost caution that he should not hear them when approaching, tying pieces of deerskin under the soles of their boots. But when they could almost lay hold of the boy he sang, " Two men are coming, one with a double jacket, the other with a foxskin jacket." Again Kalopaling pulled on the seaweed rope and the boy disappeared.

The man and his wife, however, did not give up trying. They resolved to wait near the crack, and on one occasion when the boy had just come out of the water they jumped forward from a piece of ice behind which they had been hidden and before he could give the alarm they had cut the rope and away they went with him to their huts.

The boy lived with them and became a great hunter.

THE UISSUIT.

Besides the Kalopalit there are the Uissuit, a strange people that live in the sea. They are dwarfs and are frequently seen between Iglulik and Netchillik, where the Anganidjen live, an Inuit tribe whose women are in the habit of tattooing rings around their eyes. There are men and women among the Uissuit and they live in deep water, never coming up to the surface. When the Inuit wish to see them, they go in their boats to a place where they cannot see the bottom and try to catch them by hooks which they slowly move up and down. As soon as they get a bite they draw in the line. The Uissuit are thus drawn up; but no sooner do they approach the surface than they dive down headlong again, only their legs having emerged from the water. The Inuit have never succeeded in getting one out of the water.

KIVIUNG.

An old woman lived with her grandson in a small hut. As she had no husband and no son to take care of her and the boy, they were very poor, the boy's clothing being made of skins of birds which they caught in snares. When the boy would come out of the hut and join his playfellows, the men would laugh at him and tear his outer garment. Only one man, whose name was Kiviung, was kind to the young boy; but he could not protect him from the others. Often the lad came to his grandmother crying and weeping, and she always consoled him and each time made him a new garment. She entreated the men to stop teasing the boy and tearing his clothing, but they would not listen to her prayer. At last she got angry and swore she would take revenge upon his abusers, and she could easily do so, as she was a great angakoq.

She commanded her grandson to step into a puddle which was on the floor of the hut, telling him what would happen and how he should behave. As soon as he stood in the water the earth opened and he sank out of sight, but the next moment he rose near the beach as a yearling seal with a beautiful skin and swam about lustily.

The men had barely seen the seal when they took to their kayaks, eager to secure the pretty animal. But the transformed boy quickly swam away, as his grandmother had told him, and the men continued in pursuit. Whenever he rose to breathe he took care to come up behind the kayaks, where the men could not get at him with their harpoons; there, however, he splashed and dabbled in order to attract their attention and lure them on. But before any one could turn his kayak he had dived again and swam away. The men were so interested in the pursuit that they did not observe that they were being led far from the coast and that the land was now altogether invisible.

Suddenly a gale arose; the sea foamed and roared and the waves destroyed or upset their frail vessels. After all seemed to be drowned the seal was again transformed into the lad, who went home without wetting his feet. There was nobody now to tear his clothing, all his abusers being dead.

Only Kiviung, who was a great angakoq and had never abused the boy, had escaped the wind and waves. Bravely he strove against the wild sea, but the storm did not abate. After he had drifted for many days on the wide sea, a dark mass loomed up through the mist. His hope revived and he worked hard to reach the supposed land. The nearer he came, however, the more agitated did the sea become, and he saw that he had mistaken a wild, black sea, with raging whirlpools, for land. Barely escaping he drifted again for many days, but the storm did not abate and he did not see any land. Again he saw a dark mass looming up through the mist, but he was once more deceived, for it was another whirlpool which made the sea rise in gigantic waves.

At last the storm moderated, the sea subsided, and at a great distance he saw the land. Gradually he came nearer and following the coast he at length spied a stone house in which a light was burning. He landed and entered the house. Nobody was inside but an old woman whose name was Arnaitiang. She received him kindly and at his request pulled off his boots, slippers, and stockings and dried them on the frame hanging over the lamp. Then she went out to light a fire and cook a good meal.

When the stockings were dry, Kiviung tried to take them from the frame in order to put them on, but as soon as he extended his hand to touch them the frame rose out of his reach. Having tried several times in vain, he called Arnaitiang and asked her to give him back the stockings. She answered: "Take them yourself; there they are; there they are" and went out again. The fact is she was a very bad woman and wanted to eat Kiviung.

Then he tried once more to take hold of his stockings, but with no better result. He called again for Arnaitiang and asked her to give him the boots and stockings, whereupon she said: "Sit down where I sat when you entered my house; then you can get them." After that she left him again. Kiviung tried it once more, but the frame rose as before and he could not reach it.

Now he understood that Arnaitiang meditated mischief; so he summoned his tornaq, a huge white bear, who arose roaring from under the floor of the house. At first Arnaitiang did not hear him, but as Kiviung kept on conjuring the spirit came nearer and nearer to the surface, and when she heard his loud roar she rushed in trembling with fear and gave Kiviung what he had asked for. "Here are your boots," she cried; "here are your slippers; here are your stockings. I'll help you put them on." But Kiviung would not stay any longer with this horrid witch and did not even dare to put on his boots, but took them from Arnaitiang and rushed out of the door. He had barely escaped when it clapped violently together and just caught the tail of his jacket, which was torn off. He hastened to his kayak without once stopping to look behind and paddled away. He had only gone a short distance before Arnaitiang, who had recovered from her fear, came out swinging her glittering woman's knife and threatening to kill him. He was nearly frightened to death and almost upset his kayak. However, he managed to balance it again and cried in answer, lifting up his spear: "I shall kill you with my spear." When Arnaitiang heard these words she fell down terror stricken and broke her knife. Kiviung then observed that it was made of a thin slab of fresh water ice.

He traveled on for many days and nights, following the shore. At last he came to a hut, and again a lamp was burning inside. As his clothing was wet and he was hungry, he landed and entered the house. There he found a woman who lived all alone with her daughter. Her son-in-law was a log of driftwood which had four boughs. Every day about the time of low water they carried it to the beach and when the tide came in it swam away. When night came again it returned with eight large seals, two being fastened to every bough. Thus the timber provided its wife, her mother, and Kiviung with an abundance of food. One day, however, after they had launched it as they had always done, it left and never returned.

After a short interval Kiviung married the young widow. Now he went sealing every day himself and was very successful. As he thought of leaving some day, he was anxious to get a good stock of mittens (that his hands might keep dry during the long journey?). Every night after returning from hunting he pretended to have lost his mittens. In reality he had concealed them in the hood of his jacket.

After awhile the old woman became jealous of her daughter, for the new husband of the latter was a splendid hunter and she wished to marry him herself. One day when he was away hunting, she murdered her daughter, and in order to deceive him she removed her daughter's skin and crept into it, thus changing her shape into that of the young woman. When Kiviung returned, she went to meet him, as it had been her daughter's custom, and without exciting any suspicion. But when he entered the hut and saw the bones of his wife he at once became aware of the cruel deed and of the deception that had been practiced and fled away.

He traveled on for many days and nights, always following the shore. At last he again came to a hut where a lamp was burning. As his clothing was wet and he was hungry, he landed and went up to the house. Before entering it occurred to him that it would be best to find out first who was inside. He therefore climbed up to the window and looked through the peep hole. On the bed sat an old woman, whose name was Aissivang (spider). When she saw the dark figure before the window she believed it was a cloud passing the sun, and as the light was insufficient to enable her to go on with her work she got angry. With her knife she cut away her eyebrows, ate them, and did not mind the dripping blood, but sewed on. When Kiviung saw this he thought that she must be a very bad woman and turned away.

Still he traveled on days and nights. At last he came to a land which seemed familiar to him and soon he recognized his own country. He was very glad when he saw some boats coming to meet him. They had been on a whaling excursion and were towing a great carcass to the village. In the bow of one of them stood a stout young man who had killed the whale. He was Kiviung's son, whom he had left a small boy and who was now grown up and had become a great hunter. His wife had taken a new husband, but now she returned to Kiviung.

ORIGIN OF THE NARWHAL.

A long, long time ago a widow lived with her daughter and her son in a hut. When the boy was quite young he made a bow and arrows of walrus tusks and shot birds, which they ate. Before he was grown up he accidentally became blind. From that moment his mother maltreated him in every way. She never gave him enough to eat, though he had formerly added a great deal to their sustenance, and did not allow her daughter, who loved her brother tenderly, to give him anything. Thus they lived many years and the poor boy was very unhappy.

Once upon a time a polar bear came to the hut and thrust his head right through the window. They were all very much frightened and the mother gave the boy his bow and arrows that he might kill the animal. But he said, "I cannot see the window and I shall miss him." Then the sister leveled the bow and the boy shot and killed the bear. The mother and sister went out and took the carcass down and skinned it.

After they had returned into the hut they told the boy that he had missed the bear, which had run away when it had seen him taking his bow and arrows. The bad mother had strictly ordered her daughter not to tell that the bear was dead, and she did not dare to disobey. The mother and the daughter ate the bear and had an ample supply of food, while the boy was almost starving. Sometimes, when the mother had gone away, the girl gave her brother something to eat, as she loved him dearly.

One day a loon flew over the hut and observing the poor blind boy it resolved to restore his eyesight. It sat down on the top of the roof and cried, "Come out, boy, and follow me." When he heard this he crept out and followed the bird, which flew along to a lake. There it took the boy and dived with him to the bottom. When they had risen again to the surface it asked, "Can you see anything?" The boy answered, "No, I cannot yet see." They dived again and staid a long time in the water. When they emerged, the bird asked, "Can you see now?" The boy answered, "I see a dim shimmer." Then they dived the third time and staid very long under water. When they had risen to the surface the boy had recovered his eyesight altogether.

He was very glad and thankful to the bird, which told him to return to the hut. Then he found the skin of the bear he had killed drying in the warm rays of the sun. He got very angry and cut it into small pieces. He entered the hut and asked his mother: "From whom did you get the bearskin I saw outside of the hut?" The mother was frightened when she found that her son had recovered his eyesight, and prevaricated. She said, "Come here, I will give you the best I have ; but I am very poor ; I have no supporter; come here, eat this, it is very good." The boy, however, did not comply and asked again, "From whom did you get yon bearskin I saw outside the hut?" Again she prevaricated ; but when she could no longer evade the question she said, "A boat came here with many men in it, who left it for me."

The boy did not believe the story, but was sure that it was the skin of the bear he had killed during the winter. However, he did not say a word. His mother, who was anxious to conciliate him, tried to accommodate him with food and clothing, but he did not accept anything.

He went to the other Inuit who lived in the same village, made a spear and a harpoon of the same pattern he saw in use with them, and began to catch white whales. In a short time he had become an expert hunter.

By and by he thought of taking revenge on his mother. He said to his sister, "Mother abused me when I was blind and has maltreated you for pitying me; we will revenge ourselves on her." The sister agreed and he planned a scheme for killing the mother.

When he went to hunt white whales he used to wind the harpoon line round his body and, taking a firm footing, hold the animal until it was dead. Sometimes his sister accompanied him and helped him to hold the line.

One day he told his mother to go with him and hold his line. When they came to the beach he tied the rope round her body and asked her to keep a firm footing. She was rather anxious, as she had never done this before, and told him to harpoon a small dolphin, else she might not be able to resist the strong pull. After a short time a young animal came up to breathe and the mother shouted, "Kill it, I can hold it ;" but the boy answered, "No, it is too large." Again a small dolphin came near and the mother shouted to him to spear it ; but he said, "No, it is too large." At last a huge animal rose quite near. Immediately he threw his harpoon, taking care not to kill it, and tossing his mother forward into the water cried out, "That is because you maltreated me; that is because you abused me."

The white whale dragged the mother into the sea, and whenever she rose to the surface she cried, "Louk! Louk!" and gradually she became transformed into a narwhal.

After the young man had taken revenge he began to realize that it was his mother whom he had murdered and he was haunted by remorse, and so was his sister, as she had agreed to the bad plans of her brother. They did not dare to stay any longer in their hut, but left the country and traveled many days and many nights overland. At last they came to a place where they saw a hut in which a man lived whose name was Qitua'jung. He was very bad and had horribly long nails on his fingers. The young man, being very thirsty, sent his sister into the hut to ask for some water. She entered and said to Qitua'jung, who sat on the bed place, "My brother asks for some water;" to which Qitua'jung responded, "There it stands behind the lamp. Take as much as you like." She stooped to the bucket, when he jumped up and tore her back with his long nails. Then she called to her brother for help, crying, "Brother, brother, that man is going to kill me." The young man ran to the hut immediately, broke down the roof, and killed the bad man with his spear.

Cautiously he wrapped up his sister in hares' skins, put her on his back, and traveled on. He wandered over the land for many days, until he came to a hut in which a man lived whose name was Iqignang. As the young man was very hungry, he asked him if he might eat a morsel from the stock of deer meat put up in the entrance of the hut. Iqignang answered, "Don't eat it, don't eat it." Though he had already taken a little bit, he immediately stopped. Iqignang was very kind to the brother and sister, however, and after a short time he married the girl, who had recovered from her wounds, and gave his former wife to the young man.[1]

THE VISITOR.

An old hag lived in a house with her grandson. She was a very bad woman who thought of nothing but playing mischief. She was a witch and tried to harm everybody by witchcraft. Once upon a time a stranger came to visit some friends who lived in a hut near that of the old woman. As the visitor was a good hunter and procured plenty of food for his hosts, she envied them and resolved to kill the new comer. She made a soup of wolf's and man's brains, which was the most poisonous meal she could prepare, and sent her grandson to invite the stranger. She cautioned him not to say what she had cooked, as she knew that the visitor was a great angakoq, who was by far her superior in wisdom.

The boy went to the neighboring hut and said: "Stranger, my grandmother invites you to come to her hut and to have there a good feast on a supper she has cooked. She told me not to say that it is a man's and a wolf's brains and I do not say it."

Though the angakoq understood the schemes of the old hag he followed the boy and sat down with her. She feigned to be very glad to see him and gave him a dish full of soup, which he began to eat. But by help of his tornaq the food fell right through him into a vessel which he had put between his feet on the floor of the hut. This he gave to the old witch and compelled her to eat it. She died as soon as she had brought the first spoonful to her mouth.

---

[1] See foot-note on p. 208

THE FUGITIVE WOMEN.

Once upon a time two women who were with child quarreled with their husbands and fled from their families and friends to live by themselves. After having traveled a long distance they came to a place called Igdluqdjuaq, where they resolved to stay. It was summer when they arrived. They found plenty of sod and turf and large whale ribs bleaching on the beach. They erected a firm structure of bones and filled the interstices with sod and turf. Thus they had a good house to live in. In order to obtain skins they made traps, in which they caught foxes in sufficient numbers for their dresses. Sometimes they found carcasses of ground seals or of whales which had drifted to the shore, of which they ate the meat and burnt the blubber. There was also a deep and narrow deer pass near the hut. Across this they stretched a rope and when the deer passed by they became entangled in it and strangled themselves. Besides, there was a salmon creek near the house and this likewise furnished them with an abundance of food.

In winter their fathers came in search of their lost daughters. When they saw the sledge coming they began to cry, as they were unwilling to return to their husbands. The men, however, were glad to find them comfortable, and having staid two nights at their daughters' house they returned home, where they told the strange story that two women without the company of any men lived all by themselves and were never in want.

Though this happened a long time ago the house may still be seen and therefore the place is called Igdluqdjuaq (The Large House).

QAUDJAQDJUQ.

I. STORY OF THE THREE BROTHERS.

A long time ago there lived three brothers. Two of them were grown up, but the third was a young lad whose name was Qaudjaqdjuq. The elder brothers had left their country and traveled about many years, while the youngest lived with his mother in their native village. As they had no supporter, the poor youth was abused by all the men of the village and there was nobody to protect him.

At last the elder brothers, being tired of roaming about, returned home. When they heard that the boy had been badly used by all the Inuit they became angry and thought of revenge. At first, however, they did not say anything, but built a boat, in which they intended to escape after having accomplished their designs. They were skillful boat builders and finished their work very soon. They tried the boat and found that it passed over the water as swiftly as an eider duck flies. As they were not content with their work they destroyed it again and built a new boat, which proved as swift as an ice duck. They were not yet content, destroyed this, and built a third one that was good. After having finished the boat they lived quietly with the other men. In the village there was a large singing house, which was used at every festival. One day the three brothers entered it and shut it up. Then they began dancing and singing and continued until they were exhausted. As there was no seat in the house they asked their mother to bring one, and when they opened the door to let her pass in, an ermine, which had been hidden in the house, escaped.

Near the singing house the other Inuit of the village were playing. When they saw the ermine, which ran right through the crowd, they endeavored to catch it. In the eagerness of pursuit one man, who had almost caught the little animal, stumbled over a bowlder and fell in such a manner that he was instantly killed. The ermine was sprinkled with blood, particularly about its mouth. During the ensuing confusion it escaped into the singing house, where it concealed itself again in the same corner.

The brothers, who were inside, had recommenced singing and dancing. When they were exhausted they called for their mother (to bring something to eat). When they opened the door the ermine again escaped and ran about among the Inuit, who were still playing outside.

When they saw it they believed that the brothers would induce them to pursue it again, and thus make them perish one by one. Therefore the whole crowd stormed the singing house with the intention of killing the brothers. As the door was shut they climbed on the roof and pulled it down, but when they took up their spears to pierce the three men they opened the door and rushed down to the beach. Their boat was quite near at hand and ready to be launched, while those of the other Inuit were a long distance off.

They embarked with their mother, but, when they were at a short distance and saw that the other men had not yet reached their boats, they pretended that they were unable to move theirs, though they pulled with the utmost effort. In reality, they played with the oars on the water. A few young women and girls were on the shore looking at the brothers, who seemed to exert themselves to the utmost of their strength. The eldest brother cried to the women: "Will you help us? We cannot get along alone." Two girls consented, but as soon as they had come into the boat the brothers commenced pulling as hard as possible, the boat flying along quicker than a duck, while the girls cried with fright. The other Inuit hastened up desirous to reach the fugitives, and soon their boats were manned.

The brothers were not afraid, however, as their boat was by far the swiftest. When they had almost lost sight of the pursuers they were suddenly stopped by a high, bold land rising before the boat and shutting up their way. They were quite puzzled, as they had to retrace their way for a long distance and feared they would be over-taken by the other boats.   But one of the brothers, who was a great angakoq, saved them by his art.   He said: "Shut your eyes and do not open them before I tell you, and then pull on."   They did as they were bade, and when he told them to look up they saw that they had sailed right through the land, which rose just as high and formid-able behind them as it had formerly obstructed their way.   It had opened and let them pass.

After having sailed some time they saw a long black line in the sea. On coming nearer they discovered that it was an impenetrable mass of seaweed, so compact that they could leave the boat and stand upon it.   There was no chance of pushing the boat through, though it was swifter than a duck.   The eldest brother, however, thought of his angakoq art and said to his mother, "Take your hair lace and whip the seaweed."   As soon as she did so it sank and opened the way.

After having overcome these obstacles they were troubled no more and accomplished their journey in safety.   When they arrived in their country they went ashore and erected a hut.   The two women whom they had taken from their enemies they gave to their young brother Qaudjaqdjuq.

They wanted to make him a very strong man, such as they were themselves.   For this reason they led him to a huge stone and said, "Try to lift that stone."   As Qaudjaqdjuq was unable to do so, they whipped him and said, "Try it again."   Now Qaudjaqdjuq could move it a little from its place.   The brothers were not yet content and whipped him once more.   By the last whipping he became very strong and lifted the bowlder and cast it over the hut.

Then the brothers gave him the whip and told him to beat his wives if they disobeyed him.

II. QAUDJAQDJUQ.

A long time ago there was a poor little orphan boy who had no protector and was maltreated by all the inhabitants of the village. He was not even allowed to sleep in the hut, but lay outside in the cold passage among the dogs, who were his pillows and his quilt. Neither did they give him any meat, but flung old, tough walrus hide at him, which he was compelled to eat without a knife.   A young girl was the only one who pitied him.   She gave him a very small piece of iron for a knife, but bade him conceal it well or the men would take it from him.   He did so, putting it into his urethra. Thus he led a miserable life and did not grow at all, but remained poor little Qaudjaqdjuq.   He did not even dare to join the plays of the other children, as they also maltreated and abused him on account of his weakness.

When the inhabitants assembled in the singing house Qaudjaqdjuq used to lie in the passage and peep over the threshold. Now and then a man would lift him by the nostrils into the hut and give him the large urine vessel to carry out (Fig. 148). It was so large and heavy

FIG. 148 Qaudjaqdjuq is maltreated by his enemies. Drawn by Qeqertuqdjuaq, an Oqomio.

FIG. 149. The man in the moon comes down to help Qaudjaqdjuq..

that he was obliged to take hold of it with both hands and his teeth. As he was frequently lifted by the nostrils they grew to be very large, though he remained small and weak.

FIG. 150. The man in the moon whipping Qaudjaqdjuq.

FIG. 151. Qaudjaqdjuq has become Qaudjuqdjuaq.

At last the man in the moon,[1] who had seen how badly the men behaved towards Qaudjaqdjuq, came down to help him. He harnessed his dog[2] (Fig. 149) Tirie′tiang to his sledge and drove down. When near the hut he stopped and cried, "Qaudjaqdjuq, come out." Qaudjaqdjuq answered, "I will not come out. Go away!" But when he had asked him a second and a third time to come out, he complied, though he was very much frightened. Then the man in the moon went with him to a place where some large bowlders were lying about and, having whipped him (Fig. 150), asked, "Do you feel stronger now?" Qaudjaqdjuq answered: "Yes, I feel stronger." "Then lift yon bowlder," said he. As Qaudjaqdjuq was not yet able to lift it, he gave him another whipping, and now all of a sudden he began to grow, the feet first becoming of an extraordinary size (Fig. 151). Again the man in the moon asked him: "Do you feel stronger now?" Qaudjaqdjuq answered: "Yes, I feel stronger ;" but as he could not yet lift the stone he was whipped once more, after which he had attained a very great strength and lifted the bowlder as if it were a small pebble. The man in the moon said: "That will do. To-morrow morning I shall send three bears; then you may show your strength."

He returned to the moon, but Qaudjaqdjuq, who had now become Qaudjuqdjuaq (the big Qaudjaqdjuq), returned home tossing the stones with his feet and making them fly to the right and to the left. At night he lay down again among the dogs to sleep. Next morning he awaited the bears, and, indeed, three large animals soon made their appearance, frightening all the men, who did not dare to leave the huts.

Then Qaudjuqdjuaq put on his boots and ran down to the ice. The men who looked out of the window hole said, "Look here, is

---

[1] The man in the moon is the protector of orphans.

[2] By a mistake of the Eskimo who made the drawings, four dogs are harnessed to the sledge. According to his own explanation the dappled one ought to be the only dog.

not that Qaudjaqdjuq? The bears will soon make way with him."
But he seized the first by its hind legs and smashed its head on an
iceberg, near which it happened to stand. The other one fared no
better; the third, however, he carried up to the village and slew some
of his persecutors with it. Others he pressed to death with his
hands or tore off their heads (Fig. 152), crying: "That is for abus-
ing me; that is for your maltreating me." Those whom he did not
kill ran away, never to return. Only a few who had been kind to
him while he had been poor little Qaudjaqdjuq were spared, among
them the girl who had given him the knife. Qaudjuqdjuaq lived to
be a great hunter and traveled all over the country, accomplishing
many exploits.

Fig. 152 Qaudjuqdjuaq killing his enemies.

IGIMARASUGDJUQDJUAQ THE CANNIBAL.

Igimarasugdjuqdjuaq was a very huge and bad man, who had committed many murders and eaten the victims after he had cut them
up with his knife. Once upon a time his sister-in-law came to visit
his wife, but scarcely had she entered the hut before Igimarasugdjuqdjuaq killed her and commanded his wife to cook her.

His wife was very much frightened, fearing that she herself would
be the next victim, and resolved to make her escape. When Igimarasugdjuqdjuaq had left to go hunting she gathered heather,
stuffed her jacket with it, and placed the figure in a sitting position
upon the bed. Then she ran away as fast as she could and suc-

ceeded in reaching a village. When her husband came home and saw the jacket he believed that it was a stranger who had come to visit him and stabbed him through the body. When he discovered, however, that his wife had deceived and left him, he fell into a passion and pursued her.

He came to the village and said: "Have you seen my wife? She has run away." The Inuit did not tell him that she was staying with them, but concealed her from his wrath. At last Igimarasugdjuqdjuaq gave her up for lost and returned home.

The Inuit, however, resolved to revenge the many outrages which he had wrought upon them. They went to visit him and met him on the ice just below the hut. When he told them he was going bear hunting they said: "Let us see your spear." This spear had a stout and sharp walrus tusk for a point. "Ah," said they; "that is good for bear hunting; how sharp it is. You must hit him just this way." And so saying they struck his brow, the point of the spear entering his brain, and then cut the body up with their knives.

THE TORNIT.[1]

In olden times the Inuit were not the only inhabitants of the country in which they live at the present time. Another tribe similar to them shared their hunting ground. But they were on good terms, both tribes living in harmony in the villages. The Tornit were much taller than the Inuit and had very long legs and arms. Almost all of them were blear eyed. They were extremely strong and could lift large bowlders, which were by far too heavy for the Inuit. But even the Inuit of that time were much stronger than those of to-day, and some large stones are shown on the plain of Miliaqdjuin, in Cumberland Sound, with which the ancient Inuit used to play, throwing them great distances. Even the strongest men of the present generations are scarcely able to lift them, much less to swing them or throw them any distance.

FIG. 153. Tumiujang or lamp of the Tornit. (Museum für Völkerkunde, Berlin   IV, A 6848.)

The Tornit lived on walrus, seals, and deer, just as the Eskimo do nowadays, but their methods of hunting were different. The principal part of their winter dress was a long and wide coat of deerskins,

[1] See foot-note on p. 208.

similar to the jumper of the Eskimo, but reaching down to the knees and trimmed with leather straps. When sealing in winter they wore this garment, the lower edge of which was fastened on the snow by means of pegs. Under the jacket they carried a small lamp, called tumiujang (literally, resembling a footprint) or quming (Fig. 153), over which they melted snow in a small pot. Some Eskimo say that they opened the seals as soon as they were caught and cooked some meat over these lamps. When the seal blew in the hole they whispered, "Kapatipara" (I shall stab it) and, when they had hit it, "Igdluiliq." Frequently they forgot about the lamp and in throwing the harpoon upset it and burned their skin.

All their weapons were made of stone. For the blades of their knives they used green slate (uluqsaq, literally material for women's knives), which was fastened by ivory pins to a bone or ivory handle.

The points of their harpoons were made of bone, ivory, or slate; those of their lances, of flint or quartz, which was also used for drill-heads; and they made neither kayaks nor bows.

Their method of hunting deer was remarkable. In a deer pass, where the game could not escape, they erected a file of cairns across the valley and connected them by ropes. Some of the hunters hid behind the cairns, while others drove the deer toward them. As the animals were unable to pass the rope they fled along it, looking for an exit, and while attempting to pass a cairn were lanced by the waiting hunter, who seized the body by the hind legs and drew it behind the line.

This tale is related as a proof of their enormous strength and it is said that they were able to hold a harpooned walrus as the Eskimo hold a seal.

The Tornit could not clean the sealskins so well as the Inuit, but worked them up with part of the blubber attached. Their way of preparing meat was disgusting, since they let it become putrid and placed it between the thigh and the belly to warm it.

The old stone houses of the Tornit can be seen everywhere. Generally they did not build snow houses, but lived the whole winter in stone buildings, the roofs of which were frequently supported by whale ribs. Though the Eskimo built similar structures they can be easily distinguished from one another, the bed of their huts being much larger than that of the Tornit.

Though both tribes lived on very good terms, the Inuit did not like to play at ball with the Tornit, as they were too strong and used large balls, with which they hurt their playfellows severely.

A remarkable tradition is told referring to the emigration of this people.

The Tornit did not build any kayaks, but as they were aware of the advantages afforded by their use in hunting they stole the boats from the Inuit, who did not dare to defend their property, the

Tornit being by far their superiors in strength. Once upon a time a young Tuniq had taken the kayak of a young Inung without asking him and had injured it by knocking in the bottom. The Inung got very angry and ran a knife into the nape of the Tuniq's neck while he was sleeping. (According to another tradition he drilled a hole into his head; this form is also recorded in Labrador.) The Tornit then became afraid that the Inuit would kill them all and preferred to leave the country for good. They assembled at Qernirtung (a place in Cumberland Sound), and in order to deceive any pursuers they cut off the tails of their jumpers and tied their hair into a bunch protruding from the crown of the head.

In another form of the tradition it is said that while playing with the Tornit a young Inung fell down and broke his neck. The Tornit feared that the Inuit might take revenge upon them and left the country.

Many old ditties are sung which either treat of the Tornit or are reported to have been sung by them. Some of them will be found in the linguistic account connected with my journey.

THE WOMAN AND THE SPIRIT OF THE SINGING HOUSE.

Once upon a time a woman entered the singing house when it was quite dark. For a long time she had wished to see the spirit of the house, and though the Inuit had warned her of the impending danger she had insisted upon her undertaking.

She summoned the spirit, saying, "If you are in the house, come here." As she could not see him, she cried, "No spirit is here; he will not come." But the spirit, though yet invisible, said, "Here I am; there I am." Then the woman asked, "Where are your feet; where are your shins; where are your thighs; where are your hips; where are your loins?" Every time the spirit answered, "Here they are; there they are." And she asked further, "Where is your belly?" "Here it is," answered the spirit. "Where is your breast; where are your shoulders; where is your neck; where is your head?" "Here it is; there it is;" but in touching the head the woman all of a sudden fell dead. It had no bones and no hair (p. 191).

THE CONSTELLATION UDLEQDJUN.

Three men went bear hunting with a sledge and took a young boy with them. When they approached the edge of the floe they saw a bear and went in pursuit. Though the dogs ran fast they could not get nearer and all of a sudden they observed that the bear was lifted up and their sledge followed. At this moment the boy lost one of his mittens and in the attempt to pick it up fell from the sledge. There he saw the men ascending higher and higher, finally being transformed into stars. The bear became the star Nanuqdjung

(Betelgeuse); the pursuers, Udleqdjun (Orion's belt); and the sledge, Kamutiqdjung (Orion's sword). The men continue the pursuit up to this day; the boy, however, returned to the village and told how the men were lost.

ORIGIN OF THE ADLET AND OF THE QADLUNAIT.

Savirqong, an old man, lived alone with his daughter. Her name was Niviarsiang (i. e., the girl), but as she would not take a husband she was also called Uinigumissuitung (she who would not take a husband). She refused all her suitors, but at last a dog, spotted white and red, whose name was Ijirqang, won her affection and she took him for a husband. They had ten children, five of whom were Adlet and five dogs. The lower part of the body of the Adlet was that of a dog and hairy all over, the soles excepted, while the upper part was that of a man. When the children grew up they became very voracious, and as the dog Ijirqang did not go out hunting at all, but let his father in law provide for the whole family, it was difficult for Savirqong to feed them. Moreover, the children were awfully clamorous and noisy; so at last the grandfather got tired of it, put the whole family into his boat, and carried them to a small island. He told the dog Ijirqang to come every day and fetch meat.

Niviarsiang hung a pair of boots round his neck and he swam across the narrow channel. But Savirqong, instead of giving him meat, filled the boots with heavy stones, which drowned Ijirqang when he attempted to return to the island.

The daughter thought of revenging the death of her husband. She sent the young dogs to her father's hut and let them gnaw off his feet and hands. In return Savirqong, when Niviarsiang happened to be in his boat, threw her overboard and cut off her fingers when she held to the gunwale. As they fell into the sea they were transformed into seals and whales. At last he allowed her to climb into the boat.

As she feared that her father might think of killing or maiming her children, she ordered the Adlet to go inland, where they became the ancestors of a numerous people. She made a boat for the young dogs, setting up two sticks for masts in the soles of her boots, and sent the puppies across the ocean. She sang: "Angnaijaja. When you arrive there across the ocean you will make many things giving you joy. Angnaija." They arrived in the land beyond the sea and became the ancestors of the Europeans.

THE GREAT FLOOD.

A long time ago the ocean suddenly began to rise, until it covered the whole land. The water even rose to the top of the mountains and the ice drifted over them. When the flood had subsided the ice

stranded and ever since forms an ice cap on the top of the mountains.   Many shellfish, fish, seal, and whales were left high and dry
and their shells and bones may be seen to this day.   A great number
of Inuit died during this period, but many others, who had taken to
their kayaks when the water commenced to rise, were saved.

INUGPAQDJUQDJUALUNG.[1]

In days of yore, an enormous man, whose name was Inugpaqdjuqdjualung, lived in company with many other Inuit in a village
on a large fjord.   He was so tall that he could straddle the fjord.
He used to stand thus every morning and wait for whales to pass
beneath him.   As soon as one came along he stooped and caught it,
just as another man would scoop up some little thing that had fallen
into the water, and he ate it as other men eat a small piece of meat.

One day all the natives had manned their boats to hunt a whale.
Inugpaqdjuqdjualung at the time was sitting lazily near his hut, but
when he saw the efforts of the men he scooped both whale and boats
from the water and placed them upon the beach.

At another time, being tired from running about, he lay down on
a high hill to take a nap.   The Inuit told him that a couple of huge
bears had been seen near the village, but he said he didn't care, and
told his friends to rouse him by throwing large stones upon him if
they should see the bears coming.   They did so and Inugpaqdjuqdjualung, suddenly starting up, cried: "Where are they? Where are
they?"   When the Inuit pointed them out he said: "What! those
little things?   Those are not worth the bustle; they are small foxes,
not bears," and he crushed one between his fingers, while he put the
other into the eyelet of his boot and strangled it there.

THE BEAR STORY.

This story is reprinted from Hall (II, p. 240):

Many moons ago, a woman obtained a polar bear cub but two or three days old.
Having long desired just such a pet, she gave it her closest attention, as though it
were a son, nursing it, making for it a soft warm bed alongside her own, and talking to it as a mother does to her child.   She had no living relative, and she and the
bear occupied the house alone.   Kunikdjuaq, as he grew up, proved that the woman
had not taught him in vain, for he early began to hunt seals and salmon, bringing
them to his mother before eating any himself, and receiving his share from her
hands.   She always watched from the hilltop for his return, and if she saw that he
had been unsuccessful, she begged from her neighbors blubber for his food.   She
learned how this was from her lookout, for if successful, he came back in the tracks
made on going out, but if unsuccessful always by a different route.   Learning to
excel the Inuit in hunting, he excited their envy, and, after long years of faithful
service, his death was resolved upon.   On hearing this, the old woman, overwhelmed
with grief, offered to give up her own life if they would but spare him who had so
long supported her.   Her offer was sternly refused.   Upon this, when all his ene-

---

[1] See foot-note on p. 208

mies had retired to their houses, the woman had a long talk with her son — now well grown in years — telling him that wicked men were about to kill him, and that the only way to save his life and hers was for him to go off and not return. At the same time she begged him not to go so far that she could not wander off and meet him, and get from him a seal or something else which she might need. The bear, after listening to what she said with tears streaming down her furrowed cheeks, gently placed one huge paw on her head, and then throwing both around her neck, said, ' Good mother, Kunikdjuaq will always be on the lookout for you and serve you as best he can." Saying this, he took her advice and departed, almost as much to the grief of the children of the village as to the mother.

Not long after this, being in need of food, she walked out on the sea ice to see if she could not meet her son, and soon recognized him as one of two bears who were lying down together. He ran to her, and she patted him on the head in her old familiar way, told him her wants, and begged him to hurry away and get something for her. Away ran the bear, and in a few moments the woman looked upon a terrible fight going on between him and his late companion, which, however, to her great relief, was soon ended by her son's dragging a lifeless body to her feet. With her knife she quickly skinned the dead bear, giving her son large slices of the blubber, and telling him that she would soon return for the meat, which she could not at first carry to her house, and when her supply should again fail she would come back for his help. This she continued to do for "a long, long time," the faithful bear always serving her and receiving the same unbroken love of his youth.

SUNDRY TALES.

(1) Two little girls, while playing about a cliff near Aivillik, with infants in the hoods on their backs, went into an opening between the rocks, which closed upon them before escape was possible. All attempts at rescue were unsuccessful, and the poor children, to whom for a time meat and water were passed, perished in the cliffs (Hall II, p. 222).

(2) Opposite to Niutang, a village in Kingnait, Cumberland Sound, there is a vein of diorite resembling a boot, and therefore called Kamingujang. A long time ago two enemies lived in the village. One day they stood on the beach ready to go hunting. Suddenly the one exclaimed, pointing to Kamingujang, "There he blows," making his enemy believe that a whale was passing up the fjord and inducing him to look out for it. Then he killed him from behind, piercing him with the spear.

(3) At Qognung, near the head of Nettilling Fjord, there is a large white stone on each side of the fjord, somewhat resembling a bear. It is said that these stones have been bears which, being pursued by an Eskimo in the water, escaped to the land, but were transformed into these stones.

(4) A long time ago a dead boy was buried under a large stone. Before his relatives had returned to their hut the body was transformed into a hare, which jumped forth from the tomb. All hares come from this animal.

(5) It is said that albinos of seals and deer spring from an egg of about half a foot in length, which forms itself in the earth. The seal digs an underground passage to the sea, the deer a similar one to a distant part of the country, and there they rise. The albinos are said to be very quick.

I will add here an enumeration of the fabulous tribes of which I gained intelligence, but of some of them I only know the names.

(1) The Tornit, or, as they are called by the Akudnirmiut, the Tuniqdjuait (p. 226). It is remarkable that this people is considered here, as well as in Labrador, a tribe similar to the Eskimo, with whom they formerly lived in company, but who were subsequently expelled by the latter. In Greenland they are entirely a fabulous tribe, each individual being of enormous size, living inland and seldom hunting in the upper parts of the fjords. While in the western parts of the Eskimo country a more historical form of the tradition is preserved, it is entirely mythical in Greenland.

(2) The Adlet or Erqigdlit. In the tradition treating of this tribe a similar change occurs. The Labrador Eskimo call the Indians of the interior Adlet, the tribes west of Hudson Bay call them Erqigdlit. The Baffin Land Eskimo and the Greenlanders have forgotten this relation altogether, but denote with the term a fabulous tribe with dogs' legs and a human body. The name Adla is used as far north as Cumberland Peninsula, the Akudnirmiut and the more northern tribes using the term Erqigdlit. It is difficult to account for the use of these different terms in both senses.

(3) The Ardnainiq, a tribe living in the extreme northwest. The men of this people are small, tiny, like children, but entirely covered with hair. They are carried about in the hoods of their wives, just like children. The women are of normal size. They do all the work, going out hunting in the kayaks and providing for the men.

(4) The Inuarudligang, dwarfs living in the cliffs near the shore.

(5) The Igdlungajung, a bandy legged people living inland.

(6) The Uissuit, dwarfs living in the depth of the sea (p. 213).

(7) The Ijirang.

(8) The Qailerte'tang, a people consisting of women only (p. 197).

Finally, I will mention the animals which are only known to the natives by reports of foreign tribes and are described as fabulous creatures. These are the umingmang (the musk ox), which is represented as a fierce animal with black and red streaks and larger than a bear, and the agdlaq (the black bear), which, according to their belief, is also of enormous size. It is said to live inland and to devour everything that comes near it. I am unable to decide whether the report of an enormous fish, the idluk, which is said to live in the lakes, is altogether fabulous. The natives say that if they want to catch the fish they build a snow house on the lake and cut a hole through the ice, into which they sink the hook with a deer's ham for a bait and a stout thong for a fishing line. Six men hold the line by turns, and as soon as they feel the fish has nibbled they pull it up with all their strength.

The fabulous amaroq and avignaq of the Greenlanders are unknown, but the terms denote real animals, the wolf and the lemming.

Besides traditions of this kind the Eskimo have a great number of fables. Following is an example.

THE OWL AND THE RAVEN

The owl and the raven were fast friends. One day the raven made a new dress, dappled white and black, for the owl, who in return made a pair of boots of whalebone for the raven and then began to make a white dress. . But when he was about to try it on, the raven kept hopping about and would not sit still. The owl got angry and said : " Now sit still or I shall pour out the lamp over you." As the raven continued hopping about, the owl fell into a passion and poured the oil upon it. Then the raven cried " Qaq! Qaq!" and since that day has been black all over.

COMPARISON BETWEEN BAFFIN LAND TRADITIONS AND THOSE OF OTHER TRIBES.

The similarity of the language and traditions of the Eskimo from Behring Strait to Greenland is remarkable, considering the distance which separates the tribes. Unfortunately the material from other tribes, except the Greenlanders, is very scanty, but it is probable that the same traditions or elements of traditions are known to all the tribes. In the following table the above traditions are compared with Rink's Tales and Traditions of the Greenlanders and with those of other tribes :

Traditions of Greenlanders and other tribes :	Traditions of the Central Eskimo:
Qagsaqsuq, Rink, p. 93.	Qaudjaqdjuq, p. 222
The blind man who recovered his sight, Rink, p. 99.	The origin of the narwhal, p. 217
Igimarasugsuq, Rink, p. 106.	Igimarasugdjuqdjuaq, p. 225
The man who mated himself with a sea fowl, Rink, p. 145.	Ititaujang, p. 207
Givioq, Rink, pp. 157 and 429.	Kiviung, p. 213
Tiggaq, Rink, p. 162.	The visitor, p. 219
A lamentable story, Rink, p. 239.	No. 1, sundry tales, p. 231
The sun and the moon, Rink, p. 236.	The sun and the moon, p. 189
(L'homme lunaire, Petitot, Traditions indiennes du Canada Nord-Ouest, p. 7. Also found by Simpson at Point Barrow.)	

The moon, Rink, p. 440.

The Tornit (from Labrador), Rink, p. 469.

A woman who was mated with a dog, Rink, p. 471.

(Fragmentary in J. Murdoch: "A few legendary fragments from the Point Barrow Eskimos," American Naturalist, p. 594, July, 1886.)

The angakoq's flight to the moon, p. 190

The Tornit, p. 226

Origin of the Adlet and the white men, p. 229

Some of these stories are almost identical in both countries, for instance, Qaudjaqdjuq, the origin of the narwhal, &c., and it is of great interest to learn that some passages, particularly speeches and songs, occur literally in both countries, for instance, the interesting song of Niviarsiang (page 229) and the conclusion of the Kiviung tradition. The tradition of the Tornit and the form of the second tale (origin of the narwhal) resemble much more those of Labrador than those of Greenland. The elements of which the traditions are composed are combined differently in the tales of Baffin Land and Greenland, but most of these elements are identical. I give here a comparative table.

	Greenland.	Baffin Land.
Transformation of a man into a seal.	Rink, pp. 222, 224, 469.	Kiviung, p. 213
Men walking on the surface of the water.	Rink, pp. 123, 407.	Kiviung, p. 214
Harpooning a witch.	Rink, p. 372.	Sedna, p. 196
Erqigdlit.	Rink, pp. 401 et seq.	Adlet, p. 229
Sledge of the man of the moon drawn by one dog.	Rink, pp. 441, 442.	Qaudjaqdjuq, p. 223 and The flight to the moon, p. 190
Origin of the salmon.	Cranz, p. 262.	Ititaujang, p. 209
Arnaquagsaq.	Rink, pp. 150, 326, 466.	Sedna, p. 175
Origin of the thunder.	Cranz, p. 233; Egede, p. 207.	Kadlu, p. 192

The following is a comparison between traditions from Alaska and the Mackenzie and those of the Central Eskimo·

Traditions from Alaska and the Mackenzie:	Traditions of the Central Eskimo:
Men as descendants of a dog, Murdoch, op. cit., p. 594.	Origin of the Adlet and white men, p. 229
The origin of reindeer, Murdoch, op. cit., p. 595.	Origin of the reindeer and walrus, p. 179
The origin of the fishes, Murdoch, op. cit., p. 595.	Ititaujang, p. 209
Thunder and lightning, Murdoch, op. cit., p. 595.	Kadlu the thunderer, p. 192
Sun and moon, Petitot, op. cit., p. 7.	Sun and moon, p. 189
Orion, Simpson, p. 940.	Orion, p. 228

PLATE I

Exeter Sound

Miñgejuin

CUMBERLAND PENINSULA, DRAWN BY ARANIN, A SAUMINGMIO.

The table shows that the following ideas are known to all tribes from Alaska to Greenland: The sun myth, representing the sun as the brother of the moon; the legend of the descent of man from a dog; the origin of thunder by rubbing a deerskin; the origin of fish from chips of wood; and the story of the origin of deer.

It must be regretted that very few traditions have as yet been collected in Alaska, as the study of such material would best enable us to decide upon the question of the origin of the Eskimo.

SCIENCE AND THE ARTS.

GEOGRAPHY AND NAVIGATION.

The Eskimo exhibit a thorough knowledge of the geography of their country. I have already treated of their migrations and mentioned that the area they travel over is of considerable extent. They have a very clear conception of all the countries they have seen or heard of, knowing the distances by day's journeys, or, as they say, by sleeps, and the directions by the cardinal points. So far as I know, all these tribes call true south piningnang, while the other points are called according to the weather prevailing while the wind blows from the different quarters. In Cumberland Sound uangnang is west-northwest; qaningnang (that is, snow wind), east-northeast; nigirn, southeast; and aqsardnirn, the fohn-like wind blowing from the fjords of the east coast. On Nettilling these names are the same, the east-northeast only being called qanara (that is, is it snow?) In Akudnirn uangnang is west-southwest; ikirtsuq (i. e., the wind of the open sea), east-northeast; oqurtsuq (i. e., the wind of the land Oqo or of the lee side, southeast; and avangnanirn (i. e., from the north side along the shore), the northwestern gales. According to Parry the same names as in Cumberland Sound are used in Iglulik.

If the weather is clear the Eskimo use the positions of the sun, of the dawn, or of the moon and stars for steering, and find their way pretty well, as they know the direction of their point of destination exactly. If the weather is thick they steer by the wind, or, if it is calm, they do not travel at all. After a gale they feel their way by observing the direction of the snowdrifts.

They distinguish quite a number of constellations, the most important of which are Tuktuqdjung (the deer), our Ursa Major; the Pleiades, Sakietaun; and the belt of Orion, Udleqdjun.

As their knowledge of all the directions is very detailed and they are skillful draftsmen they can draw very good charts. If a man intends to visit a country little known to him, he has a map drawn in the snow by some one well acquainted there and these maps are so good that every point can be recognized. Their way of drawing is first to mark some points the relative positions of which are well known. They like to stand on a hill and to look around in order to place these correctly. This done, the details are inserted. It is remarkable that their ideas of the relative position and direction of coasts far distant one from another are so very clear. Copies of some charts drawn by Eskimo of Cumberland Sound and Davis Strait are here introduced (Plate I , p. 234, and Figs. 154–157). A comparison between the maps and these charts will prove their correctness. Fre-

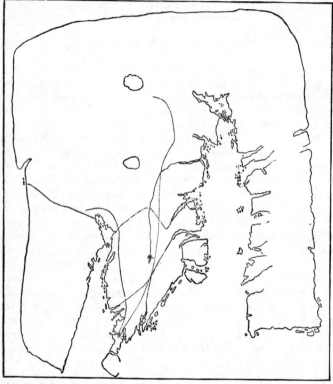

FIG. 154. Cumberland Sound and Frobisher Bay, drawn by Itu, a Nugumio. (Original in the Museum für Völkerkunde, Berlin.)

quently the draftsman makes his own country, with which he is best acquainted, too large; if some principal points are marked first, he will avoid this mistake. The distance between the extreme points represented in the first chart (Fig. 154) is about five hundred miles.

The Eskimo have a sort of calendar. They divide the year into thirteen months, the names of which vary a great deal, according to the tribes and according to the latitude of the place. The surplus is

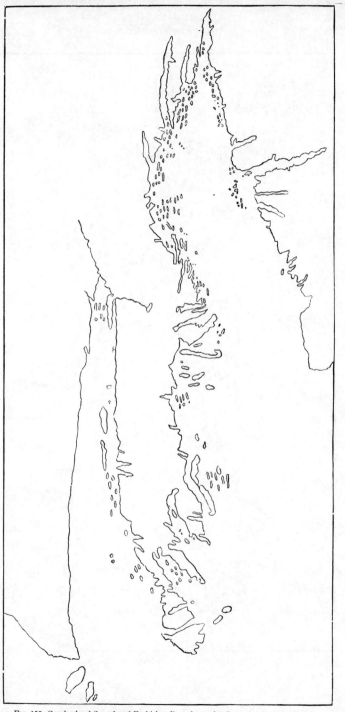

Fig. 155 Cumberland Sound and Frobisher Bay, drawn by Sunapignang, an Oqomio.

FIG. 156. Cumberland Sound, drawn by Itu, a Nugumio.

Fig. 157. Peninsula of Qivitung, drawn by Angutuqdjuaq, a Padlimio.

balanced by leaving out a month every few years, to wit, the month siringilang (without sun), which is of indefinite duration, the name covering the whole time of the year when the sun does not rise and there is scarcely any dawn. Thus every few years this month is totally omitted, when the new moon and the winter solstice coincide. The name qaumartenga is applied only to the days without sun but with dawn, while the rest of the same moon is called siriniktenga. The days of the month are very exactly designated by the age of the moon. Years are not reckoned for a longer space than two, backward and forward.

The Eskimo are excellent draftsmen and carvers. Most of the drawings are similar to the bear and deer shown on Plate II (Figs. d and q) or to the illustrations of the Qaudjaqdjuq tale (see Figs. 148–152, pp. 223–225.) The rest, on Plates III and IV, are excellently made, and by far superior to any I have seen made by other Eskimo of these regions. A number of carvings are represented on Plates V and VI. The narwhal and the whale are particularly admirable. Among the implements represented in this paper there are many of beautiful and artistic design.

I also add a number of engravings of implements plainly showing the influence of European patterns (Plate VII).

POETRY AND MUSIC.

Among the arts of the Eskimo poetry and music are by far the most prominent. The tales which have been related are only a small part of their stock of traditions. Besides the contents their form also is very interesting, as most of them have been handed down in unchanged form and their narration demands a great deal of art. Many traditions are told in a very abridged form, the substance being supposed to be known. A specimen of this kind is the Sedna tradition (p. 196). All these tales must be considered recitatives, many of them beginning with a musical phrase and continuing as a rhythmic recitation, others being recited in rhythmic phrases throughout. Other traditions are told in a more detailed and prosaic manner, songs or recitations, however, being sometimes included. Ititaujang, for instance, in traveling into the country looking for his wife, sings the song No. XIII, and in the Kalopaling tradition the boy, on seeing the two Inuit coming, sings:

PLATE II

a, b, c, e Drawn by Aisĕ'ang, a native of Nuvujen.

d, f, g Drawn by Maleki, a native of Imigen.

ESKIMO DRAWINGS.

Some Eskimo are very good narrators and understand how to express the feelings of the different persons by modulations of the voice. In addition, as a number of tales are really onomatopoetic, an artistic effect is produced. The way of reciting is always similar to the one above described by notes (p. 240).

Besides these tales, which may be called poetic prose, there are real poems of a very marked rhythm, which are not sung but recited. The following are examples:

MERRYMAKING AMONG THE TORNIT.

Pi-ka pikagning minge-pignirming qije-pignirming suka-dla.   aq!   aq!

The Eskimo reciting this song jump up and down and to the right and left with their legs bent and their hands hanging down, the palms touching each other. In crying aq! aq! they jump as high as possible.

THE LEMMING'S SONG.

I-ker-gna-pi-gen,   i-ker-gna-pi-gen   sir-dna-tu-re-nain a-χe-e-roq-tu-re-nain   na-kusungming   auk-tu-re-nain pijungma-djangi-la-tit   qi-a-lung-nua-ra-lung-nan

Besides these old songs and tales there are a great number of new ones, and, indeed, almost every man has his own tune and his own song. A few of these become great favorites among the Eskimo and are sung like our popular songs. The summer song (No. I) and "The returning hunter" (No. II) may be most frequently heard. As to the contents of the songs, they treat of almost everything imaginable: of the beauty of summer; of thoughts and feelings of the composer on any occasion, for instance, when watching a seal, when angry with somebody, &c.; or they tell of an important event, as of a long journey. Satiric songs are great favorites.

The form of both old and new songs is very strict, they being divided into verses of different length, alternating regularly. I give here some examples:

ARLUM PISSINGA (the killer's song).

Moderato.

Qian - ga - lo tai - to - χalun - ga   qo - la - ra - lo tai - to - χalun - ga Qian - ga -

-lo - ga - lo   qo - la - ra - lo - ga - lo   ai - si - nai - i - si   se - ni - le - a - ra -

- luqdjua - ra   ma - lik - si - aq - tu - aq - tu - go   u - va - na - le - u - nen au - dla -

- tsia - pi - a - ta   kingodni - dlaq - djua - gung qangatir - gakulung uai - ju - va - ra.

I. The killer's song:

   (1) Qiangalo taitoχalunga,
      Qolaralo taitoχalunga
      Qiangalogalo
      Qolarologalo
      Aisinaisi.[1]

   (2) Senilearaluqdjuara
      Maliksiaqtuaqtugo.
      Uvanaleunen
      Audlatsiapiata
      Kingodnidlaqdjuagung

   (3) Qangatirgakulunguaijuvara.

II. Summer song:

   Aja.

   (1) Ajaja adlenaipa.
      Adlenaitariva silekdjua una au-
        jaratarame
      Ajaja, Ajaja!
      Aja!

II. Summer song—Continued.

   (2) Ajaja adlenaipa
      Adlenaitariva silekdjua una tek-
        torotikelektlune.
      Ajaja, Ajaja.
      Aja!

   (3) Ajaja nipituovokpan!
      Nipituovokpan kouvodlalimokoa
        nunatine aujadle
      Ajaja, Ajaja
      Aja!
      &c.

III. Utitiaq's song:

   Aja!

   (1) Adlenaipunganema adlenait.
      Adlenaipunganema
      Adlenaipunganema adlenait,
      Aja!

---

[1] The stanza is scanned thus:

PLATE III

Drawn by Aisĕ'ang, a native of Nuvujen.

ESKIMO DRAWINGS.

PLATE IV

Drawn by Aise'ang, a native of Nuvujen

ESKIMO DRAWING

III. Utitiaq's song—Continued.
  (2) Sikuqdjualimena adlenait.
    Atoqpoqtaromena
    Tanerangitu adlenait.
    Aja!
    &c.

IV. Kadlu's song:
  '1) Odlaqē', odlaqē', odlaqē'.
    Odlaqē' saranga tutaranga atu-
    jang una ajajaja.
    Odlaqē' atedlirlungai aχigirn
    qodlusuaning aχiatungitunga
    ajaja.
    Nettiulunga iχatijetingirn pinas-
    sousirdlunirn pinasuatautlir-
    padlirunirn.

IV. Kadlu's song—Continued.
  (2) Odlaqē', odlaqē', odlaqē'.
    Odlaqē' saranga tutaranga atu-
    jang una ajajaja.
    Odlaqē' atedlirlungai aχigirn
    qodlusuaning aχiatungitunga
    ajaja.
    Ugjurutlarunirn iχatijitingirn pi-
    nassousirdlunirn pinasuataut-
    lirpadlirnunirn.
  (3) . . . . &c.

Some of these verses contain only a single word, the rhythm being brought about by the chorus aja, amna aja, &c. I add two examples of this kind:

V. S ng in the language of the Angakut:
  Ajarpaija taitlaniqdjuàq ajarpe
  aitarpik ajijaija.
  Ajarpaija ataqdjuaq ajarpe aitarpik ajijaija.
  Ajarpaija mingeriaqdjuaq ajarpe
  aitarpik ajijaija.

VI. Oχaitoq's song:
  Aja.
  (1) Tavunga tavunga tavunga tavunga
  Tavunga tavunga tavunga tavunga tavungadlo tavunga
  Aja.
  (2) Pissutaramaima tavunga tavunga.
  Pissutaramaima tavunga tavunga tavungadlo tavunga, &c.

The rhythm of the songs will best be understood by examining the melodies. Every long syllable may be replaced by two or even three short ones; other short syllables appear as unaccented parts before the accented part of a measure; in short, the rhythmic adaptation of the words to the melody is very arbitrary and interchanges frequently occur, so that it is impossible to speak of metric feet. At the same time this furnishes distinct proof that the musical rhythm is the decisive element in determining the form. The rhythmic arrangement of the words is regulated with considerable exactness by the quantity of the syllables, and not by the accent. While, for instance, in speaking, it would be "palirtu'gun," in song No. IV it is "palir'tugun'," and in No. I "tekto'roti'kelek'tlune," instead of "tektorotikelektlu'ne," &c. Such displacements of the accent, however, are avoided if possible, and in the best and most popular songs they hardly appear at all.

The construction of the songs corresponds entirely with that of the music, inasmuch as every melody and every rhythmically spoken song is made up of musical, that is, rhythmic, phrases which are divided by cæsuræ. Repetitions of the same phrases are very frequent.

The adaptation of the melodies to our divisions of time and measure is also somewhat arbitrary, as they frequently consist of a mixture of three and four part phrases. It is for this reason that I have noted down some songs without any division into bars or measures and in those cases have only marked the accented syllables.

Among the twenty melodies and rhythmic poems we find ten of binary measures, five of triple measures, and six of mixed ones. Of the whole number, nine begin on the full bar, eleven on the arsis.

The melodies move within the following range: In a fifth (No. III), one; in a minor sixth (Nos. VII, IX, X), three; in a major sixth (Nos. II, IV, XVII), three; in a seventh (Nos. XII, XIV), two; in an octave, (Nos. I, II, V, VIII, XI, XVI), six; in a minor ninth (No. VI), one; in a major ninth No. (XV), one; in a tenth (No. XIII), one.

These may be divided into two very characteristic and distinct groups. The first, which would coincide with our major key, contains the following essential tones:

The fourth and the sixth occur seldom, and then only as subordinate tones. This key is identical with the Chinese and many of the Indian ones.

In the second group, which corresponds to our minor key, we frequently find the fourth, while the sixth only appears twice and then as a subordinate tone (in No. XV). We furthermore find the major seventh in the lower position leading back to the beginning, i. e., the key note. The essential components of this key are:

Professor R. Succo calls attention to the fact that the relation of the melodies to their key note resembles that of the Gregorian chants, especially the psalmodic ones among them.

If we, in accordance with our ideas, suppose the melody — No. XIII, for example — to begin in C major, it nevertheless does not conclude in the same key, but in E. We would say that No. XIV is written in A minor; still it ends in E. We find the same in the Gregorian chants. They also resemble the songs of the Eskimo in the retention of the same note during a large number of consecutive syllables.

On the whole the melodies, even to our musical sense, can be traced to a key note. However, changes often occur as well (see No. VI). A very striking construction appears in No. XIII, where the oft-repeated E forms a new key note, while at the conclusion the melody leaps back without any modulation to C through the peculiar interval, b̲, c.

PLATE V

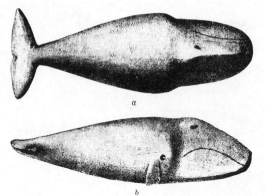

a

b

Carving representing whale. (In the possession of Mrs. Adams. Washington.) ¼

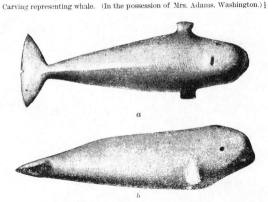

a

b

Carving representing whale. (National Museum, Washington. 29998.) ¼

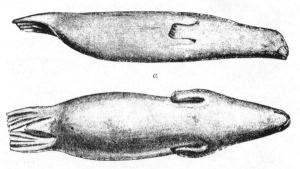

a

b

Carving representing seal. (National Museum, Washington. 29991.) ¼

ESKIMO CARVINGS

PLATE VI

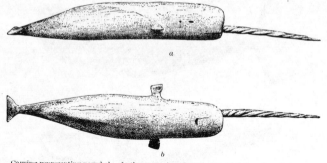

Carving representing narwhal. (In the possession of Capt. John O. Spicer, Groton, Conn.) ½

Seal. (Museum für Völkerkunde, Berlin.) ¼

Walrus head. (National Museum, Washington. 10414.) ½

Polar bear. (Museum für Völkerkunde, Berlin.) ¼

Sealskin float. (Museum für Völkerkunde, Berlin.) ¼

Seal. (Museum für Völkerkunde, Berlin.) ¼

Knife. (Museum für Völkerkunde, Berlin.) ¼

Spyglass. (Museum für Völkerkunde, Berlin.) ¼

ESKIMO CARVINGS.

I. SUMMER SONG.

Moderato.

A - ja. A - ja - ja, a - dle - nai - pa, a - dle - nai - ta - ri - va si-
lekdju - a u - na au - ja - ra - ta - ra·me. A - ja - ja, A - ja - ja, A - ja.

II. THE RETURNING HUNTER.

a.

Allegro.

Angutivun tai - na tau - nane tai ·· na, au - va - si - mame - ta a - va - va - si-
mameta ne - ri - opa - luktunga - a —, hangaanga ; hangaanga a - ga - ga.

b.

Angu - ti - vun tai - na tau - na - ne tai - na, au - va - si - mame - ta
a - va - va - si - mameta ne - ri - o - pa - luktunga ; hangaanga a - ga - ga.

III. SONG OF THE TORNIT.

Andante.

Sa - vu sau - jaqdjuin te - te - tlir - pa - vun, aqtun-
- gan. Sur - qar - mun pi - lak - tu - tu a - χi lur - pa, aqtun - gan.

IV. SONG OF THE INUIT TRAVELING TO NETTILLING.

Adagio non troppo.

A - ja. A - χa - go - dlo pa - lir - tu - gun; uang-
nangmun ti - pa - vun - ga, i - ja ji - ja a - ja - ja. A - ja.

V. OXAITOQ'S SONG.

Allegro.

A - ja. Ta-vunga tavunga tavunga tavunga. Tavunga tavunga ta - vunga ta - vunga ta - vunga - - dlo ta- vun-ga. A - ja.

VI. UTITIAQ'S SONG.

Allegro.

A - ja. A - dlenai- punga- nema a-dle - nait. A - dlenaipunganema a - dlenaipunganema adle - nait. A - ja. A

VII. SONG.

Allegro.

A - ja. A- ja- ja- ja a -ja- ja- ja a - ja - ja - ja - ja a-ja- ja- ja a - ja - ja a - ja - ja a - ja- ja- ja - ja - ja.

VIII. SONG.

Allegro.

Haja-jaja ha-ja-ja haja-jaja ha-jaja haja-jaja hajaja haja-jaja ha-jaja.

IX. SONG OF THE TORNIT.

Allegro.   FINE.

Savun - ga-ja a - ja a - ja Sa-ma a - ja- ja a - ja.

D. C. al Fine.

Nuna- ta-χa-toq sed - na ————, serser-ta- χa-toq sed - na.

PLATE VII

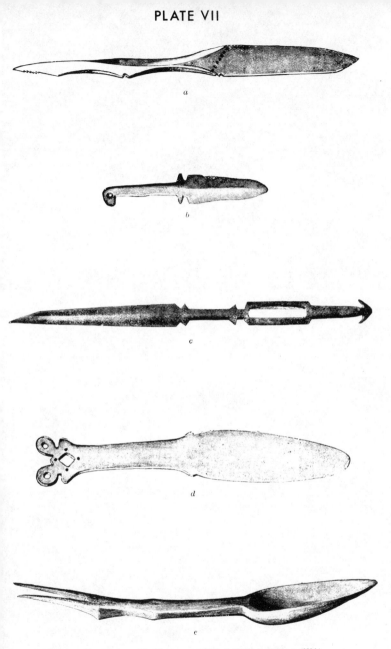

a

b

c

d

e

(National Museum, Washington. *a*, 10395 : *b*, 68146 ; *c*, 10396 ; *e*, 10394.)

MODERN IMPLEMENTS

X. THE FOX AND THE WOMAN.

So-ur - me oχome-ja-me —, kan-gedlir - piuk ta-ja-ja-ja - ja.

RECITATIVE *Slowly*.

Ir - dning—— nuχing - naq—— ujarqamo - ma——

satu-ai-ti - em—— aqbi - ran - ga pirietuki- laun - ga.

Song Da Capo.

XI. THE RAVEN SINGS.

Andantino.

A - -aja a-ja a-ja   a - ja - ja   a-ja a-ja a-ja - - ja.
A - -aja a-ja a-ja   a - ja qi - lirsi - uta - ra-ta taunane.
Ar-naq-djuqpun una qiavoqtung qi - tungnaqdju-ago nu-ting-men.

XII. SONG OF A PADLIMIO.

Moderato.

A-na-ne- ma Pa - dli unguata - ne na-unir-punga a - nane - ga oqsomik -

se - ma qi - janur - pomena ki-ju-ta - i-dle nout-lar - pu - tin kungesi-

en - ing qa-qo- a - mu - dle no- ut-lar - pu-ti - dle a - ja.

XIII. ITITAUJANG'S SONG.

Allegro.

Ta- vun- ga-vun - ga pi-supa-gasu-pun-ga pisu-pa- gasu-

rit. FINE.

-pun - ga si-la- potu-a-dnun tigmidjen nunanun tavungaja i - ja- a- ja.

RECITATIVE.

Nutitavun okoa quliqdjuaq una niguviksa- o adjirdjangirtun

qangiq-sa- o ad-jirdjangirtun kissieni okoa oχomeangitigun

D. C. al Fine.

majoar-dlunga ta - vunga imma pi- su - ta - lu - purmalirmi-junga.

XIV. PLAYING AT BALL.

Sa-ke-e-tan sungmunping-me-ta naumunping-me-ta qa-u-ja-

-ra-ju-va u-dluja-ra-ju-va am-u-ta-i qimu-ta-i

i-dlo-o-ma u-na qag-i-e-la u-na i-dnir-so-ri-va-ra

inung ikoa oaitiang ikoa au-dlertouq ikoa to-gitju-gitju-ge

to-gitju-gitju-ge se-ti-dle—— si-na-dle——

ar-na-ri-sa-i-gneman tigmi-djen arnai-ning tu-ni-go

an-e-ju-i-dla qau-sirtu-ming i-ta itjam-u-na

ma-ja-o-adle-la-tit i-ku-se-ka— a-va-si-tu-ko—

oq-su-ke-na tao-tugni-te a-ka-tao-tukta-ra

su-ga-vi-ka-na ka-na-ne-pa ilu-qio gnari-putit aaiqto-dlu-ti-dlo——

ne-ser-todlu-tidlo a-va-tirtung-giengo-dlu-ti-dlo

XV. PLAYING AT BALL.

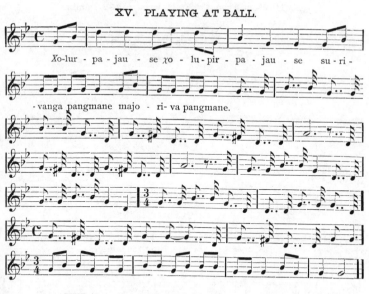

Xo-lur - pa - jau - se χo - lu-pir- pa - jau - se su - ri -

-vanga pangmane majo - ri- va pangmane.

XVI. From Parry, Second Voyage, p. 542, Iglulik.

Amna a- ya   a- ya amna   ah   amna a- ya   a- ya amna

ah   ah etc.

The sixteenth bar is probably

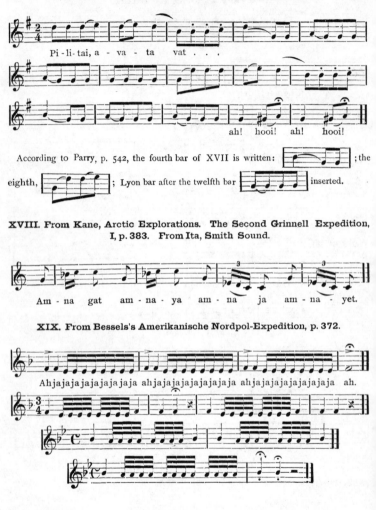

XVII. From Lyon, Private Journal, p. 135, Iglulik.

Pi - li - tai, a - va - ta   vat . . .

ah! hooi! ah!   hooi!

According to Parry, p. 542, the fourth bar of XVII is written: ; the eighth, ; Lyon bar after the twelfth bar inserted.

XVIII. From Kane, Arctic Explorations. The Second Grinnell Expedition, I, p. 383. From Ita, Smith Sound.

Am - na gat   am - na - ya   am - na   ja   am - na - yet.

XIX. From Bessels's Amerikanische Nordpol-Expedition, p. 372.

Ahjajajajajajajajaja ahjajajajajajajajaja ahjajajajajajajajaja ah.

GLOSSARY

A.

ADLIPAR'MIUT, the inhabitants of the country farthest below; from *at*, below; *-lirn*, being in a certain direction; *-päng*, superlative; *-mio* (plural, *-miut*), inhabitant of.

A'DLIRN, a small lamp on the floor of the hut; from *at*, below; *-lirn*, being in a certain direction.

ADLI'VUN, those beneath us; from *at*, below; *-lirn*, being in a certain direction; *-vun*, possessive first person plural.

A'GDLAG, black bear.

AGDLIAQ, a small spear; from *ake-*, across; *-dlivoq*, he provides with; *-aq*, past participle.

AG'GIRN, a species of duck (*Anas glacialis*).

AISS'IVANG, spider.

A'JANG, beam of kayak; from *ajaq-*, to support.

AJA'RORPOQ, he plays the game cat's cradle.

AJE'GAUNG, a game.

AJOKITARPOQ, a game.

AJUKTAQ'TUNG, batting the ball.

AKPARAIK'TUNG, hook for preventing the loss of harpoon.

AKUD'NANG, paddle handle; from *ako*, middle.

A'KUK, lateral strips of wood used in boat; from *ako*, middle.

A'LIRN, harpoon line.

A'MAROQ, wolf.

A'MING, skin of land animals, cover of boat and kayak.

ANG'AKOQ, a magician, conjurer.

ANGAKUNIRN, the art of the angakoq.

ANG'AKUT, plural of angakoq.

ANGIAQ, spirit of a murdered child (Greenland).

ANG'UN, paddle.

ANGUTA', his father.

ANGU'VIGANG, lance; from *anguvoq*, he goes sealing with the harpoon.

ANING'A, her brother (the moon).

A'NO, dog harness.

A'PUMANG, gunwale.

AQO'JANG, stern of kayak.

AQSAR'DNIRN, wind blowing down a valley.

ARAU'TAQ, snow beater (Aivillik dialect).

ARM'GOAQ, amulet.

ASE'DLUN, flat receptacle for the harpoon line on kayak.

ASIMAU'TANG, piece of board or whalebone on which skins are cleaned.

ATAU'TA, neck of sealskin float; from *atav-*, to be connected.

AUDLITI'VING, vault back of snow house.

AVANGNA'NIRN, northwestern gales along the coast of Baffin Land.

AVAU'TANG, sealskin float.

AVAUTAPĀQ', large sealskin float; from *avautang*, sealskin float; *-pāq*, superlative.

A'VIGNAQ, lemming.

AχI'GIRN, ptarmigan.

E.

EχALŪ'JANG, carved ivory fish, used as bait; from *eχaluq*, salmon; *-ujang*, similar to.

EχALUQ, salmon.

I.

IDLUK', a fabulous fish.

IGDL'U, snow house.

IGDL'UARN, a vault attached to snow hut; from *igdlu*, snow house; *-arn*, small.

IGDLUKITAQ'TUNG, playing with two balls, tossing them up alternately; from *igdlung*, both; *-kitarpoq*, he uses at the same time.

IGDLU'LING, second vault of snow house; from *igdlu*, snow house; *-ling*, with.

I'GIMANG, ball-and-socket joint of harpoon and lance ; from *igipā'*, he throws it off.

IKAN', store room supported by stone pillars; from *ikarpoq*, it stretches from one support to another.

IKIRT'SUQ, wind blowing from the open sea.

ILAGA, my friend (Netchillik).

ILUPI'QANG, lining of snow house ; from *ilo*, inner.

IMITI'JUNG, drinking water ; from *imiq*, fresh water.

INETANG, hoop with net of thongs to dry clothing etc. in snow house ; from *inivā'*, he hangs it up.

IN'UA, its man, owner ; possessive third person of *inung*, man.

INUG'SUNG, cairn : from *inung*, man.

IPAR'ANG, harpoon line.

IP'UN, oar, a s ear.

IRQATA'TUNG, a certain circuit among the huts.

ISSUMAU'TANG, a chief ; from *issu'mavoq*, he thinks.

ITIGEGA, boot (Iglulik).

ITIR'BING, cross piece abaft the hole in kayak ; from *itiq*.

K.

KAB'LIAQDJUQ, wolverine (Iglulik).

KAITIKPOQ, a game.

KAIVITI'JUNG, a game.

KAKI'VANG, fish spear.

KAKLIO'KIA, hook (Iglulik).

KALU'GIANG, a heavy lance (*qalugiang?*).

KAN'GO, a species of goose.

KA'PUN, spear ; from *kapivā'*, he stabs him.

KA'TENG, entrance to stone hut.

KENTUN, drumstick.

KIDLU'LIRN, lamp standing in the rear of the hut.

KI'GLO, boat post.

KILAUT, drum.

KOUKPARMIU'TANG, a certain amulet at point of hood.

KU'JANG, keel of kayak.

M.

MA'LING, paddle blade.

MA'MI, membrane or inner side of skin.

MA'SING, cross piece before hole in kayak.

MIR'QUN, needle.

MIRQUSS'ANG, two masked persons.

MUMIPOQ, he dances.

N.

NABI'RING, a loop ; from *nā'poq*, he hinders a motion.

NA'PO (plural *napun*), cross bar of sledge.

NAQETA'RUN, lashing for the sledge ; from *naqigpoq*, it is pressed down.

NAU'LANG, harpoon head.

NE'TIVANG, *Phoca cristata*.

NI'GIRN, southeast.

NIKSIANG, hook.

NIKSIAR'TAUNG, fish hook.

NIRT'SUN, small ropes used in sledge and house.

NIUQ'TUNG, drill bow with string ; from *niorpoq*, he drills.

NIU'TANG, hoop with skin stretched over it; beam of kayak.

NUGLU'TANG, a certain game.

NU'IRN, bird spear.

NULIANITITI'JUNG, exchange of wives.

NUNAJISAR'TUNG, a certain festival.

NUQSANG, throwing board.

NUSSUERAQTUNG, a certain festival.

O.

OQUR'TSUQ (Akudnirn), southeast, blowing from Oqo ; from *oqo*, weather side.

P.

PA, hole of kayak.

PAKIJUMIJAR'TUNG, game of hook and crook.

PA'NA, double edged knife.

PARTI'RANG, button for closing the *pitu* ; from *pārpa*, he meets him.

PAUK'TUN, pegs.

PAU'TING, double bladed kayak paddle.

PI'LAUT, large knife.

PILEK'TUNG, cutting something.

PI'MAIN, chief, he who knows everything best by practice.

PI'NINGNANG, true south.

PIR'QANG, shoeing of runners of sledge.

PITIQ'SE, bow.

PITKUSI'RARPOQ, a certain game.

PI'TU, a stout thong, consisting of two parts to fasten traces to sledge.

POVIU'TANG, pipe for inflating skins; from *pō-*, to blow.

PUKIQ, the white part of a deerskin.

Q.

QADLUNAIT, Europeans.

QAG'GI, singing house.

QAILERTE'TANG, a certain masked figure.

QAI'VUN, drill.

QA'JAQ, kayak.

QA'MUN, sledge runner.

QA'MUTING (dual of qam'un), sledge.

QANA'RA, east-northeast (Nettilling); from qaning, falling snow.

QANG'ING, a toggle.

QANG'IRN, a ventilating hole in snow house; from qa, above.

QA'NING, a certain rib of kayak.

QA'NINGNANG, east-northeast; from qaning, falling snow.

QAQ'DJUNG, arrow.

QA'REANG, annex of house for an additional family.

QAR'MANG (plural qarmat), stone or bone house.

QARMAU'JANG, similar to a qarmang; suffix, -ujang, similar to.

QASI'GIAQ, Phoca annellata.

QATILIK, a spear (Iglulik); from qatirn, ivory head of harpoon shaft; -lik, with.

QA'TIRN, ivory head of harpoon shaft.

QATU'RANG, a boot ornament.

QAUMARTENG'A, days without sun, but with dawn.

QAU'MAT, a kind of fire (?); from qauq, daylight.

QAUMATI'VUN, sun (in the sacred language of the angakut).

QAUMA'VUN, moon (in the sacred language of the angakut).

QAUQ, daylight.

QIDJA'RUNG, whirl; from qipivā', he twists it.

QIJUQTENG'Ⱥ, harpoon shaft; from qijuq, wood.

QILAQ, sky.

QILER'TUANG, clasp for holding the coils of the harpoon line; from qilerpā', he ties it with a knot.

QING'ANG, a hole to look out of snow house.

QING'MIAQ, mouth piece of drill.

QIPEKU'TANG, rod to indicate approach of seal to his hole.

QI'PIQ, blanket.

QI'QIRN, phantom in the shape of a huge, hairless dog.

QOQSIUARIVA, the ceremony of washing children with urine.

QUDLIPAR'MIUT, the inhabitants of the country farthest above; from qu, above; -lirn, being in a certain direction; -pāng, superlative; -mio (plural, -miut), inhabitant of.

QUDLIRN, a lamp; from qu, above; -lirn, being in a certain direction.

QUDLI'VUN, the uppermost ones; from qu, above; -lirn, being in a certain direction; -vun, possessive first person plural.

QUDLUQSIU'TA, ring on a paddle.

QU'MING, a certain lamp.

QUQAR'TAUN, an implement to string fish.

QUVIE'TUNG, a festival.

S.

SADNI'RIAQ, cross piece, a certain button, from sadne, side, across.

SADNI'RUN, a yard.

SĀKETĀN', roulette; from sakagpā', he pushes it.

SAKIE'TAUN, the Pleiades.

SAKURPĀNG', whale harpoon; from sako, weapon; -pāng, the largest.

SA'VING, knife.

SELIGO'UNG, scraper; from selivā', he cleans a skin.

SIAD'NIRN (plural, siadnit), lateral strip in kayak; from siaq-, to place in a row; -nirn, being.

SIAT'KO, harpoon head (Iglulik).

SIEK'TUNG, the three stars in Orion's belt: those standing in a row.

SIR'DLOANG, store room of snow house.

SIRING'ILANG, the excepted month in balancing Eskimo calendars, the month without sun; from sirinirn, sun; -ngilang, he has not.

SIRINIKTENG'A, the first days with sunlight; from sirinirn, sun; -tang, new; -a, possessive third person singular.

SIRMI'JAUNG, scraper for kayak; from sirming, thin ice.

SULUBAUT', bunch of hair projecting from forehead.

SULUI'TUNG, festival in which a knife (sulung) is used.

SU'LUNG, wing; knife shaped like a wing.

T.

TAGUSIAR'BING, eye (of harpoon).

TAGUTA', a thong (of harpoon).

TELIQ'BING, certain piece on harpoon line.

TESIR'QUN, scraper: from *tesivá'*, he stretches it.

TIGDLUIQ'DJUNG, blow with the fist (of a stranger); from *tigdlugpá'*, he strikes him with the fist.

TIKA'GUNG, support of hand in throwing harpoon.

TI'KIQ, thimble.

TIK'PING, rib of kayak.

TILUQ'TUNG, snow beater; from *tiluqpá'*, he strikes it, in order to shake something off.

TINGMI'UJANG, images of birds (used for dice); from *tingmiang*, bird; -*ujang*, similar to.

TO'KANG, harpoon head.

TOQ'SUNG, vaulted entrance to snow house.

TOR'NAQ, a guardian spirit.

TORNARSUQ, the great *tornaq*.

TO'UNG, tusk, point.

TOUNG'A, point of spear.

TUGLIGA, a tress.

TUKTUQ'DJUNG, the constellation of the Reindeer, or the Great Bear, Ursa Major; from *tukto*, caribou (deer).

TUMI'UJANG, a certain lamp resembling a footprint; from *tume*, footprint; -*ujang*, similar to.

TUNIQ'DJUNG, stern of kayak.

TU'PILAQ, spirit of a deceased person.

TU'PIQ, tent.

TUPU'TANG, plugs for closing wounds.

TUTA'REANG, a certain buckle.

TU'VING, strip in the boat nearest the gunwale; from *tuk-*, to stop a motion *tupá'*, he makes it fast.

U.

UA'DLING, first vault of snow house.

UANG'NANG, west-northwest, Cumberland Sound; west-southwest in Akudnirn.

UDLEQ'DJUNG, Sword of Orion: following one another.

UI'NIRN, head of sledge runner.

U'KUSIK, soapstone kettle.

U'LO, woman's knife.

ULUQ'SAQ, green slate, material for women's knives; from *ulo* and -*saq*, material for.

U'MIAQ, large skin boat.

UMING, beard.

U'MINGMANG, musk ox.

UMĪ'UJANG, needle case.

U'NANG, sealing harpoon.

UNAQIU'TA, ring on shaft of sealing harpoon; from *unang*; -*iarpá*, he fastens it; -*ta*, past participle.

UNARTENG'A, iron rod of sealing harpoon; from *unang*; -*tang*, belonging to; -*a*, possessive.

UQSIRN, implement for fastening traces to sledge.

USUJANG, stern projection of kayak from *usung*, penis; -*ujang*, similar to.

ESKIMO GEOGRAPHICAL NAMES USED, WITH ENGLISH SIGNIFICATIONS.

A.

AGDLINARTUNG.

AGGIRTIJUNG, abounding with ducks.

AGGO, the weather side.

AGGOMIUT, the inhabitants of Aggo.

AGPAN, loons.

AGUTIT.

AIVILLIK, with walrus.

AIVILLIRMIUT, the inhabitants of Aivillik (the walrus country).

AKUDNIRMIUT, the inhabitants of Akudnirn.

AKUDNIRN, the intervening country.

AKUGDLIRN, the central one.

AKUGDLIT, the central ones.

AKULIAχATING.

AKULIAQ.

AKULIARMIUT, the inhabitants of Akuliaq.

AMAQDJUAQ, the large place where children are carried in the hood.

AMARTUNG, a woman carrying a child in the hood.

AMITOQ, the narrow one.

ANARNITUNG, smelling of excrements.

ANARTUAJUIN, the excrements.

ANAULEREË'LING.

ANGIUQAQ; from *angivoq*, it is large.

ANGMALORTUQ, the round one.

ANGMANG, jasper.

ANGMARTUNG, the open one (not frozen over).

AQBENILING, six; so called because reached after six days' travel.

Aqbirsiarbing, a lookout for whales.
Aqbirtijung, abounding with whales.
Aqojang ; from *aqo*, stern.
Aqojartung ; from *aqo*, stern.
Arligaulik.
Audnerbing, place where seals are approached by the crawling hunter.
Augpalugtijung, with many red places.
Augpalugtung, the red one.
Aulitiving, an annex of the snow house ; hills lying at the foot of steep cliffs.
Auqardneling, with many places where the ice melts early in spring.
Avatutiaq.
Avaudjeling, with a low saddle.

E.

Eꭓaloaping, with common salmon.
Eꭓalualuin, the large salmon (plur.).
Eꭓaluaqdjuin, the small salmon (plur.).
Eꭓaluin, the salmon (plur.).
Eꭓaluqdjuaq, the shark.
Eꭓoleaqdjuin.

I.

Idjorituaqtuin, the only places with an abundance of grass.
Idjuk, the testicles.
Igdlumiut, the inhabitants of the other side.
Igdlungajung, the bandy legged man ; so called from a fabulous tribe.
Igdluqdjuaq, the large house.
Iglulik, with houses.
Iglulirmiut, the inhabitants of the place with houses.
Igpirto, with many hills.
Igpirtousirn, the smaller place with many hills.
Ijelirtüng.
Ikaroling, with a ford.
Ikerassaq, the narrow strait.
Ikerassaqdjuaq, the large narrow strait.
Iliqimisarbing, where one shakes one's head.
Imeraqdjuaq.
Imigen, with fresh water.
Ingnirn, flint.
Inugsuin, the cairns.
Inugsulik, with cairns.

Ipiuteling, with an isthmus.
Ipiuting, the isthmus ; literally, the traces of a dog.
Irtiujang.
Isiritung.
Isoa, its cover.
Issortuqdjuaq, the large one with muddy water.
Ita, food.
Itidliaping, the common pass.
Itidlirn, the pass.
Itijareling, with a small pass.
Itirbilung, the anus.
Itivimiut, the inhabitants of the coast beyond the land.
Ituatukan.
Itutonik (Etotoniq).

K.

Kaming'ujang, similar to a boot.
Kangertloa'ping, the common bay.
Kangertlua'lung, the large bay.
Kangertlukdjuaq, the large bay.
Kangertluk'siaq.
Kangertlung, the bay.
Kangia, its head, its upper part (of a bay).
Kangianga, its upper part.
Kangidliuta, nearest to the land.
Kangivamiut, inhabitants of Kangia.
Kautaq, diorite.
Kilauting, the drum.
Kingnait, the high land.
Kingnaitmiut, the inhabitants of Kingnait.
Kinipetu.
Kitigtung, the island lying farthest out toward the sea.
Kitingujang, the gorge.
Kouaqdjuaq.
Koukdjuaq the large river.
Kouksoarmiut, the inhabitants of Kouksoaq.
Koukteling, with a river.
Kugnuaq, the small nice river.

M.

Majoraridjen, the places where one has to climb up.
Maktartudjennaq, where one eats whale's hide.
Maluksilaq.
Manirigtung, with many eggs.

MANITULING, with uneven places.
METJA, the lid.
MIDLURIELING, where stones are thrown (for catching white whales).
MILIAQDJUIN, the small ones, which shut it up(?).
MILIQDJUAQ, the large one, which shuts up (?).
MINGONG, the beetle.
MISIQTUNG.
MUINGMANG.

N.

NANUQTUAQDJUNG, the little bear.
NANURAGASSAIN, abounding in young bears.
NAQOREANG.
NARPAING.
NAUJAN, the gulls.
NAUJAQDJUAQ, the large gull.
NAUJATELING, with gulls.
NEBARVIK.
NEDLUNG, peninsula from the point of which deer are driven into the water; from *nedlugpoq*, he swims.
NEDLUQSEAQ; from *nedlugpoq*, he swims.
NEQEMIARBING, where something is carried in the hand.
NERSEQDJUAQ, the large valley.
NETCHILLIK, with seals.
NETCHILLIRMIUT, the inhabitants of Netchillik (the seal country).
NETTILLING, with seals.
NIAQONAUJANG, similar to a head.
NIKOSIVING; from *nikuipoq*, it stands erect.
NIRDLIRN, the goose.
NIUTANG, hoop used in whaling.
NUDLUNG, the posteriors.
NUDNIRN, the point.
NUGUMIUT, the inhabitants of the point.
NURATA.
NURATAMIUT, the inhabitants of Nurata.
NUVUJALUNG, the large cape or point.
NUVUJEN, the points.
NUVUKDJUAQ. the great point.
NUVUKDJUARAQDJUNG, the little Nuvuk-djuaq.
NUVUKTIRPĀNG', the greatest point.
NUVUKTUALUNG, the only great point.
NUVUNG, the point.

O.

OKAN, the codfish (plural).
OKAVIT.
OPERDNIVING, place where one lives in spring.
OQO, the weather side.
OQOMIUT, the inhabitants of Oqo.
OWUTTA.

P.

PADLI, with the mouth of a river.
PADLIAQ, the little mouth of the river. (?)
PADLIMIUT, the inhabitants of Padli.
PADLOPING; from *padlorpoq* (lying on the face?).
PAMIUJANG, similar to a tail.
PANGNIRTUNG, with many bucks.
PIKIULAQ, *Uria grylle*.
PILING, with many things (i. e., game).
PILINGMIUT, the inhabitants of Piling.
PINGITKALIK.
PITIKTAUJANG.
PUJETUNG, with plenty of blubber.
PUTUKIN.

Q.

QAGGILORTUNG; from *qaggi*, singing house.
QAIROLIKTUNG, with plenty of seal (*Phoca grœnlandica*).
QAMUSIOJODLANG.
QARIAQ.
QARMANG, walls.
QARMAQDJUIN, the large walls
QARUSSUIT, the caves.
QASIGIDJEN, *Callocephali*.
QAUMAUANG; from *qauq*, daylight.
QAUMAUANGMIUT, the inhabitants of Qaumauang.
QAχODLUALUNG, the large fulmar.
QAχODLUIN, the fulmars.
QEQERTAKADLINANG; from *qeqertaq*, island.
QEQERTALUKDJUAQ, the large island.
QEQERTAQ, the island.
QEQERTAUJANG, similar to an island.
QEQERTELUNG, the large island.
QEQERTEN, the islands.
QEQERTOME ITOQ TUDLIRN, next to the island.
QEQERTUQDJUAQ, the large island.
QERNIQDJUAQ, the great black place.

QIDNELIK.

QIMISSUNG, the snow drift.

QIMUQSUQ; fiom *qimuqpoq*, he draws the sledge.

QINGASEAREANG.

QINGUA, its head.

QINGUAMIUT, the inhabitants of Qingua.

QIVITUNG, the hermit.

QOGNUNG, the narrow place.

QOGULORTUNG (Qaggilortung ?).

QORDLUVING, where the water runs in a solid stream.

QUAIIRNANG.

QUDJITARIAQ.

S.

SAGDLIRMIUT, the inhabitants of Sagdlirn.

SAGDLIRN, the island nearest the sea.

SAGDLUA, its Sagdlirn.

SAKIAQDJUNG, the little rib.

SARBAQ (*sarvaq*), the rapids.

SARBAQDJUKULU, the small rapids.

SARBAQDUALUNG, the large rapids.

SARBAUSIRN, the smaller rapids.

SARBUQDJUAQ, the large rapids.

SAUMIA, its left side.

SAUMINGMIUT, the inhabitants of Saumia.

SAUNIRTUNG, with many bones.

SAUNIRTUQDJUAQ, the great one with many bones.

SEDNIRUN, the yard.

SIEGTUNG, the scattered ones.

SIKOSUILAQ, the coast without ice.

SIKOSUILARMIUT, the inhabitants of Sikosuilaq.

SINI, the edge.

SINIMIUT, the inhabitants of Sini.

SIORELING, with sand.

SIRMILING, with a glacier.

SULUNG, the valley through which the wind blows howling.

SUROSIRN, the boy.

T.

TALIRPIA, its right side.

TALIRPINGMIUT, the inhabitants of Talirpia.

TAPPITARIAQ, the pass crossing two isthmuses.

TAPPITARIDJEN, the passes crossing two isthmuses.

TAQUIRBING.

TARIONITJOQ, the salt water basin.

TARRIONITUNG, the salt water basin.

TAχOLIDJUIN.

TESSIUJANG, similar to a pond.

TIKERAQDJUAQ, the great point.

TIKERAQDJUAUSIRN, the smaller great point.

TIKERAQDJUNG, the small point.

TIKERAQDJUQ, the small point.

TININIQDJUAQ, the large beach.

TINIQDJUARBING, the great place with a high tide.

TINIQDJUARBIUSIRN, the smaller great place with a high tide.

TORNAIT, spirits.

TOUAQDJUAQ.

TUARPUQDJUAQ.

TUDJAN.

TUDJAQDJUAQ.

TUDJAQDJUARALUNG.

TUDJARAAQDJUNG.

TUKIA, its farthest corner.

TULUKAN, the ravens.

TUNIQTEN, those lying behind it.

TUNUKUTANG.

TUNUNIRMIUT, the inhabitants of Tununirn.

TUNUNIRN, the country lying back of something.

TUNUNIRUSIRMIUT, the inhabitants of Tununirusirn.

TUNUNIRUSIRN, the smaller Tununirn.

TUNUSSUNG, the nape.

TUPIRBIKDJUIN, the tent sites.

U.

UDLIMAULITELING, with a hatchet.

UGJUKTUNG, with many ground seals.

UGJULIK, with ground seals.

UGJULIRMIUT, the inhabitants of Ugjulik (the ground seal country).

UGLARIAQ.

UGLIRN, walrus island.

UGLIT, the walrus islands.

UIBARUN, the cape.

UJARAQDJUIN, the large stones.

UJARADJIRAAITJUNG; from *ujaraq*, stone.

UKADLIQ, the hare.

UKIADLIVING, the place where one lives in the fall.

UKIUKDJUAQ, the great winter.

UKUSIKSALIK, the place with pot stone

UKUSIKSALIRMIUT, inhabitant of Ukusiksalik.

UMANAQ, the heart-like island.

UMANAQTUAQ, the great heart-like island.

UMINGMAN NUNA, the land of the musk
ox.

UNGAVA.

UNGAVAMIUT.

USSUALUNG, the large penis.

UTIQIMITUNG.

APPENDIX

After the preceding paper was in type some additional information was received from whalers who returned from Cumberland Sound in the autumn of 1887. In the following notes I give the substance of these reports:

NOTE 1.

Page 61. Since 1883 the whalers have been more successful, and consequently more ships visit the sound. In the present winter—1887-'88—one American and two Scottish whaling stations are in operation in Cumberland Sound; a new station was established in Nugumiut two years ago, and the Scottish steamers which used to fish in Baffin Bay and the northern parts of Davis Strait are beginning to visit Cumberland Sound and Hudson Strait. The whaling in Baffin Bay shows a sudden falling off and it seems that the number of ships will be greatly reduced. This cannot be without influence upon the Eskimo, who will probably begin again to flock to Cumberland Sound and Nugumiut.

NOTE 2.

Page 130. In 1884 and 1885 a lively intercourse existed between Padli and Cumberland Sound, and in the spring of the latter year the dog's disease broke out for the first time on the coast of Davis Strait, and spread, so far as is known, to the northern part of Home Bay.

NOTE 3.

Page 166. A peculiar game is sometimes played on the ice in spring. The men stand in a circle on the ice, and one of them walks, the toes turned inward, in a devious track. It is said that only a few are able to do this in the right way. Then the rest of the men have to follow him in exactly the same track.

One of their gymnastic exercises requires considerable knack and strength. A pole is tied with one end to a stone or to a piece of wood that is firmly secured in the snow. A man then lies down on his back, embracing the pole, his feet turned toward the place where the pole is tied to the rock. Then he must rise without bending his body.

In another of their gymnastic exercises they lie down on their stomachs, the arms bent so that the hands lie close together on the breast, palms turned downward. Then they have to jump forward without bending their body, using only their toes and hands. Some are said to be able to jump several feet in this manner.

NOTE 4.

Page 174. In the Report of the Hudson Bay Expedition of 1886, p. 16, Lieut. A. Gordon remarks that the same custom is reported from Port Burwell, near Cape Chidleigh, Labrador. He says: "There lived between the Cape and Aulatsivik a good Eskimo hunter whose native name is not given, but who was christened by our station men 'Old Wicked.' He was a passionate man and was continually threatening to do some bodily harm to the other more peaceably inclined natives. * * * His arrogance and petty annoyances to the other natives became at length unbearable. It appears that these unfortunates held a meeting and decided that Old Wicked was a public nuisance which must be abated, and they therefore decreed that he should be shot, and shot he was accordingly one afternoon when he was busily engaged in repairing the ravages which a storm had made in his 'igdlu' or snow house. The executioner shot him in the back, killing him instantly. The murderer or executioner (one hardly knows to which title he is more justly entitled) then takes Old Wicked's wives and all his children and agrees to keep them * * * so that they shall be no burden on the company."

The fact that the custom is found among tribes so widely separated will justify a description of those events which came under my own observation. There was a native of Padli by the name of Padlu. He had induced the wife of a Cumberland Sound native to desert her husband and follow him. The deserted husband, meditating revenge, cut off the upper part of the barrel of his gun so that he could conceal it under his jacket. He crossed the land and visited his friends in Padli, but before he could accomplish his intention of killing Padlu the latter shot him. When this news was reported in Qeqerten, the brother of the murdered man went to Padli to avenge the death of his brother; but he also was killed by Padlu. A third native of Cumberland Sound, who wished to avenge the death of his relatives, was also murdered by him. On account of all these outrages the natives wanted to get rid of Padlu, but yet they did not dare to attack him. When the pimain of the Akudnirmiut in Niaqonaujang learned of these events he started southward and asked every man in Padli whether Padlu should be killed. All agreed; so he went with the latter deer hunting in the upper part of Pangnirtung, northwest of Padli, and near the head of the fjord he shot Padlu in the back.

In another instance a man in Qeqerten had made himself odious. After it was agreed that he was a bad man an old man of Qeqerten, Pakaq, attacked him on board a Scottish whaler, but was prevented from killing him.

NOTE 5.

Page 186. The following performance was observed in Umanaqtuaq, on the southwestern coast of Cumberland Sound, in the winter of 1886–'87 : An angakoq began his incantations in a hut after the lamps were lowered. Suddenly he jumped up and rushed out of the hut to where a mounted harpoon was standing. He threw himself upon the harpoon, which penetrated his breast and came out at the back. Three men followed him and holding the harpoon line led the angakoq, bleeding profusely, to all the huts of the village. When they arrived again at the first hut he pulled out the harpoon, lay down on the bed, and was put to sleep by the songs of another angakoq. When he awoke after a while he showed to the people that he was not hurt, although his clothing was torn and they had seen him bleeding.

Another angakoq performed a similar feat on the island Utussivik in the summer of 1887. He thrust a harpoon through his body and was led by about twenty-five men through the village. It is said that he imitated the movements and voice of a walrus while on the circuit.

Still another exhibition was witnessed by the whalers in the fall of 1886 in Umanaqtuaq. An angakoq stripped off his outer jacket and began his incantations while walking about in the village. When the men heard him, one after the other came out of his hut, each carrying his gun. After a while the angakoq descended to the beach; the men followed him, and suddenly fired a volley at him. The angakoq, of course, was not hurt, and then the women each gave him a cup of water, which he drank. Then he put on his jacket, and the performance was ended. The similarity of this performance with part of the festival which is described on pp. 197 et seq. is evident.

NOTE 6.

Page 198. The same feast was celebrated in 1886 in Umanaqtuaq, in Cumberland Sound, where all the Talirpingmiut had gathered. The witnesses of this festival describe it exactly in the same way as I described it above. One thing ought to be added, which I did not mention because it seemed to me accidental, but as it was repeated in the same way in 1886 it must have some meaning. I noticed that the Qailertetang, after having invoked the wind, hop about, making a grunting noise and accosting the people. When doing so they are attacked by the natives and killed. According to the description of the whalers they imitate sometimes deer, sometimes walrus. Perhaps this fact gave rise to Kumlien's description of the "killing of the evil spirit of the deer." It is remarkable that in 1883 in Qeqerten and in 1886 in Umanaqtuaq the festival was celebrated on exactly the same day, the 10th of November. This can hardly be accidental, and does not agree with the idea sometimes advanced, that the festival refers to the winter solstice. Unfortunately Hall (I, p. 528) does not give the dates of the festival in Nugumiut. On the western coast of Hudson Bay a festival in which masks were used was celebrated about the end of January, 1866 (Hall II, p. 219), but it is hardly possible to draw conclusions from Nourse's superficial account of Hall's observations.

NOTE 7.

Page 207. It may be of interest to learn that in 1885 and 1886 two instances of this kind occurred in Cumberland Sound. There was a very old woman in Qeqerten by the name of Qaχodloaping. She was well provided for by her relatives, but it seems that one of the most influential men in Qeqerten, Pakaq, whom I mentioned above (p. 260) as the executioner of a murderer, deemed it right that she should die. So, although she resisted him, he took her out of her hut one day to a hill and buried her alive under stones. Another case was that of an old woman whose health had been failing for a number of years. She lived with her son, whose wife died late in the autumn of 1886. According to the religious ideas of the Eskimo, the young man had to throw away his clothing. When, later on, his mother felt as though she could not live through the winter, she insisted upon being killed, as she did not want to compel her son to cast away a second set of clothing. At last her son complied with her request. She stripped off her outside jacket and breeches, and was conveyed on a sledge to a near island, where she was left alone to die from cold and hunger. The son who took her there did not use his own sledge nor any other Eskimo sledge for this purpose, but borrowed that of the Scottish whaling station.